Tourism Crises: Causes, Consequences and Management

Tourism Crises: Causes, Consequences and Management

Joan C. Henderson

AMSTERDAM • BOSTON • HEIDELBERG • LONDON
NEW YORK • OXFORD • PARIS • SAN DIEGO
SAN FRANCISCO • SINGAPORE • SYDNEY • TOKYO

ELSEVIER

Butterworth-Heinemann is an imprint of Elsevier

Butterworth–Heinemann is an imprint of Elsevier
30 Corporate Drive, Suite 400, Burlington, MA 01803, USA
Linacre House, Jordan Hill, Oxford OX2 8DP, UK

Recognizing the importance of preserving what has been written, Elsevier prints its books on
acid-free paper whenever possible.

Library of Congress Cataloging-in-Publication Data
Application submitted

British Library Cataloguing-in-Publication Data
A catalogue record for this book is available from the British Library.

ISBN 13: 978-0-7506-7834-6
ISBN 10: 0-75-067834-8

For information on all Butterworth–Heinemann publications
visit our Web site at www.books.elsevier.com

Printed in the United States of America
06 07 08 09 10 11   10 9 8 7 6 5 4 3 2 1

Contents

List of Figures

List of Tables

1

Introduction

Learning Objectives

By the end of the chapter, the reader should be able to

- Recognize the different causes of tourism crises.
- Identify the characteristics of tourism crises and their various types.
- Appreciate the consequences of tourism crises.
- Understand the special features of the tourism industry which make it vulnerable to crisis.
- Explain the key components of crisis management plans and underlying principles.

Introduction

The opening of the twenty-first century was marked by a wave of terrorist attacks, outbreaks of disease and devastating natural phenomena. Many of these incidents had local, regional and global repercussions and prompted tourism crises at corporate, industry and destination levels. Although some events were unprecedented, crisis and disaster have acquired greater prominence in recent years and the modern world appears to be one of heightened uncertainty and insecurity. Tourism cannot isolate itself from these forces and developments in the external environment have the capacity to precipitate tourism crises, as do industry and organizational circumstances. Some notable examples of tourism crises in the last decade are listed in Table 1.1, and this pattern seems set to continue in the years ahead.

A growing awareness of the threat of tourism crises and their potential to inflict harm is reflected in the number of academic publications devoted to the topic, including special editions of journals, many of which are referred to in the course of this book. More manuals and handbooks for practitioners are available and industry associations, official agencies and government bodies have been involved in their

Table 1.1: **Selected tourism crises 1995–2005**

Year	Event
1995	Earthquake in the Japanese city of Kobe killed over 5,500 and disrupted transport services throughout the prefecture.
1996	Indian Airlines plane hijacked on a flight from Nepal; 178 passengers released after eight days.
1997	Asian financial crisis and falling currency values depressed demand for intra-regional travel and investment in tourism.
1997	Terrorist attack on tourists visiting an historic site at Luxor in Egypt killed 58.
1998	Abduction of 16 tourists on an organized tour in Yemen, four of whom were killed.
1999	Industrial action by Cathay Pacific pilots over a labor dispute led to flight cancellations affecting thousands of passengers.
2000	Crash of a Concord plane chartered by a German tour operator at Paris killed 113.
2001	Foot and mouth outbreak in the UK restricted access to the countryside and damaged destination images.
2002	Terrorist bombings at nightclubs on the Indonesian island of Bali killed 191 and injured 300.
2003	Severe Acute Respiratory Syndrome (SARS) virus epidemic in Asia and Canada impacted on tourist movements and air travel.
2004	Indian Ocean tsunami in which over 200,000 estimated to have died, including 2,000 tourists in Thailand.
2005	Suicide bombings at an Amman hotel in Jordan killed 57 and injured 120.

Sources: Assorted news reports.

production. It is also an increasingly popular conference theme for both business and academic communities, with a strong emphasis on understanding crises and being prepared to meet them. These themes are central to this book, which deals with causes of crises, their dynamics, consequences and approaches to management.

This first chapter provides an introduction to tourism crises and tourism crisis management. It discusses the features of such crises, their origins and evolution and recommended responses within the context of the wider literature on crisis management. Distinguishing characteristics of the tourism industry, comprising public and private actors, are outlined and shown to heighten its vulnerability to crisis, which assumes a variety of forms and is provoked by assorted catalysts. The overview stresses the significance of planning and management and sets the scene for the remainder of the book, which explores a multiplicity of tourism crises and the manner of their resolution.

Individual chapters cover tourism crises related to economic, political, socio-cultural, environmental and technological issues with additional separate chapters dedicated to questions of terrorism, health and commercial crises. The final chapter reviews the principal themes which emerge from the accounts and examines the lessons to be learned, highlighting examples of best practice and considering the challenges of implementation in an era of rapid change when the future is unknown and unpredictable. It is hoped that the book will afford new insights into the important topic of managing tourism crises, which cannot be ignored by anyone with an interest in tourism.

Tourism Crises, Causes and Consequences

There is no universally accepted definition of what constitutes a crisis and different writers present their own interpretations. These do, however, frequently correspond and it appears that "three elements must be present: a triggering event causing significant change or having the potential to cause significant change; the perceived inability to cope with this change; and a threat to the existence of the foundation of the organization" (Keown-McMullan, 1997, p. 4).

A distinction can be drawn between disasters which owe their origins to factors such as extreme weather, yet impinge on industrial activity, and crises which are products of institutional stresses (Faulkner, 2001). The latter are more amenable to control, but the two have qualities in common and are connected when catastrophes outside an organization provoke a crisis within it. Emergency is another term sometimes employed interchangeably with crisis, but it refers to a less serious and therefore more easily managed event or threat. An associated concept is that of risk pertaining to latent, rather than actual, individual or sets of conditions which can become crises if realized and of sufficient gravity. Risk assessment is a key stage in planning for crisis, involving the anticipation of what might go wrong and identification of the reasons for divergences from expectations (van Waldbeek, 2005).

Every crisis is unique, yet characteristics generally cited include unexpectedness, urgency and danger (Hermann, 1972). They are precipitated by catalysts powerful enough to undermine structures and modes of operation, with repercussions for the profitability of commercial ventures which might even be destroyed (Shrivastava and Mitroff, 1987). Lives and company and individual reputations may be put in jeopardy, thereby eroding staff morale. Participants are taken by surprise and have little time to make difficult decisions in an atmosphere of tension and instability. Crises also reach a crucial point when change, for the better or worse, is unavoidable and the experience may prove beneficial for people and organizations (Prideaux et al., 2003).

Tourism crises usually share these attributes, although certain crisis situations can be predicted and lack immediacy such as those facing destinations suffering from rising sea levels due to global warming. They are also not restricted to the corporate arena and the phrase can be extended to describe circumstances in which tourists and members of the tourism industry individually or collectively, including destinations, are faced with change, which is potentially destructive for every, or certain, parties (a concept definition which is repeated at the end of the chapter). Generalizations may, however, be misleading and tourism crises display a remarkable range and variety, which it is the intention of this book to convey.

Existing typologies of corporate crises as a whole are founded on root causes (Shrivastava and Mitroff, 1987), time (Booth, 1993), gravity (Brecher, 1978) and facets of business operation (Meyers, 1986). Specific tourism crises can be classed in these ways and domain of origin or cause is a relatively straightforward method which permits comprehensive analysis. It represents the rationale for this book's organization and a conceptual framework is presented in Figure 1.1.

Causes of many tourism crises can be traced to developments in the economic, political, socio-cultural and environmental domains, which affect demand and supply in generating and destination countries. Economic downturn and recession, fluctuating exchange rates, loss of market confidence and withdrawal of investment funds can all engender a tourism crisis. Political events such as war, military coups, deteriorating international relations, the imposition of sanctions and terrorism will have a similar outcome. Civil unrest and growing crime and violence may act as triggers and natural disasters of earthquakes, typhoons, volcanic eruptions and flooding will almost inevitably do so. Deterioration in public hygiene and infectious disease also lead to tourism crises. Crises generated within the industry too can be analyzed under the headings of economic, socio-cultural and environmental when tourism has adverse impacts in these fields.

Technological is a fifth domain in which crises are initiated when technology in an assortment of manifestations fails to perform as expected and crises of competition and industrial relations are born of corporate affairs, the sixth domain. Human error is often a compounding factor, or even a principal cause, in these and all forms of tourism crises. Table 1.2 contains a list of threats of crisis by domain and whether they are external or internal to the tourism industry. There may be overlap across the domains and the demarcation between internal and external worlds is also not always clearly discernible. A crisis beyond the industry could be a rigorous test of management competence and the financial health of an organization, with corporate and industrial commercial crises ensuing if these are found to be deficient.

Figure 1.1: Domains of Tourism Crises

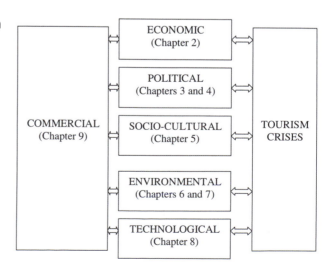

Table 1.2: **External and internal threats of crisis**

Domain	External	Internal
Economic	Recession Currency fluctuations Taxation	Rising costs Falling revenues Unprofitability
Political	Government policy International relations Instability Terrorism	
Socio-cultural	Unrest Crime	Staffing Cultural conflicts
Environmental	Natural phenomena Natural disasters Pollution Health scares	Overdevelopment Environmental degradation
Technological	Computer systems failure Mechanical failure Design faults Fire	Transport accidents
Commercial	Regulations Government intervention	Competition Labor disputes Management decisions Human error

The cause and source of a crisis will help to decide its consequences and severity can be assessed on a scale from major to minor, measured by items such as number of people implicated and costs incurred. Duration is a dimension of magnitude which embraces a short to long-term continuum, from a temporary computer systems collapse to a slowly mutating crisis linked to environmental degradation. Some crises have been likened to cobras when they erupt without warning and pythons if they reveal themselves more stealthily (Seymour and Moore, 2000). Spatial and industrial scope is another facet to take into account. The zone of crisis may be local, national, regional and international with regard to geographical area and corporate, industrial (domestic and overseas) and government (local, national and international) with regard to decision makers.

An isolated case of food poisoning at a restaurant principally concerns the manager and staff and, if managed well, will be quickly forgotten with limited financial damage. In comparison, the tourism industry and governments worldwide must respond to a pandemic of a deadly disease which could resonate for many months and have serious balance of payments implications. This range in crisis scope and, by implication, gravity is depicted in Figure 1.2.

Crises are thus rooted in a multiplicity of intrinsic and extrinsic causes originating in various domains. They occupy a spectrum, from short-lived situations confined to

Figure 1.2: Scope of Tourism Crises

single enterprises to those which involve the global industry over a prolonged period, and the manner in which crises are handled can determine their extent and life. Such observations suggest a propensity to crisis in the tourism industry which is partly derived from its distinctive features, which are summarized below.

Characteristics of the Tourism Industry

First, the tourism industry's relative immaturity and dramatic expansion are noteworthy. Tourism has a long history, but modern mass tourism and the industry which supports it date from after the Second World War. International arrivals rose from 25 million in 1950 to 760 million by 2004, although geographical imbalances persist and most tourists and their spending circulate within the developed world (WTO, 2005). The World Tourism Organization (WTO) predicts that there will be 1.6 billion international tourists in 2020 (WTO, 1999) and domestic tourism, estimated to be 10 times greater in volume (Weaver and Lawton, 2002), must not be overlooked. Growth has been fueled by new product development, aggressive marketing and intense competition.

Looking to the future, the WTO is not alone in its optimistic forecasts and analysts concur that tourists demonstrate considerable resilience in the face of setbacks. Any downturns ahead for whatever reason, including crises, could therefore be quickly overcome. However, there is also an appreciation that tourists can be fickle

6

in their decision making and behavior. Leisure tourism demand is renowned for its elasticity, seasonality and volatility whereby a change in price will produce a disproportionate change in demand, movement is often heavily concentrated in certain months and flows can fluctuate wildly (Bull, 1998). It is driven by economics, subject to fashion trends and deterred by social and political upheaval. Tourists are unlikely to cease traveling in reaction to negative forces, but could shift their direction of travel and choice of destination. Business tourism is more stable, as perhaps is tourism for purposes of education and health care, but most markets are sensitive to uncertainties.

The tourism industry, which has grown to meet the needs of all these travelers, is unusual because of its size and structure, with a number of components playing a part. It consists of all the commercial and non-commercial enterprises and agencies which make tourism possible, encourage it and deal with the consequences. Collectively, they form a network made up of inputs from a series of individual industries, rather than a discrete and homogenous industry, and some of the participants may have customers who are not tourists such as excursionists and local residents.

Core industry sectors are tourism administration and development, passenger transportation, hospitality, attractions, tour operation and retail travel. The tourism administration segment determines the environment within which the overall industry works while transport, hospitality and attractions sell the services essential to the tourist experience. These may reach tourists directly or indirectly through intermediaries of tour operators, who combine separate ingredients into single products, and travel agents, who are the retailers in the distribution chain. An additional miscellaneous category includes providers of travel insurance, currency exchange and travelers' checks and travel literature.

Conventional structures and ways of doing business are, however, changing. Intermediaries are being challenged by new channels of distribution and especially Internet technology, which facilitates direct communications and transactions between customers and suppliers. This has resulted in the threat of disintermediation, raising questions about the prospects of "bricks and mortar" travel agents in particular. Vertically integrated giant travel groups are another power reshaping industry systems, especially in Europe where companies like TUI have their own hotels, airlines, travel agents and tour operators. Nevertheless, the various functional elements still depend on one or more of the others to a greater or lesser degree and are bound together by assorted ties, represented by alliances and partnerships. Any significant occurrence in one unit and country of tourist arrival or departure thus has implications for them all.

The tourism industry caters to nationals traveling within their country of residence (domestic tourists), residents crossing international borders (outbound tourists) and visitors entering from another country (inbound tourists). Transport, hospitality and attractions sectors supply domestic and inbound tourists, and tour operators and travel agents deal mainly with residents going overseas, with some sales of domestic products. However, outbound and inbound tourists travel by foreign air and surface transport carriers and the latter may buy from overseas agents and operators. Linkages thus transcend national boundaries to create an international network or industry. Some of the largest organizations operate globally and the tourism industry is an outcome of globalization as well as a vehicle for its diffusion, creating opportunities and constraints.

It is not only markets that exhibit great diversity, but also tourism products. While encompassing some physical elements, tourism also has a psychological and socio-logical meaning (Krippendorf, 1987) and the industry has to aim to understand and satisfy both emotional and material requirements. In addition, its products possess the inseparability, variability, perishability and intangibility which characterize all services (Kotler et al., 1999). They comprise encounters among individuals in which the tourist is part of the production process. Maintaining the desired standard and consistency is thus made difficult, aggravated by the fact that suppliers of one constituent rely on others to deliver the complete experience. Sales and marketing are further complicated by perishability whereby lost revenue from unsold airline seats and hotel rooms cannot be recovered at a later date so that yields must be managed effectively.

Vulnerability of the Tourism Industry to Crisis

The above comments indicate why and how the tourism industry is prone to crisis. It has a complex structure and sells experiential products which are the collective work of several suppliers, leading to possible problems of fragmentation and control. Relationships of mutual dependence among components also mean that a crisis for one may spread to another. Such contagion is evident in destination crises when a precipitating event leads to a sudden fall in arrivals which has repercussions for accommodation, attraction and transport providers as well as government agencies and tour operators and travel agents at home and abroad.

There is fierce competition among destinations and within sectors, with a trend toward concentration and consolidation. Extremely large and powerful companies have emerged and commercial pressures can result in corporate crises, often related to financial matters. It must also be remembered that the industry is not the preserve of large corporations and small businesses are very active; some of these are particularly vulnerable and may be ill equipped to handle crises (Cushnahan, 2004).

There are striking contrasts between tourist products and other consumer goods which elevate the probability of crisis. The industry must move people to the primary place of consumption and accommodate and entertain them on arrival, the journey itself being one aspect of production. These visits could be marred and tourist safety compromised by a host of incidents which may or may not be the fault of those making the practical arrangements. Examples include transport accidents, hotel fires, street riots in which tourists are caught up and their victimization by criminals. Destinations where there are doubts about safety and security are near to a crisis of a tarnished image, official warnings against travel and a decline in visitors.

Tourism has also expanded at a rapid rate to become one of the world's leading industries, but movement on such a scale and development at such a pace have had economic, socio-cultural and environmental impacts. These impacts have inspired debate about the costs and benefits of tourism, not least for Third World countries, and strong opposition in some instances. The industry has been criticized for its pursuit of short-term economic gains and exploitation of resources which have impeded progress toward more sustainable tourism (Tourism Concern, 2005). The presence of tourists and their capacity to act as an instrument of destructive change are reasons underlying certain types of destination crises.

At the same time, national and international events unconnected to tourism can curtail demand and the working of the industry, and it has been argued that the result is a state of "dynamic chaos and turbulence" (Laws et al., 1998, p. 5). Given this apparent predisposition to many types of crises, warnings about the inevitability of confrontation (Blaikie et al., 1994; Kash and Darling, 1998) are especially apposite for the tourism industry. The question is not whether a crisis will have to be faced, but when and what the reaction should be. Investment in planning and management are therefore vital and the next section outlines key tasks to be performed before and during the evolution of a crisis.

Managing Tourism Crises

Crisis management is perhaps a self-explanatory term and there is, again, no standard definition. Santana (2004, p. 308) did, however, capture its scope and intentions when he wrote of an "ongoing integrated and comprehensive effort that organizations effectively put into place in an attempt to first and foremost understand and prevent crisis, and to effectively manage those that occur, taking into account in each and every step of their planning and training activities, the interests of their stakeholders." Such an outline is applicable to tourism crisis management, which is described in the list of concept definitions at the end of the chapter as planning for and managing tourism crises in order to protect the interests of the industry, tourists and other stakeholders involved and contain any long-term damage. It should be stressed that the industry incorporates public bodies with tourism planning, development and promotion functions as well as commercial operators.

General theories postulate that crises advance in stages which have been labeled prodromal (warning), acute (at the height of the crisis), chronic (aftermath), and resolution (Fink, 1986). They can be conceived of as circular journeys which begin and end at normality after moving through incubation; precipitating event; immediate consequences; rescue, salvage and first stage of adjustment; and full cultural adjustment (Turner, 1976). Essentially, these authors depicted three intervals of pre-crisis, crisis and post-crisis which are likely to be of varying lengths. There may be no, or very little, time for action prior to crises which arrive without warning and duration will depend on the particular case, as will the speed of recovery. Nevertheless, complete restoration of the status quo may be impossible because people and organizations are permanently altered by crisis and sometimes do not survive.

The evolution of a crisis can also be viewed as a set of tasks for managers who must detect signals, prepare and try to prevent, contain, limit damage and pursue recovery (Pauchant and Mitroff, 1992). These tasks imply the assumption of either a reactive or proactive stance while interactivity permits learning, knowledge gained helping to ensure that organizations are better placed to withstand or avert future crises (Burling and Hyle, 1997). Practical measures to reduce the chances of a similar crisis recurring or another emerging should also be seen to be taken in order to reassure and restore confidence amongst tourists, industry partners and investors. Managers must anticipate and evaluate the likelihood of crises, devise policies designed to prevent them and formulate strategies for coping when they do happen (Regester and Larkin, 1998). The main aims are therefore to reduce risks, get ready, respond and recover (Heath, 1998).

Documented and tested crisis plans, detailing actions and staff roles and responsibilities, occupy a central place in crisis management (Smith, 1990; Smith and Sipika, 1993). Teams need to be identified in advance and duties allocated accordingly. Plans should be informed by comprehensive research into, and understanding of, national and global trends of relevance to operations. Risk awareness is fundamental to preparation and prevention and more serious situations require mechanisms for industry-wide and perhaps international cooperation. Internal and external communications is a key area, with many audiences to address. The plan does not end with publication and circulation and it should be monitored and revised in the light of new circumstances. It also cannot be relied on alone and organizations should strive to foster a suitable culture with competent staff able to rise to the most difficult and demanding of occasions.

Specific studies of tourism organizations, industry sectors and destinations in crisis echo these conclusions about crisis evolution and management while acknowledging tourism's distinctiveness as a human, administrative and commercial activity (Atkas and Gunlu, 2005; Brewton, 1987; Doeg, 1995; Evans and Elphick, 2005; Henderson, 1999; Pottorff and Neal, 1994). For example, the parameters of initial risk assessment or environmental scanning exercises must be comparatively broad for the tourism industry in view of the importance of developments in outside arenas. Marketers cannot recall faulty tourism products and lives are endangered in the worst examples of service failure, necessitating appropriate safety procedures. Tourists may have to be repatriated or moved from destinations struck by crisis and arrangements made for those whose departure is imminent, with logistical and resource implications to be planned for. There is also recognition that certain tourism crises unfold in ways that cannot be forecast. Reality is more confused than logical models imply, those in charge may be unable to adhere to prearranged programs and managers have to struggle with formidable dilemmas for which they have no instructions.

Faulkner's (2001) conceptual framework pertains to a tourist destination hit by a natural disaster and is one of the most commonly quoted. It has been employed, with and without amendment, in analyses of other types of tourism crises. The process commences with an initial pre-event phase, when avoiding a disaster or containing its consequences is still feasible, and moves on to a prodromal state in which this is no longer an option. The emergency period is a time for action to protect life and property and is followed by intermediate and long-term recovery before ultimate resolution. A list of responses to match each phase is presented, alongside management strategies founded on thorough and continuously reviewed and updated risk assessment and contingency plans.

Overall, prerequisites of success in managing a tourism crisis are maximum preparedness, a willingness to accept responsibility, rapid action, transparency and good communications. Realizing these objectives is facilitated by a plan setting the direction for all personnel; some examples are discussed in the final chapter.

Researching Tourism Crises

Research exploring tourism crises and their management is often grounded in the wider literature about corporate crises which is extensive (Barton, 2001; Booth, 1993; Mitroff, 2004; Shiva, 2000). This draws on empirical data and personal experience, commentators coming from different management sciences and other disciplines such as psychology, sociology and economics. The strong interest in communications means that it is now a sub-field, indicative of the crucial influence of the media on the intensity and duration of crises (ten Berg, 1990; Bland, 1998; Ogrizek and Guillery, 1999). Many publications are targeted at business executives and several cite illustrations from the tourism industry, especially transport accidents (Harvard Business School, 2004; Lagadec, 1993; Laye, 2002; Levitt, 1997).

However, the spate of tourism crises in the past decade and predictions of more to come have meant that the subject is attracting much greater attention among tourism academics (Beirman, 2003; Faulkner and Russell, 1997; Glaesser, 2005; McKercher, 1999; Nankervis, 2000; Ritchie, 2004; Santana, 2001; Wilks et al., 2005) alongside practitioners (PATA, 2003; WTO, 1996 and 2002; WTO and WMO, 1998). Indeed, it appears to be emerging as a distinct stream in the tourism literature. Much of this work is centered on case studies and concentrates on recovery marketing and management, demonstrating both good and bad practice. There is perhaps an emphasis on extrinsic causes of crisis rather than intrinsic organizational weaknesses and on destination perspectives. Tourism crises are shown to generate widespread, and potentially very damaging, publicity (Gonzalez-Herrero and Pratt, 1998; Lehrman, 1986).

Findings reveal some evidence of reluctance on the part of the tourism industry in the past to accept the possibility of crisis and prepare for it. Actual and potential hazards facing tourists have tended to be downplayed because of fears about adverse media coverage and commercial losses. For example, a Pacific Asia Travel Association (PATA) survey undertaken in 1991 disclosed that only a minority of members included crisis management in strategic planning, despite the 40% chance of them facing a crisis (Cassedy, 1991). The formulation and execution of crisis management strategies do not seem to have become universal in the intervening years (Prideaux, 2003) and plans that do exist have their limitations (de Sausmarez, 2003; Drabek, 1995).

However, the major tourism crises experienced recently and described in this book are leading to a re-assessment of attitudes toward crisis management planning and the topic is now taken more seriously within the tourism industry. It is being allocated a much higher priority with a search for flexible plans which strike a balance between being too precise and overly generic and are capable of accommodating envisaged scenarios.

Summary and Conclusions

Crises and their management are thus matters of great importance generally and with specific reference to tourism. Tourism crises display a striking diversity and have a variety of causes founded in economic, political, socio-cultural, environmental, technological and corporate domains. Patterns of evolution differ in terms of speed and the duration of each crisis stage and consequences are felt at multiple levels of industry and geographical area, with corresponding contrasts in gravity. It appears that the tourism industry is susceptible to crisis, with defining qualities which set it apart from other industries, and that the incidence of crisis will intensify.

Knowledge about crises and preparing for them is advancing and those responsible have perhaps more information at their disposal than ever before to assist in decision and policy making. However, despite the enlarged body of literature devoted to theoretical and more practical themes, there is still a lack of quantitative and qualitative data about the extent, composition and effectiveness of formal crisis management planning within the tourism industry.

Opportunities for research are likely to grow as both crises and crisis management activity increase. Avenues for further study are discussed in the final chapter of this book, which also returns to questions of the efficacy of tourism crisis management plans. Nevertheless, it is hoped that the following chapters on the separate domains of crisis will contribute to an improved understanding of the reasons underlying tourism crises, the ensuing results and processes of resolution.

Concept Definitions

- Crisis: A situation in which an individual or organization is faced with the prospect of fundamental change, usually sudden and unforeseen, which threatens to disrupt and overturn prevailing philosophies and practices.
- Crisis management: Preparing for and managing the process of crisis from inception to resolution with the primary objective of minimizing damage.

- Tourism crisis: Circumstances in which tourists and members of the tourism industry individually or collectively, including destinations, are faced with change which is potentially destructive for every, or certain, parties.
- Tourism crisis management: Planning for and managing tourism crises in order to protect the interests of the industry, tourists and other stakeholders involved and contain any long-term damage.
- The tourism industry: The public and private organizations which provide tourist products and services, market them and deal with development and planning.

Review Questions

1. What are the main causes of tourism crises?
2. How can tourism crises be classified?
3. Is tourism more prone to crisis than other industries?
4. What are the main stages in the evolution of crises in general?
5. Do tourism crises always conform to the general pattern of evolution?
6. What are the most important components of a tourism crisis management plan?
7. Could a tourism crisis management plan prevent an industry crisis occurring?

Additional Readings

Beirman, D. (2003). *Restoring tourism destinations in crisis: A strategic marketing approach*. Wallingford: CABI Publishing.

Faulkner, B. (2001). Towards a framework for tourism disaster management. *Tourism Management, 22*, 134–147.

Glaesser, D. (2005). *Crisis management in the tourism industry* (2nd ed.). Oxford: Butterworth-Heinemann.

Ritchie, B.W. (2004). Chaos, crises and disasters: A strategic approach to crisis management. *Tourism Management, 25*(6), 669–683.

References

Aktas, G. and Gunlu, E.A. (2005). Crisis management in tourist destinations. In W.F. Theobald (Ed.), *Global tourism* (3rd ed., pp. 440–457). Amsterdam: Elsevier.

Barton, L. (2001). *Crisis in organizations II*. Cincinnati: South-Western College.

Beirman, D. (2003). *Restoring tourism destinations in crisis: A strategic marketing approach*. Wallingford: CABI Publishing.

Blaikie, P., Cannon, T., Davis, I., and Wisner, B. (1994). *At risk: Natural hazards, people's vulnerability and disasters*. London: Routledge.

Bland, M. (1998). *Communicating out of a crisis*. Basingstoke: Macmillan Business.

Booth, S.A. (1993). *Crisis management strategy: Competition and change in modern enterprises*. London and New York: Routledge.

Brecher, M. (1978). A theoretical approach to international crisis behavior. *Jerusalem Journal of International Relations, 3*(2–3), 5–24.

Brewton, C. (1987). Managing a crisis: A model for the lodging industry. *The Cornell Hotel and Restaurant Administration Quarterly, 28*(3), 10–15.

Bull, A. (1998). *The economics of travel and tourism* (2nd ed.). Melbourne: Addison Wesley Longman.

Burling, W.K. and Hyle, A. (1997). Disaster preparedness planning policy and leadership issues. *Disaster Prevention and Management, 64*, 234–244.

Cassedy, K. (1991). *Crisis management planning in the travel and tourism industry: A study of three destination cases and a crisis management planning manual.* San Francisco: Pacific Asia Travel Association.

Cushnahan, G. (2004). Crisis management in small-scale tourism. *Journal of Travel and Tourism Marketing, 15*(4), 323–338.

de Sausmarez, N. (2003). Malaysia's response to the Asian financial crisis: Implications for tourism and sectoral crisis management. *Journal of Travel and Tourism Marketing, 15*(4), 217–231.

Doeg, C. (1995). *Crisis management in the food and drinks industry.* London: Chapman and Hall.

Drabek, T.E. (1995). Disaster responses within the tourism industry. *International Journal of Mass Emergencies and Disasters, 13*(1), 7–23.

Evans, N. and Elphick, S. (2005). Models of crisis management: An evaluation of their value for strategic planning in the international travel industry. *International Journal of Tourism Research, 7*, 135–150.

Faulkner, B. (2001). Towards a framework for tourism disaster management. *Tourism Management, 22*, 134–147.

Faulkner, B. and Russell, R. (1997). Chaos and complexity in tourism: In search of a new perspective. *Pacific Tourism Review, 1*, 93–102.

Fink, S. (1986). *Crisis management.* New York: American Association of Management.

Glaesser, D. (2005). *Crisis management in the tourism industry* (2nd ed.). Oxford: Butterworth-Heinemann.

Gonzalez-Herrero, A.G. and Pratt, C.B. (1998). Marketing crisis in tourism: Communication strategies in the United States and Japan. *Public Relations Review, 24*(1), 83–97.

Harvard Business School. (2004). *Harvard business essentials: Crisis management: Master the skills to prevent disasters.* Boston: Harvard Business School.

Heath, R. (1998). *Crisis management for managers and executives: Business crisis: The definitive handbook to reduction, readiness, response and recovery.* London: Financial Times Publishing.

Henderson, J.C. (1999). Tourism management and the Southeast Asian economic and environmental crisis: A Singapore perspective. *Managing Leisure, 4*, 107–120.

Hermann, C.F. (1972). *International crises: Insights from behavior research.* New York: The Free Press.

Kash, T.J. and Darling, J. (1998). Crisis management: Prevention, diagnosis and intervention. *Leadership and Organization Development Journal, 19*(4), 179–186.

Keown-McMullan, C. (1997). Crisis: When does a molehill become a mountain? *Disaster Prevention and Management, 6*(1), 4–10.

Kotler, P., Bowen, J., and Makens, J. (1999). *Marketing for hospitality and tourism* (2nd ed.). New York: Prentice Hall.

Krippendorf, J. (1987). *The holidaymakers: Understanding the impact of leisure and travel.* London: Heinemann.

Lagadec, P. (1993). *Preventing chaos in a crisis: Strategies for prevention control and damage limitation.* London: McGraw-Hill.

Laws, E., Faulkner, B., and Moscardo, G. (1998). *Embracing and managing change in tourism.* London: Routledge.

Laye, J. (2002). *Avoiding disaster: How to keep your business going when catastrophe strikes.* New York: Wiley.

Lehrman, C.K. (1986). When fact and fantasy collide: Crisis management in the travel industry. *Public Relations Journal, 41*(4), 25–28.

Levitt, A.M. (1997). *Disaster planning and recovery: A guide for facility professionals.* New York: John Wiley.

McKercher, B. (1999). A chaos approach to tourism. *Tourism Management, 20,* 425–434.

Meyers, G.C. (1986). *When it hits the fan: Managing the nine crises of business.* New York: Mentor.

Mitroff, I. (2004). *Crisis leadership: Planning for the unthinkable.* New York: Wiley.

Nankervis, A. (2000). Dreams and realities: Vulnerability and the tourism industry in Southeast Asia: A framework for analyzing and adapting tourism management toward 2000. In K.S. Chon (Ed.), *Tourism in Southeast Asia: A new direction* (pp. 49–63). New York: Haworth Hospitality Press.

Ogrizek, M. and Guillery, J.M. (1999). *Communicating in a crisis.* New York: Aldine de Gruyter.

PATA. (2003). *Crisis: It won't happen to us.* Bangkok: Pacific Asia Travel Association.

Pauchant, T.C. and Mitroff, I. (1992). *Transforming the crisis-prone organization: Preventing individual, organizational and environmental tragedies.* San Francisco: Jossey-Bass.

Pottorff, S.M. and Neal, D.M. (1994). Marketing implications for post-disaster tourism destinations. *Journal of Travel and Tourism Marketing, 3*(1), 115–122.

Prideaux, B. (2003). The need to use disaster planning frameworks to respond to major tourism disasters: Analysis of Australia's response to tourism disasters in 2001. *Journal of Travel and Tourism Marketing, 3*(1), 281–298.

Prideaux, B., Laws, E., and Faulkner, B. (2003). Events in Indonesia: Exploring the limits to formal tourism trends forecasting methods in complex crisis situations. *Tourism Management, 24,* 475–487.

Regester, M. and Larkin, J. (1998). *Risk issues and crisis management: A casebook of best practice.* London: Kogan Page.

Ritchie, B.W. (2004). Chaos, crises and disasters: A strategic approach to crisis management. *Tourism Management, 25*(6), 669–683.

Santana, G. (2001). Global safety and national security. In S. Wahab and C. Cooper (Eds.), *Tourism in the age of globalization* (pp. 213–241). London: Routledge.

Santana, G. (2004). Crisis management and tourism: Beyond the rhetoric. In C.M. Hall, D.J. Timothy, and D.T. Duval (Eds.), *Safety and security in tourism: Relationships, management and marketing* (pp. 299–322). New York: Haworth Press.

Seymour, M. and Moore, S. (2000). *Effective crisis management: Worldwide principles and practice*. London: Cassell.

Shiva, R.S. (2000). *Corporate crisis management: Challenges for survival*. Thousand Oaks: Sage.

Shrivastava, P. and Mitroff, I. (1987, Spring). Strategic management of corporate crises. *Columbia Journal of World Business*, 5–11.

Smith, D. (1990). Beyond contingency planning: Towards a model of crisis management. *Industrial Crisis Quarterly*, 4, 263–275.

Smith, D. and Sipika, C. (1993). Back from the brink: Post crisis management. *Long Range Planning*, 261, 23–28.

ten Berg, D. (1990). *The first 24 hours: A comprehensive guide to successful crisis communications*. Oxford: Basil Blackwell.

Tourism Concern. (2005). Campaigns. Tourism Concern website at http://www. tourismconcern.org.uk/, accessed 21 November 2005.

Turner, B.A. (1976). The organizational and inter-organizational development of disasters. *Administrative Science Quarterly*, 21, 378–397.

van Waldbeek, B. (2005). What else can go wrong? Hospitality Net-Article. Hospitality net website at http://www.hospitalitynet.org, accessed 29 August 2005.

Weaver, D. and Lawton, L. (2002). *Tourism management*. Sydney: Wiley.

Wilks, J., Pendergast, D., and Leggat, P. (Eds.). (2005). *Tourism in turbulent times: Towards safe experience for visitors*. Oxford: Elsevier.

WTO. (1996). *Tourist safety and security: Practical measures for destinations*. Madrid: World Tourism Organization.

WTO. (1999). *Tourism 2020 vision: Executive summary updated*. Madrid: World Tourism Organization.

WTO. (2002). *Tourism after 11 September 2001: Analysis, remedial actions and prospects*. Madrid: World Tourism Organization.

WTO. (2005). *Tourism highlights. Edition 2004*. Madrid: World Tourism Organization.

WTO and WMO. (1998). World Tourism Organization and World Meteorological Organization. *Handbook on natural disaster reduction in tourist areas*. Madrid: World Tourism Organization.

2

Economic Tourism Crises

By the end of the chapter, the reader should be able to

- Appreciate some of the important connections between economics and tourism of relevance to tourism crises and their management.
- Understand how economic changes in generating and destination countries may create conditions of crisis for the tourism industry.
- Recognize how tourism's economic impacts can be a primary or secondary cause of crises.
- Identify the means by which the likelihood of a tourism crisis related to economics can be reduced and appropriate actions to take should such a crisis occur.

Introduction

Economics is a key influence on both the demand for tourism and supply of facilities and services. Economic circumstances in generating and receiving countries help to shape flows of tourists and their spending patterns and the nature and speed of development, which also react to general economic movements. Such economic forces may operate to create both opportunities and problems for the tourism industry, certain of the latter having the potential to evolve into a crisis.

Tourism crises of an economic origin are discussed in this chapter, which examines tourism's vulnerability to economic conditions in the wider environment and approaches to alleviating any damage arising from these conditions. Attention is also given to how the economic impacts of tourism may themselves be a cause or catalyst of crises and measures that can be adopted to lessen the risk of these occurring. Case studies at the end of the chapter explain how outbound tourism from Japan has been damaged by economic uncertainty and describe the repercussions of the 1997 Asian financial crisis for tourist activity, both indicative of the linkages which connect tourism and economics.

The Economics of Tourism

Characteristics of local, national and international economies and any alterations in them exercise a crucial influence on the tourism industry (Bull, 1998) which has its own internal economic dynamics (Lundberg et al., 1995). Depending on the nature of change, it will stimulate or depress demand in source markets and make destinations more or less attractive regarding prices and products. Costs of travel and perceptions of these costs, as well as an individual's financial position, also play an important part in vacation decisions. The health of an economy additionally helps to determine resources available for investment at home and abroad in the transport, accommodation and attractions sectors which are essential to tourism. Business travel too benefits from the heightened trading which is generated by economic progress (Davidson and Cope, 2003).

Income is a key variable of levels of participation in leisure tourism and there appears to be a close relationship between economic prosperity and a buoyant market. This was evident during the years following the Second World War in the West when rises in personal disposable income allowed lower and middle income groups to spend more on tourism than ever before. Destination choices expanded from nearby locations to more distant centers with a corresponding shift from national to intra-regional and then inter-regional travel (Murphy, 1985). Such a trend was later apparent amongst the Asian "tiger" economies of Korea, Taiwan and Singapore and is now spreading to other countries experiencing development. Affluent middle classes of consumers are emerging, notably in China which has seen rapid expansion in domestic and international tourism fueled by its exceptional economic achievements (Zhang et al., 2000).

However, economic downturn can undermine demand and possibly result in crises for industries in origin and destination countries if the slump is sufficiently intense or prolonged. The recession of the 1990s on the US mainland contributed to a decline in Hawaii's tourism from 1990 to 1993, and Japan's economic difficulties had adverse consequences for its outbound tourism in the same decade, including travel to Hawaii (see Case One). Deterioration in the global economy at the end of the twentieth century was considered partly responsible for a slowing down in worldwide tourism, recovery believed to be driven partly by the economic cycle. At the same time, domestic industries can gain from these reversals as it seems that many tourists choose less expensive options and remain closer to home when anxious about monetary and employment matters. Such a pattern of response suggests the importance of drawing tourists from a range of overseas markets, rather than relying on only a few, together with the need for domestic promotion.

It should also be noted that much of the world's population is debarred from tourism because of poverty, although there may be great disparities in income distribution with the presence of a wealthy elite of international travelers in the poorest of countries. A less advanced stage of development does not preclude countries from receiving visitors, but a certain amount of finance is required to permit the construction and maintenance of the necessary tourism infrastructure. One reason the African continent as a whole has been prevented from reaching its tourism potential is the parlous state of the economy (Christie and Crompton, 2001) and similar barriers apply in parts of Central and South America and Asia. An absence of funds and uncertain investment climate could lead to a crisis for the tourism industry, compounded by the political and social tensions that frequently accompany economic turbulence.

Government economic programs and fiscal policies can impinge on travel behavior and the operation of the industry directly and indirectly, not least in the arena of taxation. The World Travel and Tourism Council (WTTC) uses the four indices of car rental, lodging, meals and air passenger charges to monitor taxes levied. It claims that these have steadily increased around the world in recent years (WTTC, 2002) and cities with the highest rates are depicted in Table 2.1. There are also departure taxes applicable to all modes of transport and visa fees are another official

Table 2.1: **Highest taxation rates in selected cities**

Barometer	City	Tax rate (as % of overall costs)
Car rental		
	Vienna	33.22
	Brussels	32.90
	London	30.08
Lodging		
	Copenhagen	20.00
	Buenos Aries	17.35
	New Delhi	16.67
Meals		
	Copenhagen	20.00
	Stockholm	20.00
	Mumbai	19.03
Airport		
	Miami	7.66
	Los Angeles	6.95
	San Francisco	5.19
Total		
	Copenhagen	24.25
	London	21.26
	Vienna	20.65
	Brussels	20.17
	Miami	19.51

Source: WTTC, 2002.

revenue earner. Such financial burdens are opposed by commercial practitioners and destination marketers who argue that they project a poor image, alienate visitors and may undermine the financial viability of tourism enterprises (Lipman, 1997). Their sudden imposition and deficiencies in administration can be disruptive and there is scope for corrupt practices in certain instances.

Currency Rates and Controls

Currency values and their fluctuation are an additional determinant of tourist trends and investment. Substantial alterations are felt by tourists and reflected in the prices charged by operators and agents with consequences for demand. An exceptionally strong currency may deter inbound visitors but encourage outbound travel, as demonstrated by Switzerland, where the hotel industry confronted a crisis due to uncompetitive prices in the 1990s. Switzerland became an expensive destination for foreigners while its nationals were lured abroad to take advantage of their enhanced purchasing power there, accommodation occupancy levels declining as a result. Hotels were advised to be more creative and energetic in their marketing in order to regain lost market share and attract more mature travelers interested in escaping from the stresses of everyday life to the delights of an alpine environment (Marvel and Johnson, 1997). A markedly appreciating currency and prevailing notions of the costliness of locations are thus challenges for the tourism industry, which must strive to offset a drop in arrivals by stimulating greater expenditure among those who do elect to visit.

A currency which is falling dramatically in value does not inevitably boost arrivals and excessive volatility may deter investors and make tour operators and travel agents cautious about selling places thus afflicted. The Turkish lira depreciated by 70% over a few days at the beginning of 2001, but this did not have a favorable effect on inbound tourism and severely curtailed departures (Okumus et al., 2005). Brazil's 2002 currency crisis led to an overall contraction in inbound visitors, especially from other Latin American countries (Euromonitor, 2004) like Argentina where there was also economic and political turmoil. Visitors caught up in the chaos were seriously inconvenienced and tourists in Buenos Aries described being unable to cash travelers checks or use credit cards because of emergency banking measures intended to stem cash withdrawals. Surcharges were imposed and retailers raised prices in anticipation of a continuation in the collapse of the peso. Outbreaks of violence were reported (BBC News, 2002b), indicative of how economic anxieties can fuel broader unrest which might endanger tourist safety.

The Asian financial crisis and its aftermath have been well documented and the case provides insights into the complex dynamics of an economic tourism crisis initiated by currency volatility (see Case Two). Studies suggest different experiences and the presence of success factors which enabled some destinations to manage the crisis better than others. While at the heart of the economic turbulence, Thailand exhibited an ability to weather the storm attributable to its long-standing reputation as a tourist destination, range of attractions and amenities and intensive advertising. Indeed, the crisis was exploited as an opportunity to reposition Thailand as a country of nature-based, cultural and MICE (meetings, incentives, conferences and exhibitions) tourism rather than mass tourism coastal resorts. Indonesia lacked these advantages and the economic crisis there was a source of a social and political agitation, posing a more serious threat to tourism and impeding effective action and the pace of recovery (Henderson, 1999a).

The introduction of the euro as the common currency for most members of the European Commission in 2001 created a single market of 300 million residents who, alongside visitors, no longer had to worry about currency transactions when traveling within the euro zone. However, it was a threat to some destinations where a lack of price competitiveness was revealed by comparisons which were easier for tourists to make. There was negative publicity about struggles with software and price hikes, particularly in Italy, where it was reported that visitors had to pay more for public transport and museum admission. The adoption of the euro also meant a drastic loss of currency exchange business and a doubtful future for smaller scale providers of this service (BBC News, 2002a).

Official attempts to control balance of payments deficits may incorporate limits on money taken out of a country and the purchase of foreign currency. Some countries also enforce compulsory currency exchange, insisting that visitors convert a minimum sum of local currency and restricting amounts they can leave with. In an example of the former, an individual's foreign travel allowance was set at £50 in the UK in the late 1960s. The decision proved beneficial for the domestic industry and companies selling all-inclusive foreign package holidays (Holloway, 1998), but constrained aspects of independent international travel.

Escalating Costs

Certain sectors of the tourism industry are characterized by the intensity of competition which is often expressed in terms of price. Minimization of costs is therefore essential, and significant rises can precipitate crisis, especially if unexpected and beyond the control of management. This is demonstrated by rapidly rising oil prices, which have the capacity to slow down growth in global, domestic and tourism economies. Economic recession damages consumer and investor confidence in general and within the context of tourism, as already noted, while all businesses have to contend with higher fuel bills. Transport companies and especially airlines are likely to be among the worst hit with fuel accounting for between 10% and 20% of the latter's costs, the second highest after labor.

The issue acquired greater urgency when a surge in prices for crude oil added to the problems of airlines in the early years of the twenty-first century (see Boxed Case One). Business had already slumped because of terrorism, the Iraq war and the Severe Acute Respiratory Syndrome (SARS) virus which resulted in a number of airline bankruptcies worldwide and government intervention and financial aid

---

Boxed Case One: Rising Airline Fuel Costs

When fuel costs spiraled at the beginning of the current decade, certain airlines were in a stronger position than others. This partly depended on the extent of hedging, which is a term used to describe buying fuel in advance at a set rate. The practice does, however, carry the risk of prices falling below those agreed on.

European companies appeared to be better protected than others and also gained from the weakness of the US dollar, in which oil is traded, against the euro. British Airways had hedged 45% of its fuel needs for 2004 at US$28.50 a barrel and Lufthansa had covered 89% of its requirements for 2004 and 35% for 2005. Delta and Continental in the USA were reported not to have hedged for 2005; American Airlines had hedged 15% for the first quarter of 2005, reduced to 5% thereafter. The limited activity in the USA was attributed to a belief that excessively high oil prices would eventually drop, credit ratings which discouraged the purchase of oil on the futures market and a need for cash which had led to the disbanding of former hedging arrangements. The exception was Southwest, which had hedged 85% of its demands for 2005 at US$26.00 a barrel and a proportion in subsequent years up to 2009 as part of a long-term cost control strategy.

In response to the crisis, several companies started to hedge again and some waited in anticipation of a price fall while all tried to cut costs. A common reaction was the introduction of fuel surcharges which was supported by IATA and price hikes. Nevertheless, these surcharges could not apply to advance bookings and over capacity and intense rivalry among American carriers made it difficult for them to increase fares significantly compared to their European counterparts, although undercutting by budget carriers was a concern in the latter case. There were additional concerns about effects on demand.

Sources: Airwise News, 2005; Daniel, 2005; USA Today, 2004.

---

to prevent further collapses (BBC News, 2004). Oil, trading at US$30 a barrel at the start of 2004, reached US$50 in September with the Organization of Petroleum Export Countries (OPEC) talking about the possibility of US$80 by 2007. The International Air Transport Association (IATA) anticipated that these prices would lead to an overall loss of US$7.4 billion in 2005 as fuel bills doubled from 2003, "robbing the industry of a return to profitability" (IATA, 2005b).

Volatile oil prices seem set to continue, but the civil aviation industry appears to have learned lessons from recent experiences about the necessity of planning ahead and taking action to reduce exposure to escalating charges. These charges cannot always be passed on to customers in their entirety for fear of compounding the original crisis by alienating passengers and depressing demand. IATA also launched a "fuel action campaign" to help member airlines by promoting greater efficiency in fuel usage, a reduction in taxes and lower hedging costs (IATA, 2005a).

Tourism's Economic Impacts

The potential economic gains from tourism are widely recognized and a powerful rationale underlying growth strategies in many countries at differing stages of development. However, there are also negative economic outcomes (Dwyer et al., 2004; Mathieson and Wall, 1996; UNEP, 2002) which may precipitate crisis or play a part in its emergence. Major problems are outlined below and are particularly acute in the less-developed world, where several states may be looking to tourism to diversify their export base and earn hard currency, yet are not always able to secure these goals and are vulnerable to the hazards of over-dependence.

While income is generated by tourism, the public sector also has to spend in order to develop and support the industry. National and sub-national governments have responsibilities for the building and running of the necessary infrastructure, including communications and utilities such as water and power. They may also be providers of amenities like museums and parks and owners, or part owners, of transport companies. There are other less obvious areas of expenditure. Frechtling (1994, p. 395) identified life quality and fiscal costs borne by communities and officials which are depicted in Table 2.2. Such environmental damage must be factored into

Table 2.2: **Life quality and fiscal costs of tourism**

Life quality costs	Fiscal costs
Traffic congestion	Highway construction, police services, public transportation, port and terminal facilities
Crime	Police services, justice system
Fire emergencies	Fire protection
Water pollution	Water supply and sewage treatment
Air pollution	Police services, public transportation
Litter	Solid waste disposal, police services
Noise pollution	Police services, zoning
Destruction of wildlife	Police services, park and recreation facilities, forestry maintenance, fish and game regulation
Destruction of scenic beauty	Park and recreation facilities, police services
Destruction of social/cultural heritage	Maintenance of museums and historic sites, police services
Disease	Hospital and other health maintenance facilities, food service regulation
Vehicular accidents	Police services, justice system

Source: Frechtling, 1994. Reproduced with permission from the publishers, John Wiley & Sons, Inc.

any analysis which attempts to calculate the overall value of tourism for destinations (Tisdell, 2001).

There will be additional spending on administration, planning and marketing and authorities may offer an assortment of subsidies and rebates to developers and operators in a bid to win projects and investment. In some situations, host communities appear to be subsidizing tourism and this could provoke hostility which is aggravated when tourist demand inflates prices for goods and services. Land and property may become more expensive and perhaps exceed the reach of the local population. Outsiders from second home owners to foreign hotel developers are thus privileged at the expense of residents and these issues can be a matter of political contention, any disputes interfering with the functioning and prospects of the tourism industry.

As tourism grows so do the costs and more money leaves the economy to pay for imported equipment, materials, and goods as well as interest on loans. Design, consulting and management fees of external agencies may have to be paid and not all profits and salaries will be retained. Leakages are heaviest in smaller economies and the magnitude of multipliers too depends on the size of the economy, resources, access to supplies, diversity, import substitution possibilities, local skills and labor availability. When these aspects are unfavorable, multipliers may be extremely low and caution should be exercised about the priority allocated to tourism. There are also opportunity costs associated with tourism when it draws capital, land and labor away from other sectors. Traditional economic structures may thereby be weakened and social welfare projects deprived of funding, provoking criticism of tourism.

In less-developed countries, indigenous businesses may not possess the capital requirements for entry into parts of the tourism industry so that there is a reliance on foreign direct investment and multinational enterprises. These companies are often based in tourist generating countries and in a position to exercise considerable control. Such economic relationships can erode the authority of local decision makers and the profitability of the private sector, leaving residents feeling excluded and alienated. Enclave tourism typifies these tensions with its self-contained resorts designed so that guests do not have to leave the compound, restricting their contribution to the surrounding formal and informal economies. These economic impacts can incite animosity which has the potential to erupt into crisis, especially if reinforced by social and political grievances.

Tourism employment is another controversial matter and its merits have been questioned due to work which is largely low skilled and poorly paid. Other limitations relate to unsociable hours, seasonality and seasonal unemployment, inflows of migrant labor and workforce displacement. Nationals in less-developed countries also are likely to occupy menial posts while expatriates are found in management positions; this also means the drain of their salaries being remitted home. Strikes over pay are rare among hotels, especially in the Third World, but there was an example in Cambodia in 2004 (see Boxed Case Two). In another unusual case, three aggrieved employees set fire to a hotel in San Juan, Puerto Rico, on New Year's Eve 1986, killing 98, to protest against their low wages and working conditions. Inequalities of income between tourists and those who serve them are symptomatic

Boxed Case Two: Striking Over Pay

An international hotel management company included two luxury properties in Cambodia among its portfolio. Staff from both hotels first went on strike at the end of 2003 and industrial action continued into 2004 in a dispute over the 10% service charge levied on customer bills. Workers wanted to receive the money thus collected directly whereas the hotel management preferred distributing it indirectly through set monthly allowances and meals and training. Cambodian law required that employees receive the service charge, but did not specify in what manner and the issue had become a cause of disagreement between local unions and foreign hotels in particular.

Two judges ruled the strikes illegal in April and the company sacked about 300 personnel who were participating. However, other judges found in favor of the workers and an Arbitration Council later advised that those who had been dismissed should be re-employed. There were demands for a boycott from the Cambodian Tourism and Services Workers Federation (CTSWF) which was supported by international unions and labor agencies. Protestors, sometimes as many as 200, gathered regularly outside the hotels and a loss of business was reported. For example, the US Embassy changed its plans to hold a July 4 reception at one hotel and the other was closed for much of April.

Press articles commented on the extent of poverty in a country where 45% of the population existed on US$1 per day with government estimating that a family needed an average monthly income of US$300 and US$200 in order to live comfortably in the capital and other areas, respectively. Average monthly salaries at the hotels were said to be US$160 and US$210, but the CTSWF argued that some staff were paid only US$1 or US$2 daily. Guest rates for a double room ranged from US$176 to US$276 in 2004. A representative of the company claimed its actions were legal and that "we just need to step out and walk the streets to be reminded what wonderful employment it is to work in a hotel."

A settlement was reached between the company and CTSWF in September 2004 when it was agreed that 60% of those sacked would be reinstated and receive 75% of their salaries for the previous six months. Others had found alternative employment, but would get redundancy pay. The agreement was to last one year and the service charge question had still to be resolved by the Labor Ministry.

Sources: Asian Labour News, 2004; Associated Press, 2004; Dow Jones, 2004; Far Eastern Economic Review, 2004; New Frontiers, 2004.

of the gulf which can separate visitors and residents, disparities which may lead to crises of a socio-economic nature if inappropriately managed.

Addressing the Problem of Adverse Economic Impacts

Tourism can make a positive difference to economies of contrasting size and character, but there are also constraints which destination authorities need to acknowledge. Plus, it may not be the best solution to economic problems or the most suitable vehicle for general development. A heavy reliance on tourism could lead to economic weaknesses, so an effort must be made to integrate it into a wider economic program which incorporates diversification. These imperatives are more pressing in less-developed countries which are striving to overcome what is often a relationship of dependency on wealthy tourist markets (Harrison, 2001).

There are, however, signs of movement in the direction of achieving more equitable relations between Third World governments and the international tourism industry. Some of the former now insist that hotel companies from overseas purchase a specific amount of materials locally, hire a proportion of local labor, train a number of these employees for management positions, contribute to an improved infrastructure and donate to natural and cultural heritage conservation schemes (Kusluvan and Karamustafa, 2001). Such undertakings may be a prerequisite to gain approval to do business, but organizations should be prepared to take these actions voluntarily and exercise corporate social responsibility which incorporates a "triple bottom line" of environmental, social and economic returns (Zadek, 2002).

The efficacy of tourism taxation remains debatable. It can be both a factor underlying crisis and a possible remedy. The WTTC has campaigned against fiscal measures that harm the competitiveness of the industry, calling for participation by the private sector in tax policy formation. Nevertheless, there is support for the principle that those who enjoy a product or service should pay for it (Lipman, 1997).

A similar argument can be applied to meeting the expense of environmental pollution and other damage caused by tourism, acceptance of these obligations by tourists and the tourism industry providing useful funding and helping to avert local opposition to tourism. The industry can also seek to communicate the many economic advantages of tourism to communities, interest groups and politicians; this is especially important in circumstances in which development might be fiercely resisted. Adopting such a measure and the others noted above could assist in the amelioration of some of tourism's negative economic outcomes, frustrating the evolution of crises connected to the costs of tourism and criticism of these costs.

Summary and Conclusions

Participation in tourism and public and private sector activity is closely related to prevailing economic circumstances in countries which generate and receive visitors. Economic growth stimulates demand and new investment, but its absence may result in crises for outbound and inbound industries. Tourism development can itself harm economies, especially those of less-developed nations, and such repercussions may trigger crises. External economic structures and processes are beyond the control of the tourism industry which can only react to changes which occur, although some can be anticipated and planned for. In comparison, appropriate measures can help to minimize economic disruption due to tourism and thereby lessen the intensity of related crises or avoid those which might otherwise evolve.

Case One: The Japanese Outbound Market in the 1990s

Japan saw substantial growth in overseas travel after government restrictions were relaxed in the 1960s. International outbound travelers increased from approximately 2.5 million in 1975 to just under five million in 1985, over 10 million in 1990, and 16.7 million in 1996. The main factors accounting for this strong upward trend were greater prosperity, more leisure time, and the availability of package tours. Expenditure also rose at a corresponding rate to produce what has been described as one of the most spectacular success stories of the modern tourist era, the volume of Japanese tourists and their high per capita spend attracting the attention of many destination marketers.

The onset of recession and a decline in value of the yen started to have an impact by the middle of the 1990s, and over 40% of respondents cited costs as a barrier to international travel in a 1995 Japan Travel Bureau survey. As the Asian financial crisis unfolded, the Japanese economy deteriorated further with problems in the banking sector, fluctuating stock exchange prices and unemployment. Tourism figures, already showing much slower growth, responded by entering a decline for the first time in 20 years. Numbers fell from 16.8 million in 1997 to 15.8 million in 1998 and travel agency bankruptcies rose by about 40%. An official of the All Nippon Travel Agents Association described the industry as a casualty of the economic situation, with the emergence of a new type of budget traveler who was looking for value for money and likely to travel independently rather than in the traditionally organized tour group. Japan did, however, manage to retain its third position in the list of the world's top 40 tourism spenders in 1997, even though expenditure had shrunk by over 10% compared to 1996. Nevertheless, the yen lost a third of its value in US dollar terms between 1995 and 1997.

These trends were of concern to many centers which were heavily reliant on Japanese tourists such as Hawaii where they comprised two-thirds of the eastbound visitors on which tourism, and the economy as a whole, depended. Japan's faltering economy and stagnation in demand caused a revision of forecasts and reassessment of the segment's significance, prompting diversification with regard to new markets and products. The Bank of Hawaii recommended stressing the state's function as a center for business and conferences, exploiting its location and access to other Asian Pacific and Latin American markets.

Sources: Bank of Hawaii, 2003; JNTO, 1999; JTB, 1999.

Case Two: The Asian Financial Crisis

The Asian financial crisis was centered on South East Asia and had its origins in a combination of factors which included structural economic weaknesses, inappropriate government policies and global liquidity problems. Difficulties started in Thailand, which devalued its currency in the middle of 1997 and asked for help from the International Monetary Fund, and quickly spread to neighboring countries. Currencies declined sharply, Indonesia's losing 70% of its value against the US dollar with a figure of 40% in the case of Malaysia and Thailand. There was also intense speculation on stock markets and recessions ensued. The stronger economies of Hong Kong, Singapore, South Korea and Taiwan were not spared and there was a general erosion of confidence. Many investors in the region decided to withdraw funds and postponed planned investment or channeled it elsewhere. Excessive economic volatility was followed by mounting unemployment, rising prices and business failures. Such conditions were accompanied by social disturbances and some political unrest, notably in Indonesia, and all of these developments had consequences for tourism.

Unprecedented exchange rates were attractive to some long-haul visitors from countries unaffected by the economic turmoil, but travel within the region declined sharply. Asian Pacific countries as a whole recorded a fall in arrivals and spending from within and outside the region by the end of 1997. There were exceptions to the trend; Thailand and South Korea, for example, reported an expansion in volume. Nevertheless, income generated was disappointing when converted into US dollars. The spending power and confidence of Asian consumers, who traditionally account for about 75% of the region's tourists, had been badly hit by the crisis which depressed their demand for travel. The slight growth seen in European and North American arrivals in some destinations was unable to offset the contraction of the regional market.

Economic uncertainty inhibited tourism investment and planning by both public and private sectors. Financial constraints delayed existing and new projects, some of which were abandoned. There were doubts about the survival of some businesses and a number of hotels chose to charge in US dollars so that guests were denied the advantages of lower prices due to weak currencies. Events attracted widespread media coverage around the world and several stories were devoted to the social and political tensions associated with economic collapse. Such material served to communicate negative images and a sense of risk.

There was a common pattern of response to the crisis by tourism industries and authorities, although circumstances did differ from country to country. Emphasis was given particularly to increased domestic and international promotion. Attempts were made at innovation in pursuit of a more diversified product offering and wider market. However, National Tourism Organizations (NTOs) found that the purchasing power of their budgets was substantially reduced outside Asia and therefore explored possibilities of partnerships and greater private sponsorship. The financial allocation of marketers was cut in some cases and they had to cope with this alongside rationalization of air services due to declining passenger traffic, higher accommodation costs and a heavier taxation burden on tourists.

There had been some discussion at the height of the financial crisis about whether it was the beginning of the disintegration of the world economy due to a contagion effect, but such dire forecasts were not realized. Conditions were more ordered by mid-1998 and economies were expanding again by 1999. Most of the tourist destinations which had been hit were also returning to normality and actually drawing more international arrivals than they had been prior to the onset of the crisis. Nevertheless, tourism was revealed to be very vulnerable to economic change and its full recovery was also dependent upon economic improvement. Confidence in the region as a whole had been badly shaken and the crisis had a lingering impact.

Sources: de Sausmarez, 2003; Henderson, 1999a, 1999b and 1999c; Muqbil, 1998; Prideaux, 1999; Roubino, 2002; WTO, 1999.

Concept Definitions

- Economic tourism crisis: A crisis for the tourism industry which arises from economic changes within the tourism system or wider economy.
- Tourism economic impacts: The consequences of tourism for a destination economy.
- Over-dependence: A situation in which destinations are economically reliant on the tourism industry.
- Tourism taxation: Taxes levied on individual tourists and the tourism industry which can be both general charges and those specific to tourism.
- Leakages: Money flowing out of a destination economy in assorted forms in order to develop and maintain inbound tourism.

Review Questions

1. How might demand for tourism be adversely affected by economic movements?
2. Why might economic conditions in destination countries result in tourism crises?
3. Which economic impacts of tourism could result in a crisis for the industry?
4. Can the industry exercise any control over crises which owe their origins to developments in the wider economy?

5. What steps can destination authorities take to reduce the likelihood of a crisis related to tourism's damaging economic consequences?
6. In what ways was the slowdown in Japanese outbound travel a potential crisis for some tourist destinations?
7. What does the Asian financial crisis reveal about the relationship between economics and tourism?

Additional Readings

Dwyer, L., Forsyth, P., and Spurr, R. (2004). Evaluating tourism's economic effects: New and old approaches. *Tourism Management*, *25*, 307–317.

Muqbil, I. (1998). The fall-out from the Asian economic crises. *Travel and Tourism Analyst*, *6*, 78–95.

UNEP. (2002). Economic impacts of tourism. UNEP website at http://www.uneptie. org, accessed 11 March 2005.

References

Airwise News. (2005). European airlines review hedging as oil prices rise. Airwise News website at http://news.airwise.com, accessed 28 March 2005.

Asian Labour News. (2004). Cambodia: Staff woes at Raffles hotels in Cambodia drag on. Asian Labour News website at http://www.asianlabour.org, accessed 18 March 2005.

Associated Press. (2004, 17 August). Hotel workers in Cambodia jobless over claim to tips. Associated Press Newswires.

Bank of Hawaii. (2003). Hawaii Annual Economic Report. Bank of Hawaii website at http://www.boh.com, accessed 23 March 2005.

BBC News. (2002a, 10 January). Tourist gripes in Italy. BBC News website at http://www.bbc.co.uk, accessed 15 March 2005.

BBC News. (2002b, 11 January). Unwitting victims of crisis. BBC News website at http://www.bbc.co.uk, accessed 15 March 2005.

BBC News. (2004, 7 June). Oil prices to hit airline profits. BBC News website at http://newsvote.bbc.co.uk, accessed 28 March 2005.

Bull, A. (1998). *The economics of travel and tourism*. Melbourne: Addison Wesley Longman.

Christie, I.T. and Crompton, D.E. (2001). *Tourism in Africa*. World Bank Working Paper. New York: World Bank.

Daniel, C. (2005, 25 March). From Financial Times. Economist Intelligence Unit Executive Briefing. EIU Client Access website at http://db.eiu.com, accessed 28 March 2005.

Davidson, R. and Cope, B. (2003). *Business travel*. London: Pearson.

de Sausmarez, N. (2003). Malaysia's response to the Asian financial crisis: Implications for tourism and sectoral crisis management. *Journal of Travel and Tourism Marketing*, *15*(4), 217–231.

Dow Jones. (2004, 7 May). Raffles Cambodia staff OK deal. Dow Jones Newswires.

Dwyer, L., Forsyth, P., and Spurr, R. (2004). Evaluating tourism's economic effects: New and old approaches. *Tourism Management, 25,* 307–317.

Euromonitor. (2004). *Travel and tourism in Brazil.* London: Euromonitor.

Far Eastern Economic Review. (2004, 8 July). Raffles Cambodia campaign bites.

Frechtling, D.C. (1994). Assessing the impacts of travel and tourism: Measuring economic costs. In J.R. Brent Ritchie (Ed.), *Travel, tourism and hospitality research: A handbook for managers and researchers* (pp. 393–402). New York: Wiley.

Harrison, D. (Ed.). (2001). *Tourism and the less developed world: Issues and cases.* New York: CABI.

Henderson, J.C. (1999a). Southeast Asian tourism and the financial crisis: Indonesia and Thailand compared. *Current Issues in Tourism, 2*(4), 294–303.

Henderson, J.C. (1999b). The Asian financial crisis and tourism. *Insights, 7*(January), A99–A105.

Henderson, J.C. (1999c). Tourism management and the Southeast Asian economic and environmental crisis: A Singapore perspective. *Managing Leisure, 4,* 107–120.

Holloway, C. (1998). *The business of tourism.* London: Longman.

IATA. (2005a). Fuel action campaign. International Air Transport Association Information sheet. IATA website at http://www.iata.org/pressroom, accessed 1 December 2005.

IATA. (2005b, 12 September). US$7.4 billion losses for global aviation in 2005. International Air Transport Association Press release, 26. IATA website at http://www.iata.org/pressroom, accessed 1 December 2005.

JNTO. (1999). Statistics. Japan National Tourism Organization. JNTO website at www.jnto.go.jp, accessed 23 July 1999.

JTB. (1999). *All about Japanese overseas travelers.* Tokyo: Japan Travel Bureau.

Kusluvan, G. and Karamustafa, K. (2001). Multinational hotel development in developing countries. *International Journal of Tourism Research, 3,* 179–197.

Lipman, G.H. (1997). Rethinking travel and tourism tax policy. *WTTC's Travel & Tourism Tax Barometer, 4,* 8–16.

Lundberg, D.E., Krishnamoorthy, M., and Stavenga, M.H. (1995). *Tourism economics.* New York: Wiley.

Marvel, M. and Johnson, C. (1997). A crisis of currency or creativity? Problems and prospects for the Swiss hotel industry. *International Journal of Hospitality Management, 16*(3), 279–288.

Mathieson, A. and Wall, G. (1996). *Tourism: Economic, physical and social impacts.* London: Longman.

Muqbil, I. (1998). The fall-out from the Asian economic crises. *Travel and Tourism Analyst, 6,* 78–95.

Murphy, P. (1985). *Tourism: A community approach.* New York and London: Methuen.

New Frontiers. (2004). Raffles Hotel gives in to workers. *New Frontiers, 10*(5), 5.

Okumus, F., Altinay, M., and Arasli, H. (2005). The impact of Turkey's economic crisis of February 2001 on the tourism industry in Northern Cyprus. *Tourism Management, 26,* 95–104.

Prideaux, B. (1999). Tourism perspectives on the Asian financial crisis. *Current Issues in Tourism, 2*(4), 279–293.

Roubino, N. (2002). Global macroeconomic and financial policy site: The Asian crisis. http://pages.stern.nyu.edu/~nroubini/asia, accessed 7 November 2002.

Tisdell, C.A. (Ed.). (2001). *Tourism economics, the environment and development: Analysis and policy.* Northampton, MA: Edward Elgar.

UNEP. (2002). Economic impacts of tourism. United Nations Economic Programme. UNEP website at http://www.uneptie.org, accessed 11 March 2005.

USA Today. (2004, 10 December). Airlines hike fares, brace for turbulence as oil prices soar USA Today website at http://www.usatoday.com, accessed 28 March 2005.

WTO. (1999). *Impacts of the financial crisis on Asia's tourism sector.* Madrid: World Tourism Organization.

WTTC. (2002). *World travel and tourism tax barometer.* London: World Travel and Tourism Council.

Zadek, S. (2002). Third generation corporate citizenship. AccountAbility website at www.accountability.org.uk, accessed 2 August 2005.

Zhang, G., Pine, R., and Hanqin, Q.Z. (2000). China's international tourism development: Present and future. *International Journal of Contemporary Hospitality Management, 12*(5), 282–290.

3

Political Tourism Crises

Learning Objectives

By the end of the chapter, the reader should be able to

- Appreciate the close relationship between politics and tourism.
- Understand how political cultures, conditions and developments affect tourism and can be a source of crises for the industry.
- Recognize different types of political instability, their consequences and significance as causes of crises.
- Identify and evaluate tools for dealing with politically inspired tourism crises.

Introduction

This chapter is concerned with the political domain of tourism crises and begins with a brief summary of selected aspects of the relationship between politics and tourism, including the role of government in tourism policy making. These aspects have implications for tourism crises as governments may be authors of crises in addition to key actors in their management and resolution. Forms of political instability are then identified and their capacity to precipitate tourism crises is discussed, using a variety of illustrations from around the world. Possible responses to difficult circumstances are finally reviewed, but the industry is shown to have little control over adverse political forces. Case studies at the end of the chapter describe political circumstances in Myanmar/Burma, which have led to calls for a tourism boycott, and Yemen where tourist safety has been threatened by challenges to government authority. The differing situations represent tourism crises initiated by politics which have industry-wide repercussions.

Politics, Governments and Tourism

The study of tourism, and tourism crises, cannot be divorced from that of politics and tourism itself is an issue of political debate and contention (Cheong and Miller, 2000). Tourism movements and the operation of the industry at home and abroad are shaped by government structures and processes at national and international levels. Nearly all governments around the world have some interest in tourism and participate in various ways. Decision making and policy making by official agencies and the drafting and enforcement of laws and regulations can affect tourism, which in turn impinges on the institutions of the state (Hall, 1994).

NTOs are usually given specific responsibility for tourism matters and financed by central government, although often having a degree of independence from it, and engage in marketing and development activities. Other formal agencies such as those dealing with customs and immigration and transport infrastructure contribute to the administration of tourism and affect the functioning of the industry. Sub-national tiers of government also participate in policy making and the allocation of resources and can be very influential in larger countries with a federal style of government. Politicians and civil servants are thus important in determining approaches to tourism, whether it merits special attention and assistance, amounts of public funding allocated, the nature of any public-private or international partnership arrangements and growth targets.

Such deliberations about tourism are usually framed within the context of broader policies and wider objectives, especially related to economics. These incorporate a commitment to economic growth and prosperity, a healthy balance of payments surplus, maximization of foreign exchange earnings and foreign direct investment, employment generation and regional development which extends to rural areas. Obligations regarding the welfare of nationals at home and overseas, the protection of consumers, the conservation and preservation of natural and cultural heritage and the construction and communication of favorable national images also involve governments in tourism directly and indirectly. They may also be suppliers of attractions, transport and assorted amenities and services which are used by tourists. International relations and foreign policy, sometimes leading to the imposition of barriers to travel, are further determinants of tourist volumes and flows. Developments have implications for the way nationals perceive other countries and their residents, with consequences for destination choice.

The specific stance adopted by governments and the steps they undertake are an outcome of overall political circumstances, the power of the state and the ways in which this power is distributed and the socio-cultural environment (Hall and Jenkins, 1995). Stages of tourism and general development are also of relevance regarding the priority given to the former and its place in political systems and agendas. The result is that contrasts are discernible within and between developed and less-developed countries in terms of how tourism interests and responsibilities are defined, interpreted and exercised. The subject tends to have greater prominence in the Third World, where the potential benefits of international tourism are likely to be more keenly appreciated and urgently required.

While differences do exist, tourism's economic rewards appeal to most governments whatever their current circumstances or geographical location (Go and Jenkins, 1997; Williams and Shaw, 1998). There is a common view that tourism is an industry to be taken seriously and one that can be a vehicle for economic development and diversification. It also serves useful purposes in other arenas such as nation building, representations assisting in the articulation of national and cultural identities which is of particular value for young nations of mixed ethnicity. Tourism can thus be exploited politically and employed in reinforcing government authority and demonstrating its legitimacy to the world (Richter, 1994). Growth is therefore highly desirable, although there is an appreciation of the importance of sustainable tourism development. This is frequently made reference to in official statements, yet cynics may question the extent of meaningful commitment to the concept and its implementation.

Political dynamics as a whole act to encourage or discourage tourism, with a distinction to be made between the domestic and international theaters. Domestic politics impacts on destination attributes and attractiveness and industry operations, as well as on demand for travel. National policies inform global happenings and good relations between countries facilitate tourist flows. The reverse applies and international tensions tend to depress or redirect travel. Such relationships and widespread interest mean that governments have an essential part to play in the management of tourism crises and are sometimes a primary or secondary cause of their evolution.

Political Ideologies and Tourism

Politics are partly a consequence of prevailing ideologies and more liberal democratic political philosophies might be seen as best suited to tourism because they favor the unimpeded circulation of people, goods and capital and place stress on individual freedoms. However, such models are not critical to the popularity of tourist destinations and totalitarianism may be compatible with success (Hall and Oehlers, 2000). One noteworthy example is Spain, the coastline of which became the holiday playground for large numbers of Europeans during the 1960s when mass inbound tourism boomed under the dictatorship of General Franco.

At the same time, there have been regimes reliant on force and lacking democratic credentials which have found it difficult to promote their territories as international tourism centers. The clash between disturbing political realities and enticing destination images is illustrated by Myanmar/Burma, where visitor arrivals have been severely damaged by the attitudes and actions of its military rulers. Opponents of the government have championed a boycott of tourism, leading to a crisis of its politicization encompassing practical and ethical dilemmas for the tourism industry and tourists to settle (see Case One).

Nevertheless, their distinctive political ideology and mode of operation are not discouraging the authorities in Myanmar/Burma from pursuing tourism growth.

They seem to be motivated by a combination of economic and political factors which have been exhibited by other authoritarian states of the right and left. In what is now an historic illustration, with the exception of North Korea, communist bloc countries of Europe and Asia were reluctant to expose their citizens to subversive values and behavior epitomized by outbound tourists from Western markets. However, there was an awareness of possible gains from tourism and a willingness to allow controlled entry and regulated internal movement. Most tourists had to travel in parties under the strict supervision of a local guide and follow a set route, minimizing contacts with the local population which were carefully managed. The visitor experience became an exercise in political propaganda, often unconvincing, designed to showcase governments and their achievements.

Political reforms around the world have since led to a relaxation of such restrictions, but there are still concerns among some governments about the capacity of forms of modern tourism to undermine orthodox beliefs and ways of life. This is evident in parts of the Muslim world, although attitudes are changing even there with a growing appreciation of the advantages of tourism in diversifying oil-dependent economies. Overt and covert anti-Western feeling, commonly directed against Americans, is another powerful political sentiment in many Islamic and other communities. Muslim travelers to non-Muslim destinations may also confront suspicion and hostility with which the industry and individuals have to contend. These conflicts have a socio-cultural dimension which is explored more fully in a later chapter, but they echo political disputes and can result in tourists becoming objects of verbal abuse and physical violence.

Political Instability and Tourism Crises

Political philosophies and practices in destination and generating countries therefore have repercussions for tourism and can engender crises, especially when instability is generated. A regime can be defined as stable when it is "durable, violence and turmoil are limited and the leaders stay in office for several years" (Wilson, 1996, p. 25). By contrast, instability implies constant and unpredictable change and disruption to the established political order, including by external parties which use illegitimate tactics (Poirier, 1997). Media reports and popular conceptions of such instability are key determinants of decisions made by travelers, the industry and investors who generally show an aversion to risk. Relatively peaceful locations where there are few perceived threats to personal safety and security and least commercial uncertainty are preferred by all parties.

Political instability has numerous manifestations and six types of "international wars, civil wars, coups, terrorism, riots and political and social unrest, and strikes" have been proposed (Hall and O'Sullivan, 1996, p. 109). A more detailed list of 28 instances is reproduced below and further indicates the range of political events to which tourism is vulnerable (Seddighi et al., 2001, p. 185). Corruption could perhaps be added to the inventory as proper planning and the conduct of business is made difficult in countries where it is endemic. Issues of the adverse consequences of terrorism have dominated discussions about political security and tourism in recent years due to a series of unprecedented attacks which have severely damaged tourism; the next chapter is devoted to this topic.

- Terrorist attacks involving tourists as victims
- Armed attack events
- Assassinations (political)
- Bombings
- Change in the government
- Change in the political party governing a country
- Civil war
- Guerrilla warfare
- Hijackings
- Kidnappings
- Peaceful demonstrations
- Peaceful strikes
- Riots
- Successful coup d'etat
- Mass arrests
- Political instability in neighboring countries
- Threat of war with other countries
- Terrorist attacks to tourism industry related targets (site seeing, transportation, accommodation)
- Unsuccessful coup d'etat
- War
- Censoring of media
- Imposition of martial law
- Restriction of political rights
- Wars in a neighboring country
- Arrests of significant persons
- Terrorist attacks or threats of attacks to nontourist targets (foiled bombing, sabotage)
- Army attacks beyond the country's borders
- Political illegal executions

Source: Reprinted from *Tourism Management*, *22*, Seddighi, H., Nuttall, M., and Theocharous, A. Does cultural background of tourists influence the destination choice? An empirical study with special reference to political instability, p. 185. Copyright (2001), with permission from Elsevier.

Many of these factors can be hazardous for tourists, or regarded as such, resulting in the outright rejection or avoidance of areas where they occur by visitors and the tourism industry. Foreign governments may also intervene and publish advisories which recommend against non-essential travel in order to protect their citizens from the dangers associated with political upheaval; this issue is returned to in the next chapter.

There is a spectrum of intensity regarding the phenomena cited and warfare is perhaps the most catastrophic for tourism, illustrated by Croatia and Sri Lanka. The former experienced a sharp fall in arrivals due to regional conflicts (see Boxed Case One) while the latter was similarly affected by civil war (see Boxed Case Two). Strikes or riots, especially if confined to a particular site, have less impact and some visitors will be prepared to put up with the inconvenience if they are sufficiently eager to visit. Nevertheless, unusually aggressive protests in 2005 against Japan's

---

Boxed Case One: Selling Croatia amid Turmoil in the Balkans

Yugoslavia under socialist rule was a popular holiday destination for many Europeans, especially its coastal resorts on the Adriatic Sea. Its fragmentation into a series of separate republics and internal and external strife proved a crisis for the tourism industry, especially Slovenia and Croatia, where visitors had been concentrated in the past. Citizens of several European nations were warned by their governments not to travel to the region at the height of the 1991 peak season. Tour operators had to evacuate their customers and stopped selling and promoting former Yugoslavian centers. International visitors fell from in excess of seven million in 1990 to 1.3 million in 1992.

Croatia did not appear in the 1992 and 1993 summer programs of any foreign tour operators, but the country's tourism industry maintained contact and encouraged companies to return to those places unaffected by the war which were numerous. Representatives of the national tour operator, acting as an NTO, attended all the main travel trade fairs in Europe and supported overseas tour operators and travel agents in restarting business in the country. The foreign media were also kept informed, accurate press releases being prepared and distributed, and educational visits were arranged for journalists and travel agents.

Companies and tourists from the main generating markets were slow to return and visitors from most markets had still had not reached 1990 levels by 1998. Continuing uncertainty in the region, illustrated by the NATO action against Serbia in 1999 and war in Kosovo, had repercussions for Croatia which again saw falling arrivals and rising cancellations. The "Kosovo effect" meant that several tour operators omitted Croatia from their 2000 summer programs. Croatia thus confronted the double challenge of creating and communicating a distinct tourist identity as a new country and developing a favorable destination image against a background of regional turmoil.

Source: Cavlek, 2002.

Boxed Case Two: Civil War and Ceasefire Opportunities in Sri Lanka

The 2002 ceasefire in Sri Lanka followed 20 years of civil war and, as a consequence, the Tourism Board expected that visitors would rise by 25% in 2003 to half a million. During the war, the north and east of the country were isolated as the Liberation Tigers of Tamil Eelam conducted a violent campaign for an independent Tamil homeland. Many citizens died in the conflict, sometimes due to suicide bombings.

The ceasefire was an opportunity for the tourism industry, but government and investors were reluctant to act due to doubts about whether the peace agreement would hold. Some Tamil businessmen and expatriates were prepared to invest, favoring more exclusive hotel resorts with an ecotourism theme. The Tourism Ministry also offered preferential loans to small hotels in the east to allow them to repair war damage. However, the authorities were reported as "lagging behind" with "little tangible planning to back up the vague rhetoric of the Tourism Board about the potential of the north east for tourism . . . The old attitudes of riding out the war crisis needs to be replaced with a new vision of turning war zones into tourist zones."

Tour operators in Britain, one of the key source markets alongside India, expressed cautious optimism about the future in 2003 and described how Sri Lanka was actually benefiting from political instability elsewhere such as the terrorist bombings in Bali and Kenya as well as the Asian SARS outbreak. Nevertheless, subsequent developments (including the President's decision to declare a state of emergency in late 2003) were unsettling and led to the adoption of a "wait-and-see" attitude by travelers and the industry.

Sources: BBC News, 2003a; BBC News 2003b; BBC News 2003c.

---

reluctance to apologize for war crimes committed in formerly occupied countries such as China and Korea were monitored by the tourism industry, anxious about their ramifications for demand from lucrative Japanese travelers. The importance of such contentious and politically sensitive questions and those of media censorship and violation of human rights varies with the individual tourist, company and government of the generating markets.

However, relatively localized incidents may ultimately inflict serious damage on the country as a whole, the wider region and even the world in what has been termed the "generalization effect" (Lepp and Gibson, 2003, p. 607). The Gulf War in 1999, although limited in time and space, triggered a significant slowdown in international tourism globally with a shift to domestic tourism and locations closer to home. A similar pattern was observed during the Kosovo conflict in Central Europe in 1999

(Cavlek, 2002) and the expansion rate of European outbound tourism fell by 50% (WTO, 2002). It should be noted that outcomes of political disturbance may be more serious for international activity and the domestic market is often comparatively resilient. Nationals are less likely to be deterred by the distorted perceptions of risk which may circulate overseas and are aggravated by inaccurate and incomplete information, distance and unfamiliarity.

It is not just actual eruptions of political turbulence which tarnish destination image and erode tourist and industry confidence, but also worries about their possibility. Periods of political transition give rise to doubts about existing and future stability which may discourage visitors and investment, exemplified by some countries in Eastern Europe after the collapse of communism (Light and Dumbraveanu, 1999).

Partition is another source of uncertainty and travel to and across borders of divided countries may be inhibited by administrative and physical barriers. Cyprus was partitioned after many years of unrest between Turkish and Greek Cypriots and the lack of international recognition of the Turkish Republic of North Cyprus, including political and economic embargoes, has impeded promotion of the territory and its tourism growth (Altinay et al., 2002). Another divided state is Korea, North and South embarking on separate journeys generally and in tourism terms after the 1953 cease-fire. Inter-Korean travel remains extremely limited and at the mercy of the evolving and tense relationships between the two countries themselves and world powers (Kim and Prideaux, 2003).

History and ongoing political tensions between the People's Republic of China and Taiwan have also disrupted tourism movements between the two and regular talk of war is a destabilizing element in the region. Disagreements between India and Pakistan over the predominantly Muslim state of Jammu and Kashmir, which became a part of Hindu-dominated India after its independence in 1947, have had similar effects, compounded by terrorist campaigns.

Tourists can accidentally find themselves in the midst of political troubles, necessitating a response from the industry and authorities. Western travelers may be targeted directly and prey to politically motivated kidnappings in some areas of the world. Increasing numbers of independent tourists determined to get off the beaten track and tour companies selling such packages have intensified the chance of such crises in which governments of the tourist's country of origin can be implicated. For example, there were reports of German officials paying a ransom to secure the release of nine of their citizens held in Western Sahara in 2003, with another 23 Europeans seized by insurgents in Algeria. A total of 15 tourists were finally freed and one German died. The alleged deal provoked heavy criticism of the German government and discussion about "whether the taxpayer should end up paying for adventure holidays that go horribly wrong" (BBC News, 2003d).

Terrorist attacks are examined in greater detail in another chapter, but events in Yemen are made reference to here in order to demonstrate what can happen when a government is no longer fully in control of its territory (see Case Two). The ability of authorities to guarantee a certain level of tourist safety is thus compromised by political instability, to the detriment of the industry and well-being of visitors.

Questions of Timescale and Geography

Timescale is a major determinant of the significance of political instability for tourism and three categories based on this measure can be recognized. They are described in a report dating from the mid-1990s with appropriate illustrations from that period (EIU, 1994), a selection of which follows. Arrivals drop sharply and remain at very low levels when there is "fundamental long term disruption" (Lebanon, Northern Ireland and Uganda), numbers responding to any advances or setbacks on the road toward peace. Tourist volumes are constrained by "ongoing volatility and uncertainty" (Cambodia, Jamaica and the Philippines) and interest shifts according to events and media coverage. Third, "disruption due to isolated incidents" (Tiananmen Square demonstrations in China and London's Heathrow Airport bombings) can reduce inbound tourism for a period extending to two years. Recovery is decided by the severity of the occasion, the ways in which it is handled by the industry and publicity. Single, short-term, instances are more quickly resolved and forgotten than persistent and widespread problems.

Unfortunately, many of the EIU examples are still apt and unrest continues to be prevalent around the world. Certain regions have acquired a reputation for political volatility, often accompanied by economic unpredictability, which is reflected in a comparatively small share of global tourists and their spending. The latter decades of the twentieth century in South America were marked by disputes, insurgency and coups with countries ruled by dictators or military juntas. The situation was made worse by incompetent economic policies and extensive corruption within governments (Santana, 2000). Central America has exhibited similar traits, including Mexico in the 1990s when a rebel group specifically targeted tourists at the Huatulco and Acapulco resorts and warned of attacks on Cancun (Cothran and Cothran, 1998). Chronic or occasional instability in some Caribbean islands such as Haiti and Jamaica have also handicapped their development as tourist destinations.

Political disturbance and violence are associated too with sub-Saharan Africa and constitute one obstacle to the realization of its immense tourism potential (Christie and Crompton, 2001). The Middle East, one of the world's least-developed tourism regions, is yet another case. Additional weaknesses of a lack of infrastructure, planning and marketing cannot be overlooked (Mintel, 2002), but inbound regional tourism is inextricably linked to the degree of peace prevailing. This applies to relatively popular countries such as Egypt and tourist arrivals in Israel are tied to progress in negotiations with its Arab neighbors (see Boxed Case Three). Certain South East Asian states like Indonesia and the Philippines have under-performed as tourist destinations, in part because of their history of poor governance and struggles to attain a greater degree of order and stability (Hall and Page, 2000; Richter, 1992).

Boxed Case Three: Middle East Uncertainties and Israel's Tourism

International tourism is of economic significance in Israel and earned 2% of GDP (US$2.1 billion) in 2002, but income had fallen substantially after the Palestinian uprising and progress toward realizing its potential has been hindered by damaging political developments in the wider region and concerns about security issues. Inbound tourism performance reflects these factors and numbers doubled between 1991 and 1995 when there seemed to be movement toward peace. A fall in 1996–1998 was arrested by slight growth in 1999–2000 to almost three million and arrivals then dropped below one million in 2002. There was recovery again in 2003 because of renewed optimism about negotiations with Palestine and the end of the war in Iraq. The upward trend continued in 2004, although whether it could be sustained remained in doubt.

Religious pilgrims and European holidaymakers were important markets, but there was strong competition for the latter from less expensive Eastern Mediterranean destinations. Prior to 2000, residents comprised about 40% of hotel visitors and many hotels focused their attention on selling to residents in the 2000–2001 season to compensate for the shortage of overseas visitors. As a result, 86% of guests in 2002 were Israelis, but increased outbound travel was eroding the domestic market and this share seemed likely to contract.

Source: EIU (2004).

Review

Whether reputations are deserved or undeserved, occurrences and expectations of instability are detrimental to tourism and can lead to crisis. This was stressed by Richter and Waugh (1986, p. 320) who contended that "tourism may decline precipitously when political conditions appear unsettled. Tourists simply choose alternative destinations. Unfortunately, many national leaders and planners either do not understand or will not accept the fact that political serenity, not scenic or cultural attractions, constitute the first and central requirement of tourism."

Perceptions are perhaps as important as realities and they are partly the product of media reporting which has a vital role in destination image formation. In an era of mass communications technology, alarming pictures and accounts of political disturbance can be transmitted instantly around the world. Even isolated locations like remote South Pacific islands are part of this global village where access to markets is opened up, but problems cannot be hidden and may be exaggerated in transmission. Information about coups in Fiji in 1987 and 2000 reached a worldwide audience, contradicting conventional marketing messages of an idyllic retreat (see Boxed Case Four). Bad news stories may attract considerable attention, especially

---

Boxed Case Four: Responding to Coups in Fiji

The South Pacific island of Fiji was the scene of two coups in 1987 and one in 2000 which had a notable effect on the tourism industry. The 1987 incidents were without violence and comparatively short-lived, but resulted in the setting up of a Tourism Action Group (TAG) which was in operation for about three months. It concentrated on the lifting of travel warnings imposed by authorities from Australian and New Zealand (Fiji's principal markets) and marketing, the budget for which was doubled. Study trips for industry representatives were arranged and special deals for air transport and vacations were offered to customers from major generating countries.

The 2000 coup was more serious as the Prime Minister and other officials were held hostage for 56 days and there were 10 deaths. Land rights became an issue and a number of popular resorts were occupied by aggrieved landowners. The media played a more prominent role, with Internet technology providing a worldwide audience with news of events. A TAG 2000 was established and devised a plan to work toward recovery. It sought to cooperate with the private sector to generate marketing funding, involve the industry overseas, conduct a series of marketing campaigns and communicate the message that Fiji was not dangerous. Contact was made with various parties, including consulates, to press for the removal of travel warnings which had been restored, and promotional packages were organized. A private firm of consultants dealing with public relations and media management was also employed.

Although the effectiveness of the crisis action plan was offset by ongoing unrest, it did achieve some success and helped to limit the fall in arrivals to 30% in 2000 which was better than initially expected. Nevertheless, Fiji's image as a tropical island paradise had been damaged and marketers had to revise their traditional approach, accommodating the new realities.

Source: Berno and King, 2001.

---

if there are fatalities, and it may take time and resources to combat unattractive images and negative associations once they have been established.

However, some tourists disregard certain types of instability in return for a cheap, or expensive, holiday. Tourism's resilience in the worst of cases also suggests a general willingness to return to formerly troubled areas, provided there have been no recurrences of violence or constant reminders in the media. Some individuals are even courting the excitement and danger found in unsafe areas and war zones. These people, as well as armchair travelers, are perhaps readers of books which promise tips for travel in the "world's most dangerous places" (Pelton et al., 1997) like Afghanistan and Chechnya. Such tourists may be drawn to political crises, representing an interesting topic for a study of motivation, but they are a small minority with little commercial significance for the mainstream industry.

For most tourists and tourism businesses as well as investors, political upheaval is a strong deterrent and one that is set to persist. Unfortunately, finding answers to the conflicts which underlie continuous or sporadic outbreaks of instability appears some way off. The task for the tourism industry is therefore to devise strategies for dealing with the difficult challenges that ensue.

Responding to Political Tourism Crises

Appropriate management strategies depend on the gravity and scale of the tourism crisis. The most serious tourism crises linked to instability are potentially devastating for destinations with serious economic and social ramifications locally and nationally. Strong pressures are therefore exerted on governments to take action with a view to supporting the industry and leading recovery. Companies and officials from generating countries also have to cope with the aftermath, necessitating the repatriation of tourists already overseas and cancellation of schedules. Other firms have the option of doing business elsewhere, although last-minute changes of plan and withdrawal of the destination from programs may be required.

Some incidents are isolated and unlikely to be repeated, but others may be a symptom of persistent instability rooted in economic, social and political conditions which interact to create sometimes intractable problems defying resolution. The EIU (1994) suggested, however, that the industry can help by addressing fundamental causes. It should aim to cultivate sustainable tourism in which tourism is integrated into the wider economy. Local communities should be protected and involved in planning, benefiting as much as possible from jobs and income created. The industry should also be seen to be a friend to the environment, active in conservation and preservation. Such an approach could facilitate general growth and obviate political unrest as well as give residents a vested interest in a prosperous tourism sector.

These measures may, nevertheless, prove ineffective and the industry is powerless in the face of some political situations. Places suffering from violent upheaval are best avoided by the industry overseas, although this is obviously not an alternative for the authorities and businesses of these destinations.

In the most extreme instances where locations have been devastated by warfare, facilities and infrastructure must be rebuilt or repaired and new investment attracted. Richter (1999) advised against overambitious and hasty timetables which fail to acknowledge existing political circumstances and probable scenarios. She quoted the example of Cambodia which tried to use tourism as a catalyst for economic development before the complete clearance of land mines at sites to be promoted to tourists. However, some action is necessary to prevent missed opportunities, which it was feared might have happened in Sri Lanka. Countries ravaged by war have to plan a steady recovery founded on the most suitable forms of tourism. They need to be realistic in their assessment of political developments ahead and the future prospects of tourism. The media and industry abroad are partners in recovery, as was appreciated by the Croatian industry, and must be kept informed with up-to-date facts.

With regard to crises which are more confined in scope and where tourists have been the victims of politically motivated violence, either purposely or by chance, the tasks are more immediate. Priority must be given to dealing with those directly affected and their next of kin, in addition to relations with the media, following the example of the tour operator in Yemen. Attempts should be made to communicate with all stakeholders, including the media, and disseminate complete and credible information which gives a fair and realistic assessment of risks. Organizations might consider employing specialist companies with expertise in areas where they themselves lack the necessary skills. The EIU (1994) wrote about a damage limitation exercise which directs visitors away from likely centers of trouble and takes practical steps to make them less vulnerable, such as providing more police, lights, signposts, tourist information and codes of conduct.

Marketing has an important role, although it is necessary to be cautious about what it can achieve and when it should be undertaken. Conventional destination advertising should be suspended in many crises, but authorities can still maintain contact with industry representatives overseas. Great care should be exercised over the timing of any campaigns following a crisis and their content, especially assertions about safety and business as usual, and messages of reassurance must be communicated. Themes and images will need to be revisited and revised, as happened in Fiji, taking into account altered perceptions of the destination as a result of political changes. Opportunities to sell to the domestic market may arise during and immediately after a crisis and it may also be possible to attract more intrepid international travelers in the interim period before a return to full or near normality.

Discounting of the prices of separate components and package holidays is another tool, although it is unlikely to be effective as a response to severe disturbance and few tourists would be prepared to put their lives at risk for the sake of a travel bargain. Nevertheless, reduced prices can be a useful way of stimulating interest and it does seem that some customers will put aside concerns about personal safety if they feel that they are getting exceptional value for money in an offer which might never be repeated.

Summary and Conclusions

Tourism and politics thus have a close, if somewhat uneasy, relationship in which domestic and international political conditions and developments shape tourism flows and the environment in which the industry operates. Tourism also impacts on political structures and processes and it is a policy making area of importance to most governments which seek to fully exploit the economic opportunities, as well as the social and political uses, it affords. However, government actions, ideologies and political events are capable of triggering a range of crises and political instability is a common catalyst.

The industry in generating countries can implement a system of monitoring, allowing for the identification and avoidance of danger zones, and procedures for dealing with emergencies which do occur. Destination authorities must try to build and maintain good relations with the media and circulate accurate details to all relevant parties so that they can make properly informed decisions. Countries which display profound instability are unlikely to prosper as tourist destinations in the short term, although they can plan for long-term recovery and growth.

Restoration of normality or near normality is a team effort and may take a number of years. Many tourism crises which are political in origin also demand political solutions, at national and international levels, and this influences their evolution and resolution. It also acts as a constraint on the formulation of industry responses and their efficacy.

Case One: The Government, Tourism and Boycott Debate in Myanmar/Burma

Myanmar/Burma managed to attract only 208,676 visitors in 2000, despite a wealth of natural and cultural tourism resources. This poor performance contrasts markedly with the achievements of its South East Asian neighbors and is mainly attributable to the political situation. A coup in 1962 installed a military government which has retained power since, establishing the State Law and Order Restoration Council (SLORC) following civil unrest in 1988. Colonial place names were changed and Burma became Myanmar. The National League for Democracy (NLD) secured over 80% of the votes in the 1990 elections, but was prevented from taking office in a move that was widely condemned abroad. The NLD is led by Aung San Suu Kyi, a Nobel Peace Prize laureate, whose personal treatment was also a cause for concern. The SLORC was renamed the State Peace and Development Council (SPDC) in 1997, but the system of government was essentially unchanged.

The regime was initially xenophobic and isolationist, but revised this stance and began to actively promote and develop tourism. However, perceptions of brutal army leaders and their repressive policies proved to be a weakness. There were reports of the suppression of ethnic minorities and violations of human rights, the latter linked to tourism. Critics claimed forced labor had been used in the construction of infrastructure and other projects. Figures of a million were quoted and these were said to include children, pregnant women and the elderly. It was also suggested that people had been compelled to leave their homes in order to make way for new developments.

These topics attracted worldwide attention and publicity with stories appearing in the American, Australian and European media. Various agencies called for a general boycott of the country, extending to tourism, as an expression of opposition to the regime and in an effort to induce change. Supporters maintained that tourism served to legitimize the authorities and endow them with a respectability they did not deserve. It was also a source of revenue which strengthened the position of the government and reduced the likelihood of democratic reforms. This position was also taken by Aung San Suu Kyi who expressed her wish that tourists should delay any visits until democratic reforms had begun, although it was not clear if the NLD as a whole adhered to this view.

Advocates of the ban targeted officials, tour operators and travel agents and tourists in generating countries with mixed results. A number of operators did cease doing business in the country, citing security problems and falling sales as well as solidarity with Aung San Suu Kyi. Others informed the government of their difficulties in running tours in the face of instability and critical human rights reports. Statements made by some operators indicated that a place's politics was not an issue for them unless it impacted on the safety of their customers and practical arrangements.

It was argued that there was no convincing proof of the worst accusations of human rights abuses and that other nations were guilty of violations and yet had escaped such censure. There was a strong feeling that tourists should be free to visit and decide for themselves. Tourism was also a force for change for the better, improving living standards of the very poor population. These sentiments were reflected in marketing literature where the political situation was either ignored or referred to in passing, the country described as opening its doors after a reclusive period. Some brochures noted that the government had its opponents, but stressed that Burma should be seen at first hand.

Publishers of travel guides were also forced to take a stand. Lonely Planet was criticized for publishing a Myanmar edition which did include two pages discussing the politics of Myanmar. The account acknowledged the dilemmas, but advised those who elected to visit to try and ensure that their spending benefited locals, rather than the state. Tourists should also write to the government and complain about the human rights situation. The publisher claimed that tourism was good for many ordinary Burmese, most of whom did not agree with any boycott, and that it alone could not be blamed for practices such as forced labor. It was unlikely that decisions by tourists not to travel would ease repression. However, the Rough Guide series of publications excluded Myanmar.

Source: Henderson, 2003.

Case Two: The Kidnapping and Release of Tour Operator Customers in Yemen

The Middle Eastern state of Yemen has a complicated and troubled history and reunification of the North and South in 1990 generated new tensions. Different political and administrative systems had to be reconciled, one of which was oriented towards Marxism-Leninism. Nevertheless, there was some tourism planning and development and 84,000 foreign visitors arrived in 1997.

Hostage taking was not unknown and over 100 Westerners were abducted between 1992 and 1998, usually by tribesmen in remote mountainous areas of the country. However, there had been no deaths and captives were released after the payment of a ransom or discussions about infrastructure improvements or better welfare conditions. Then, 16 tourists (12 from Britain and two from both America and Australia) were seized on 28 December 1998 by 20 armed men belonging to Islamic Jihad, an Islamic militant organization. They had been traveling in a convoy of four-wheel-drive vehicles with a police escort on a 15-day holiday; this was organized by an English-based company which specialized in hotel and camping trips to relatively remote locations. The hostages were moved to an isolated southern town and a rescue attempt by security forces the following day resulted in the deaths of three British tourists and one Australian, three other Westerners sustaining injuries. A policeman and two kidnappers were killed and five others injured, conflicting accounts being given about the exact circumstances of the confrontation.

The event was widely reported in the British media, including *The Times* newspaper which described how a "spokesperson for the holiday firm insisted that the company had followed Foreign Office advice to register at the embassy, take a knowledgeable guide and keep in touch with developments." The representative was quoted as saying that the company was "supreme specialists in operating in such countries. They followed Foreign Office advice to the letter. I do not think anyone could have foreseen this. There was no inkling of anything on this particular stretch of road."

An article in a trade publication related events from the perspective of the Operations Director who was told immediately about the kidnappings in a telephone call from the tour leader in Yemen. Other managers and the firm's public relations agency were informed, an emergency meeting was held and a crisis action plan was implemented. The Operations Director said that the "key to dealing efficiently with a problem, however large or small, is communicating and planning. Tour leaders are instructed to contact the duty manager as soon as a problem arises and to inform the British Embassy and ground handlers." Talks began with airlines and Yemeni hotels in anticipation of the release of the hostages. Next of kin were informed, although this was made difficult by the Christmas holiday season and the fact that the tourists came from three regions of the world with different time zones. Travel agents who had sold the packages and relevant authorities were also notified.

After the rescue, survivors remained in Yemen for two days to allow time for recovery and discussions with Yemeni and British officials. They then flew to Gatwick Airport in England where arrangements had been made regarding special customs clearance and coach transport to an airport hotel, two injured tourists following two days later. The company met the costs of travel and accommodation for relatives and the Australian tourist left for home the next day. Summing up, the Operations Director observed that "if there is a message for other operators who find themselves in a similar position it is to plan ahead—and hire a decent PR agency. Letting someone else handle the press allows you to get on with the job of getting people home."

Sources: BBC News, 2004; Burns and Cooper, 1997; *The Times*, 1998; Travel Weekly, 2004.

Concept Definitions

- Political ideology: The prevailing belief system and values which underlie political positions and actions.
- Political instability: A situation in which the established political order is threatened by internal or external forces, resulting in change and uncertainty.
- Political tourism crisis: A crisis for tourists and the tourism industry which is political in its origins.
- Tourism policy making: Decisions made by governments with regard to tourism which may or may not form an explicit strategy.

Review Questions

1. In what ways are governments involved in tourism and what are the reasons for this involvement?
2. How might the political ideology of a government affect the country's tourism and official tourism policy?
3. What forms of political instability are most damaging for tourism?
4. Can tourism crises linked to political disturbance be avoided?
5. What role do the media play in creating and resolving politically inspired tourism crises?
6. What strategies should public and private sector tourism agencies adopt to deal with crises arising from (a) civil war and (b) mass demonstrations in major cities against a legitimately elected government?
7. Debate the effectiveness of a tourism boycott of Myanmar/Burma as a means of promoting political change.
8. Should the risk of kidnapping deter tour operators from including remote locations in their itineraries?

Additional Readings

EIU. (1994). The impact of political unrest and security concerns on international tourism. *Travel & Tourism Analyst, 2*, 69–82.

Hall, C.M. and O'Sullivan, V. (1996). Tourism, political stability and violence. In A. Pizam and Y. Mansfeld (Eds.), *Tourism, crime and international security issues* (pp. 105–121). Chichester: Wiley.

Richter, L. (1999). After political turmoil: The lessons of rebuilding tourism in three Asian countries. *Journal of Travel Research, 48*(August), 41–45.

References

Alitinay, L., Altinay, M., and Bicak, H. (2002). Political scenarios: The future of the North Cyprus tourism industry. *International Journal of Contemporary Hospitality Management, 14*(4), 176–182.

BBC News. (2003a. 19 September). Boom time for Sri Lanka tourism. BBC News website at http://newsvote.bbc.com, accessed 23 November 2004.

BBC News. (2003b. 17 November). Sri Lanka crisis hits tourism. BBC News website at http://newsvote.bbc.com, accessed 23 November 2004.

BBC News. (2003c. 5 November). Sri Lanka tries to calm tourism fears. BBC News website at http://newsvote.bbc.com, accessed 23 November 2004.

BBC News. (2003d. 8 December). Western tourists abducted in Iran. BBC News website at http://newsvote.bbc.com, accessed 23 November 2004.

BBC News. (2004, 27 May). Flashback: Yemen kidnapping. BBC News website at http://newsvote.bbc.co.uk, accessed 23 November 2004.

Berno, T. and King, B. (2001). Tourism in Fiji after the coups. *Travel and Tourism Analyst, 2*, 75–91.

Burns, P. and Cooper, C. (1997). Yemen: Marxism and a tribal-Marxist dichotomy. *Tourism Management, 18*(8), 555–563.

Cavlek, N. (2002). Tour operators and destination safety. *Annals of Tourism Research, 29*(2), 478–496.

Cheong, S.M. and Miller, M.L. (2000). Power and tourism: A Foucaldian observation. *Annals of Tourism Research, 27*(2), 371–390.

Christie, I. and Crompton, D. (2001). *Tourism in Africa*. World Bank Working Paper. New York: World Bank.

Cothran, D. and Cothran, C. (1998). Promise or political risk for Mexican tourism. *Annals of Tourism Research, 25*(2), 477–497.

EIU. (1994). The impact of political unrest and security concerns on international tourism. *Travel and Tourism Analyst, 2*, 69–82.

EIU. (2004). Israel: Tourism. *Economist Intelligence Unit Viewswire, 52*(301).

Go, F.M. and Jenkins, C.L. (Eds.). (1997). *Tourism and economic development in Asia and Australasia*. London: Cassell.

Hall, C.M. (1994). *Tourism and politics: Policy, power and place*. New York: Wiley.

Hall, C.M. and Jenkins, J.M. (1995). *Tourism and public policy*. London and New York: Routledge.

Hall, C.M. and Oehlers, A.L. (2000). Tourism and politics in South and Southeast Asia: Political instability and policy. In C.M. Hall and S. Page (Eds.), *Tourism in South and Southeast Asia: Issues and cases* (pp. 77–93). Oxford: Butterworth-Heinemann.

Hall, C.M. and O'Sullivan, V. (1996). Tourism, political stability and violence. In A. Pizam and Y. Mansfeld (Eds.), *Tourism, crime and international security issues* (pp. 105–121). Chichester: Wiley.

Hall, C.M. and Page, S. (Eds.). (2000). *Tourism in South and Southeast Asia: Issues and cases*. Oxford: Butterworth-Heinemann.

Henderson, J.C. (2003). The politics of tourism in Myanmar. *Current Issues in Tourism*, 6(2), 97–118.

Kim, S. and Prideaux, B. (2003). Tourism, peace, politics and ideology: Impacts of the Mt. Gumgang tour project in the Korean peninsula. *Tourism Management*, 24(6), 675–685.

Lepp, A. and Gibson, H. (2003). Tourist roles, perceived risk and international tourism. *Annals of Tourism Research*, 30(3), 606–624.

Light, D. and Dumbraveanu, D. (1999). Romanian tourism in the post-communist period. *Annals of Tourism Research*, 26(4), 898–927.

Mintel. (2002). The Middle East. *Country Reports*, 4, 221–235.

Pelton, R., Aral, C., and Dulles, W. (1997). *Fielding's the world's most dangerous places*. Redondo Beach, CA: Fielding Worldwide.

Poirier, R.A. (1997). Political risk analysis and tourism. *Annals of Tourism Research*, 24(3), 675–686.

Richter, L. (1999, August). After political turmoil: The lessons of rebuilding tourism in three Asian countries. *Journal of Travel Research*, 48, 41–45.

Richter, L.K. (1992). Political instability and tourism in the Third World. In D. Harrison (Ed.), *Tourism and the less developed countries* (pp. 35–46). London: Belhaven Press.

Richter, L.K. (1994). The political dimensions of tourism. In J.R. Brent Ritchie and C.R. Goeldner (Eds.), *Travel, tourism and hospitality research* (pp. 219–231). New York: Wiley.

Richter, L.K. and Waugh, W.L. (1986). Terrorism and tourism as logical companions. *Tourism Management*, 7(4), 230–238.

Santana, G. (2000). An overview of contemporary tourism development in Brazil. *International Journal of Contemporary Hospitality Management*, 12(7), 424–430.

Seddighi, H., Nuttall, M., and Theocharous, A. (2001). Does cultural background of tourists influence the destination choice? An empirical study with special reference to political instability. *Tourism Management*, 22, 181–191.

The Times. (1998, 30 December). Three Britons killed in shoot-out. http://nextdada. hostit.be/travel/kidnap, accessed 23 November 2004.

Travel Weekly. (2004). Contingency plan limits damage for Yemen operator. Travel Weekly website at http://www.travelweekly.co.uk/Article 8930.html, accessed 23 November 2004.

Williams, A.M. and Shaw, G. (1998). *Tourism and economic development*. Chichester: Wiley.

Wilson, F.L. (1996). *Concepts and issues in comparative politics*. Englewood Cliffs, NJ: Prentice Hall.

WTO. (2002). *Tourism after 11 September 2001: Analysis, remedial actions and prospects*. Madrid: World Tourism Organization.

4

Terrorism and Tourism

Learning Objectives

By the end of the chapter, the reader should be able to

- Appreciate the significance of terrorism and the threat of terrorism in the modern world.
- Understand the direct and indirect consequences of acts of terrorism and fears about these consequences for tourism demand and the operation of the industry.
- Identify appropriate strategies that destination authorities and tourism businesses can use to deal with incidences of terrorism and anxieties about the possibility of their occurring.

Introduction

The preceding chapter revealed the unwelcome outcomes for tourism of political instability, one serious expression of which is terrorism. The impact of terrorism on tourism at the particular location where it occurs, or is threatened, and its broader implications are examined in this chapter. After an opening summary of the nature and extent of terrorism and its linkages with tourism, responses of commercial operators and tourism authorities are reviewed. A final section outlines possible preventive measures and strategies.

The discussion affords insights into approaches to managing the aftermath of terrorist violence and fears of its occurrence, as well as questions of avoidance and containment. Terrorism and tourism are shown to be a topic of mounting interest as terrorist extremism and awareness of the threat of terrorism appear to have heightened in recent decades. The twenty-first century has already seen numerous examples which have had ramifications for global tourism and two of these, the events of 11 September 2001 and the Bali bombings in 2002, constitute the chapter case studies.

The Global Threat of Terrorism

There is no standard definition of terrorism and the concept is a contested one with a variety of meanings, partly depending on perspective. The observation that one man's terrorist is another's freedom fighter may be a cliché, but it does pertain in many situations in which there are differing interpretations of the motives and objectives of participants. However, terrorism commonly describes "premeditated, politically motivated violence perpetrated against noncombatant targets by subnational groups or clandestine agents, usually intended to influence an audience. The term international terrorism means involving citizens or the territory of more than one country" (US Department of State, 2004). The extent of "influence" being pursued is substantial and may incorporate the overthrow of ruling governments as part of a radical political agenda. A distinction is sometimes drawn between domestic and international operations, but random attacks can harm both national and overseas interests and individuals so that differentiation is not always valid. State terrorism is another label applied to governments which engage in oppression at home and may sponsor subversion overseas (Thackrah, 2004).

Published statistics regarding the scale of activity vary, but there were signs of a rapid increase in the number of terrorist acts between the 1970s and 1980s. The volume of incidents then fell, but deaths and injuries have continued to grow (Thackrah, 2004). There are also regional disparities with American official figures indicating substantial rises in fatalities in Asia, the Middle East and Western Europe between 1998 and 2003 (US Department of State, 2004). Principal targets in the latter year were business (30%), government (8%), diplomatic (7%), military (1.5%) and others (53%). Another trend is the expansion in magnitude of individual attacks and their spread which has given rise to a feeling that they are part of an organized conspiracy, rather than isolated happenings, and that everyone is vulnerable (Horner and Swarbrooke, 2004).

Notions of nationalism and separatism, alongside an assortment of political ideologies, have conventionally underpinned terrorism. One common objective is to create homelands for people who are stateless or have been dispossessed. Terrorists frequently embrace a revolutionary philosophy concerned with establishing a new order and the perpetration of a particular political philosophy. However, religion now plays a more dominant role, especially Islam, and Islamic revivalism has led to a new phase in its politicization. The harnessing of Islam to terrorism is demonstrated by the Al-Qaeda movement which originated in Afghanistan in the late 1970s in opposition to the occupying Soviet forces. Led by Osama bin Laden, it became a machine for the promotion of jihad, usually and perhaps controversially translated from the original Arabic as "holy war." The intention is to promote the supremacy of a particular view of Islam and establish theocratic states throughout the Middle East and elsewhere, destroying contrary governments and belief systems (Foreign and Commonwealth Office, 2004).

International jihadists attached to Al-Qaeda or in sympathy with its cause have become more visible, not least in Southeast Asia where an organization named

Jemaah Islamiah (JI) has a presence (Desker, 2002). These groupings have been responsible for a series of attacks since the mid-1990s in America, Europe and the Middle and Far East. Anti-Western feeling is a defining characteristic and has been fueled by the 2003 war in Iraq and its aftermath. Such animosity has been directed at international tourism and Al-Qaeda has admitted the aim of "assassinating enemy personnel as well as foreign tourists" (The Straits Times, 2002). Even if they are not specific targets, domestic tourists are also at risk from assaults in public places as well as those on transport, hotels and leisure amenities.

Current circumstances are thus somewhat different from previous decades when terrorists were less ambitious and more geographically confined. British officials note how the ideas of prominent figures are "taken up transnationally by others who find them compelling and attractive, and who use the tools of globalization to realize their aims, such as the Internet, mobile communications, the media, the easy covert international movement of people and funds and opportunities for identity theft. As a result the threat has become fluid, global and relatively unpredictable" (Foreign and Commonwealth Office, 2004). Terrorist groups also seem to have made contact and forged loose affiliations, moving away from a domestic to an international orientation. Several emerging alliances claim some connections with Al-Qaeda, albeit tenuous, and their danger is thereby enhanced (CDI, 2002). Consequences are therefore no longer local or national, but global and the world as a whole seems more unsafe to many of its inhabitants who include potential tourists.

Islamic extremism has come to dominate discussions of terrorism, but other forms exist around the world and should not be overlooked. In Europe, members of Euskadi ta Askatsuna (ETA) or Basque Fatherland and Freedom in Spain continue to press for their own state and Chechens are seeking independence for the former Soviet Republic of Chechnya, which was incorporated into Russia after the breakup of the USSR. Kurdish groups operate in Central Asia, Kashmiri separatists in the Indian subcontinent and Maoists in Nepal. New styles of terrorism are also evident which employ tools such as suicide bombings, industrial poisons, chemicals and biological weapons. These tools allow terrorists to access more sites and launch larger scale attacks, with correspondingly high casualties. Recent anxieties relate to the possibility of terrorists acquiring disease pathogens, more and deadlier toxic substances and even a nuclear capability (Henderson, 2004; Thackrah, 2004).

Tourism and Terrorism

Terrorism represents a serious threat to law and order and undermines stability and security in political, economic and social arenas. Tourism is not spared from these effects and has been seen to be especially exposed and sensitive to incidents of terrorism, whether directed at visitors specifically or the wider community (Aziz, 1995; Pizam and Smith, 2000; Richter, 1999; Richter and Waugh, 1986; Sonmez, 1998; Sonmez and Graefe, 1998; Sonmez et al., 1999). Demand is adversely affected, destination attractiveness is tarnished and industry operations are disrupted. Such consequences can linger, dislocation and depressed visitor arrivals harming economies, and may have social and political ramifications which compound the original crisis. Terrorism is only one determinant among many of tourist flows, but it is unusually potent and can help to restructure volumes and patterns of distribution in the short term.

There are several explanations of why tourists and tourism businesses are sometimes deliberately targeted, one reason being the publicity generated worldwide and especially in the countries of origin of international visitors caught up in events. A fall in tourists and their spending also weakens economies and may cause social tensions, placing governments under stress and contributing to realizing the terrorist goal of general destabilization. It has been argued that tourists may be unpopular in the local community, leading to a condoning of the action by residents who themselves are spared. Enmity toward tourists can be acute in developing countries where tourism symbolizes the inequalities between the developed and Third World. Finally, the sector is a relatively straightforward target because of its size, diversity and extent. Many tourists are easily recognizable and tend to gather in large numbers at identifiable sites such as famous attraction venues, beaches, hotels and transport termini (Dimanche, 2004; Horner and Swarbrooke, 2004; Richter and Waugh, 1986).

Manifestations of terrorism aimed at tourism include suicide missions, hijackings, bombings and shootings which can take place in an assortment of environments. There is a history of moves against aircraft and airports, illustrated by the crash of a Pan-Am flight in Scotland in 1988 due to a bomb on board with the deaths of 249 people on the plane and 11 on the ground. Surface travelers are also deemed to be at greater risk now, although the Achille Lauro cruise ship was taken over by the Palestinian Liberation Front in 1985. An elderly wheelchair-bound passenger from the USA was thrown overboard and this was estimated to have dampened American enthusiasm for European cruising for at least five years (Weaver and Lawton, 2002). Trains were hijacked in the Netherlands in 1976 and 1977 by Republik Maluku Selatan (RMS), a group dedicated to founding a South Moluccas Republic independent of the former Dutch colony of Indonesia. Passengers were held hostage and a total of five died. Railways were also selected as objects of attack in London and Madrid in 2005 with heavy loss of life, for which Al-Qaeda sympathizers claimed responsibility.

Hotels appear to be regarded as comparatively "soft" targets. Islamic militants killed 16 Greek tourists in front of an Egyptian property in 1996; some subsequent atrocities are recorded in Table 4.1. Popular attractions are vulnerable and over 50 tourists were murdered at one of Egypt's ancient temples in 1997 (see Boxed Case One). Bombs were detonated at nightclubs known to be frequented by tourists in Bali in 2002 (see Case One) and again at restaurants in 2005. The Maoist Sender Luminoso (Shining Path) kidnapped and killed tourists in the mid-1980s and early 1990s in Peru (Ryan, 1991), some of these traveling on popular trekking routes. ETA has struck coastal tourist resorts in Spain and Kurdish groups have done so in Turkey. Visitors are also exposed to the hazards of terrorism by chance when in the

Table 4.1: **Significant terrorist attacks since 2002**

Date	Attack
November 2002	Suicide bombing at the Israeli-owned Paradise Hotel in Mombassa (Kenya) killed 15 people and injured 40. Anti-aircraft missiles also launched at Israeli charter flight from Mombassa. Al-Qaeda and Palestinian groups claimed responsibility.
February 2003	Beginning of series of kidnappings of European tourists in the Sahara Desert (Algeria) by the Salafist Group for Call and Combat (GSPC). A total of 32 hostages were taken and released by August, except one who died from heat stroke. The GSPC is linked indirectly to Al-Qaeda.
March 2003	Bomb in airport terminal in the Philippines killed 21 and wounded 149. Police blamed the Moro Islamic Liberation Front (MILF), an Islamic separatist group.
May 2003	Bombs in Casablanca (Morocco) at a Spanish restaurant, a five-star hotel and Jewish community center killed 45 and wounded 101. Salafiya Jihadiya with possible links to Al-Qaeda considered responsible.
August 2003	Suicide car bombing outside the Marriott hotel in Jakarta (Indonesia) left 12 dead and 149 wounded. JI claimed responsibility.
September 2003	Cabins in a Colombia National Park attacked and eight visitors kidnapped. One escaped and others later released. National Liberation Army claimed responsibility.
October 2003	Six people kidnapped from a resort in Sabah (Malaysia) near Philippine waters. One escaped and others executed. Abu Sayyaf Group (ASG), which split from the MILF in the early 1990s, suspected.
February 2004	Explosion led to sinking of ferry in the Philippines with 116 deaths. ASG believed to be responsible.
March 2004	Simultaneous bomb attacks on commuter trains in Madrid (Spain) resulted in 191 deaths and over 2,000 injured. Al-Qaeda claimed responsibility.
August 2004	Simultaneous explosions aboard two commercial aircraft in Russia killed 89. Believed to be the work of Chechen separatists.
October 2004	Bomb attacks at hotels in the Sinai Peninsula (Egypt) killed 34 and injured 159. Al-Qaeda network suspected.
July 2005	Suicide bombers on a London bus and underground trains killed 70 and injured 700. They appeared linked to Al-Qaeda.
July 2005	Car bombs at Egyptian resort of Sharm el-Sheikh killed 88 and wounded 100. Various Islamic militant groups claimed responsibility.
September 2005	Bombs at beach restaurants in Bali killed 23 and injured 150. JI suspected.
October 2005	Bombs in New Delhi (India) killed 61 and injured 200. Uncertainty about responsibility.
November 2005	Suicide bombers at hotels in Amman (Jordan) killed 57 and injured 120. Insurgents with Al-Qaeda connections suspected.

Sources: BBC News assorted reports; US Department of State, 2004; Wikipedia, 2005.

Boxed Case One: Tourist Attractions in Egypt as Terrorist Targets

In November 1997, militants armed with machine guns and swords arrived in a stolen tourist bus at Egypt's Queen Hatshupset temple in the Valley of Queens near the town of Luxor. They opened fire on people on the steps leading to the temple and nearly 70 were killed, 58 of whom were tourists. It was reported that the terrorists spent at least 45 minutes shooting before they were challenged. Knives were also used to kill some of the wounded and mutilate the bodies. The victims included 35 Swiss, nine Japanese, six Britons and four Germans. Egypt's Gama's al-Islamiya, dedicated to the creation of an Islamic state in Egypt, claimed responsibility and warned of further attacks to coincide with the beginning of the critical winter tourist season.

The dead and wounded were repatriated with the assistance of the various embassies and tourists hurried to leave as countries warned their nationals against travel to the south of the country. Many tour operators canceled their programs until the end of the year and there was a slump in arrivals. The event attracted global publicity with numerous human interest stories and a British paper ran an article about how three generations of the same family had died. One hotel saw occupancies decline to 8% and management summarized the crisis in terms of human, public relations and economic dimensions. Fearful guests and employees had to be dealt with and a crisis communication strategy executed in cooperation with the head office. Financial imperatives included pursuing cost savings, halting advertising temporarily, reducing the labor force and honoring the management contract agreed with the owner.

The Egyptian President blamed the attack on inadequate security and a new Interior Minister and Security Committee were appointed. It was announced that anti-terrorist squads would accompany tour groups, checkpoints and patrols would be increased near ancient sites and communications would be improved. The police presence was immediately heightened at popular sites such as the Pyramids and Sphinx and the surrounding desert areas. Authorities sought to convey the message that Egypt was as safe as any other destination and a month of discounted prices on transport, accommodation and attractions was planned for early 1998 to lure tourists back. The hotel made reference to above spoke of the need to keep a balanced perspective, focus on a return to normalcy and develop a clear crisis plan.

Events were reflected in Egypt's international tourism statistics. Arrivals in 1998 fell by 13.8% over 1997 and tourism receipts by 45.4%, although arrivals and revenue had recovered in 1999 when 1997 figures were exceeded. However, Luxor hotels failed to reach 1997 occupancy levels in 1999 with an average of 53%, although this was significantly higher than in 1998. It was reported that

> Egypt as a whole had successfully overcome the "Luxor effect" by 2000, perhaps assisted by the exceptional quality of its tourist attractions.
>
> *Sources:* Arthur Andersen, 2000; Oshins and Sonnabend, 1998; Assorted press reports.

vicinity of bombs detonated in busy markets and other crowded public spaces, often chosen as appropriate venues in order to maximize casualties.

Death and destruction are not, however, always the goals of terrorists and tourists can be employed as political pawns in cases of hostage taking and kidnapping. Overseas nationals are considered especially valuable because they can be used to extract concessions from destination governments which are put under strong pressure to act from the authorities of the tourist's home state. The example of a group of package tourists held hostage in Yemen was quoted in Chapter 3 and, although this ended in fatalities, it is not certain that this was the original intention of the perpetrators.

Sonmez and Graefe (1998) cited some of the above occurrences and additional illustrations from the 1970s through to the 1990s, linking their frequency to mass communications technologies. These technologies offer sophisticated and comprehensive channels through which to draw the world's attention to the cause being espoused by terrorists, the media sometimes being accused of complicity in providing a stage to present the stories of terrorism to eager audiences in the interests of stimulating sales and ratings. The twenty-first century continues to provide examples and the Al-Qaeda onslaught on New York and Washington in 2001 was unprecedented (see Case Two), ushering in a new era of insecurity. Other terrorist incidents of significance since 2002 which had a direct bearing on the tourism industry are listed in Table 4.1.

Terrorism unrelated to travel and tourism can also engender a mood of fear and foreboding among tourists and the tourism industry. Worries about being an accidental victim and negative images of places where outrages have occurred influence travel behavior and commercial decisions; this is exemplified by the troubled history of Northern Ireland as a tourist destination (see Boxed Case Two).

The tourism industry not only has to deal with horrific events and their aftermath, but also media interest which is usually very high. A great deal of attention and space will be devoted in print and broadcast materials to the topic, intensifying fears and heightening the sense of continuing danger. The influence of media reports generally is widely appreciated (Hall and O'Sullivan, 1996) and this perhaps increases during a tourism crisis related to terrorism. Exhaustive publicity can lead to distortion and exaggeration with a tendency to dramatize events, thereby escalating perceptions of risk out of proportion to realities. Images of violence and human misery are communicated immediately and repeatedly, creating negative destination images which it is extremely difficult for the tourism industry to counter. The chal-

Boxed Case Two: Tourism in Northern Ireland

Tourists to Northern Ireland, formally part of the United Kingdom and separated from the south after a civil war and intervention of British forces in 1920, attained a record 1.1 million in 1968. This number had fallen to 435,000 in 1972 and remained under a million until 1989. Growth was very slow thereafter, but reached 1.7 million in 2002 and 1.95 million in 2003.

The erratic pattern of arrivals and relatively low volumes mirror the political situation in the state and the activities of terrorist groups. The Irish Republican Army (IRA) and its various factions, dedicated to reunion with the predominantly Roman Catholic south, was the most active. Their aspirations were resisted by the majority Protestant population who wished to preserve the status quo, some supporting paramilitary groups such as the Ulster Volunteer Force of Protestant loyalists. The IRA has a long history, but its campaign was originally confined to the north-south border area. It intensified in the 1970s and spread to other parts of the north and later to the mainland where a series of major bombings also damaged the British international tourism industry. Although the Irish incidents mainly involved residents and British troops and were largely restricted to specific areas, they resulted in adverse publicity and negative associations which served to discourage tourists. Violence persisted for almost two decades.

The Tourist Board acknowledged the difficulties of trying to promote the territory generally in the worst periods. Nevertheless, it did make efforts to develop special-interest tourism such as river cruising, angling and travel by those of Irish ancestry wanting to discover their ancestral home. Most tourism was, however, motivated by visiting friends and relatives. Marketing and arrivals started to increase in the late twentieth century due to an easing of the security situation and progress in peace negotiations among the British and Irish governments and the IRA. There were, however, several outstanding issues to resolve such as the decommissioning of IRA arms.

Sources: Northern Ireland Tourist Board, 2004; Thackrah, 2004; Witt and Moore, 1992.

lenge is made worse when accompanied by the imposition of formal advisories which are discussed in the next section.

However, there may be variations in how these messages are received and responded to according to cultural background (Seddighi et al., 2001) and some tourists are less risk averse than others. Philippine Abu Sayyaf terrorists have been guilty of abductions in some Malaysian islands, but dive companies reported more customers after kidnappings in 2000. Mainly young divers professed themselves adventurous and unafraid, some visiting in expectation of bargain prices due to the unrest, and still attracted by the reputation of the area as an outstanding diving spot (The Straits Times, 2000).

Such individuals are perhaps unusual and considerations of personal safety play a crucial part in destination choice for most tourists (Sonmez and Graefe, 1998). Planned vacations are likely to be canceled after a terrorist attack, and tourists will substitute locations they believe to be safer. It does not make commercial sense for travel agents and tour operators in generating markets to promote places which are perceived as high risk. Hotel companies may reconsider planned developments and airlines rationalize services as demand falls in the most severe of cases, leading to an overall decline in investment and prolonged slump in tourism. Such a scenario is partly dependent on the recurrence of terrorism and government competence in managing it. Pizam and Fleischer (2002) argued that the repetition of any violence is more pertinent than the gravity of the first incident. This accounts for industry anxiety about the second bombings in Bali in 2005 which reminded the world of those in 2002, making it harder to dismiss the latter as an exceptional incident unlikely to be repeated. Depictions of Bali as a paradise lost were thereby reinforced and the recovery process interrupted.

Nevertheless, while talk of a "war on terror" was ubiquitous in the opening years of the present century, the might of terrorists should not be inflated. Some politicians have been accused of playing the politics of fear by overstating risks in order to strengthen their argument for the imposition of draconian measures which might otherwise be unacceptable on the grounds of an infringement of civil liberties. It must be remembered that injuries and fatalities due to terrorism remain extremely low in comparison to those due to more prosaic causes such as road traffic accidents. Recovery may also be fairly rapid and there are signs that society at large could be growing more resistant to the terrorist threat as a consequence of familiarity and adaptation, demonstrated by popular assertions that living life as normal represents a gesture of defiance against terrorists and may contribute to their ultimate defeat.

Travel Advisories

As already indicated, action undertaken by states to protect their citizens abroad may aggravate conditions of crisis or ameliorate them. Official embargos on travel are uncommon, but many governments do have a system of travel advisories which warn about actual and possible problems (Santana, 2001). These advisories increasingly include references to terrorist activity and urge vigilance. Messages are aimed at nationals and organizations with the intention of advising and instructions are not mandatory, but obviously carry the weight of official opinion. Places described as unsafe, or where there are doubts about safety, are likely to be shunned. There are also legal questions to consider and tour operators and travel agents may choose not to sell nations cited because of issues of liability and insurance coverage in the event of an incident.

Whether the advice constitutes a realistic evaluation or magnification of danger is a topic for debate, critics frequently maintaining that warnings only lead to unnecessary alarm. They are also often general and apply to a country as a whole, even though any disturbances may be confined to specific areas. This means that the national industry is affected and there is sometimes a spillover effect on the wider region. States previously seen as stable and safe may thus be sullied by their proximity to neighbors where terrorists are active. Singapore, renowned for its order and security, found itself included in advisories covering South East Asia following the Bali bombings in 2002 (Henderson, 2003a). Destination images of neighboring states can thus be damaged by such notices with adverse economic consequences, not least a fall in tourist arrivals and their spending.

Advisories may therefore have serious repercussions and are fiercely resisted by governments and tourism industries as a result, becoming a political issue which can mar international relations. The impartiality of some material has been questioned and there is a feeling among some observers that official statements reflect political interests and agendas (Sharpley et al., 1996). Governments are sometimes quick to promulgate warnings, but less eager to do so when dealing with close allies or regimes with which they are seeking an improved relationship. Tourism Concern, the UK-based pressure group, has been lobbying the British government to exercise much greater caution in any public announcements because of their potentially harmful consequences in the developing world (Tourism Concern, 2004).

Some authorities have responded to the above concerns and are seeking to work more closely with industry partners to ensure that information is accurate, appropriate and properly disseminated. The Australian Department of Foreign Affairs and Trade launched a "Smartraveller" public awareness campaign in 2003 accompanied by a Charter for Safe Travel in which the tourism industry is cooperating with government to safeguard Australian travelers abroad (Kemish, 2004). Revisions in 2005 sought to clarify risks further by adding a five-level scale and graphic table (DFAT, 2005). The British have a similar initiative dating from 2001, titled "Know Before You Go," designed to encourage safe and enjoyable travel by nationals. A Travel Advice Review Group was also set up and includes industry members. One participant is the PATA, which has consistently argued for greater industry consultation and representation in decision making on this topic (PATA, 2005).

The system of travel advisories thus has its weaknesses and there may be room for review and improvement to avoid unnecessary and alarmist pronouncements. However, it does serve an important purpose and allows governments to exercise their responsibilities concerning protecting the welfare of citizens and promoting their well-being when overseas which are essential duties in an era of mass international travel. The data contained in such bulletins are also of commercial interest and can be utilized by the tourism industry in tasks of environmental scanning and risk assessment which are key aspects of crisis planning.

Responding to Terrorism

Whether the threat of terrorism, either generalized or specific, leads to crisis partly depends on how it is handled with a need to strike a balance between action and over-reaction. Photographs of tanks stationed at London's Heathrow Airport after intelligence reports of a planned missile attack on a passenger plane in 2003 were deemed a "public relations disaster" for the UK industry. An impression was given that the country was under siege, frightening visitors away (BBC News, 2003).

In contrast, tourism crises following actual attacks are inescapable for the destination where they take place and will reverberate across a wider area. They are most acute for accommodation, attraction and transport services at the place hit as well as its marketers with the particular site having to cope with physical damage and perhaps total destruction. Violence against surface or air transport facilities and services is also a crisis for the regulatory authorities and governments at home and abroad must react to both the terrorist menace and damage to the tourism industry.

Acceptance of responsibilities and prompt action emerge as essential, as do effective communications, and Pan Am's deficiencies in this area exacerbated the airline's difficulties following the Lockerbie bombing. The company was reluctant to talk to the media, made no public apology and the CEO was not present at a memorial service. The official enquiry revealed that there had been specific warnings about a Pan Am plane being targeted and that the airline's security had been lax (Regester and Larkin, 1998; Thackrah, 2004). A tourist exodus and mass cancellations can be met by rationalization, capacity reduction and staff redundancies. Repatriation of tourists may have to be organized and arrangements made about customers who have already booked. Subsequent preferred industry tactics are intensified marketing, discounting, cultivation of favorable media coverage and upgrading of security which were all pursued by American airlines and hotels in the aftermath of 11 September 2001.

Official tourism marketing and development bodies play a vital part in leading the overall response and recovery at destination and industry levels. They are a focus and coordinator and would be expected to act as a spokesperson. Policy options correspond to those selected by Egyptian and Indonesian agencies after the mass murders at Luxor and Bali, respectively, such as the arrangement of special promotions and demonstrations of a commitment to tourist safety. Other proactive steps include encouraging the development of new products and markets and improvements in product quality, competitiveness and research. Crisis is a time of opportunity when moves toward efficiency, flexibility and desirable changes can be accelerated (WTO, 2002).

Traditional NTO promotion is unlikely to be appropriate or effective in the short term and marketing activity needs to be revised in light of the stage reached in progress toward rehabilitation. Major amendments are imperative if campaigns were previously centered on promises of tranquility in idyllic settings. Neighboring NTOs must also respond to serious outrages in ways designed to restore confidence. Many decide to concentrate on domestic and regional tourism which are likely to yield better immediate returns, but attempts are also made to transmit positive and reassuring messages about the destination in longer haul markets. However, it is not enough to only proffer assurances and practical measures to augment security should be implemented and advertised.

The collection of relevant and accurate information and its communication to key audiences are necessary to prevent distortion and combat irrational fears. However, many prospective visitors might be rather dismayed to see a lengthy bulletin on terrorist activities featured on the same official website which advertises the "Tourist Paradise" of Jammu and Kashmir in India (Government of J & K, 2004). The dissonance reveals the importance of an objective analysis of conditions and an acceptance that chronic instability due to terrorism may render tourism and its promotion temporarily unviable, a factor appreciated by the Northern Ireland Tourism Board in the most acute phase of its prolonged tourism crisis.

In the worst of circumstances, governments must be prepared to intervene to assist troubled businesses, boost confidence within and outside the industry and help in promotion as the US authorities tried to do after 11 September 2001. Security is obviously a government concern and there will always be room for advances, ideally in consultation with industry experts within the context of tourism. Senior officials can strive for fairness in travel advisories and lobby their foreign counterparts to limit and lift formal warnings. There is also scope for international initiatives, exploiting existing structures or installing new machinery for joint discussion and collaboration.

While schemes launched by public and private sector tourism bodies are crucial to recovery, its pace and final outcomes will depend upon a range of determinants beyond their control. They include media reporting and the attitudes of and actions by the international community. Terrorism is a political issue with its own complicated dynamics and underlying problems must be addressed in the search for compromise and workable political answers to ensure its ultimate defeat and a return to stability.

Prevention Strategies

Minimizing the chances of terrorism occurring is an important element of crisis planning with regard to tourism. Terrorism thrives on unpredictability and surprise, but this should not stop endeavors to understand and anticipate its dangers. Risk management can be practiced and consists of the stages of recognition, evaluation, avoidance and threat reduction (Thackrah, 2004). It does, however, partly depend upon sensitive and secret information in the context of terrorism which may not be readily obtainable. The business community must therefore rely on governments to share as much data as they can, but it is possible to identify many of the insecure areas of the world. Rejecting these areas for places which are comparatively safe is a practice already being followed by the international tourism industry and tourists.

Effective security is an aspect of prevention and recommended steps to reinforce post-crisis safety can be a means of averting another disaster (WTO, 1996). Airlines and airports have taken the lead in this arena, compelled by the security lapses revealed by the 11 September 2001 hijackings. Air marshals, impregnable cockpit doors, armed pilots, more thorough screening of passengers and luggage, bans on sharp objects in hand luggage and a military presence at airports have all been introduced. Immigration and passport controls have also been reformed and made stricter, with experiments in sophisticated biometric techniques to confirm identities.

Many hotel companies are now considering an airport style approach to deter terrorists. The Karachi Sheraton Hotel and Tower in Pakistan, which was attacked in May 2002 and remains a target, has a system of checking all vehicles and screening packages and luggage. The entrances are equipped with metal detectors and bullet-proof glass has been installed while the grounds are monitored by security cameras and armed guards are on duty. It was suggested by some commentators that the quick response of the security team at the Jakarta Marriott in 2003 led to the bomber panicking and detonating the explosive earlier than planned. Although there were human casualties, they might have been greater. The hotel experienced no structural damage and was able to reopen in a few weeks. The trade press argues that security is now a way for hotels and other tourism businesses to achieve competitive advantage and no longer a topic to be wary of when marketing (Hotels, 2003).

Operators and agents in generating countries, as well as governments, also have an obligation to educate travelers about security matters and what to do when faced with suspicious behavior. Optimal security regimes are determined by the particular enterprise and destination circumstances and arrangements suitable for a Karachi hotel, for example, may be excessive elsewhere. Facilities such as hotels, attractions and transport termini are also public spaces which must be accessible and allow people to move around with some freedom internally. Management has only limited authority over the terrain beyond its own boundaries, especially in city centers, and must therefore work with government organizations regarding perimeter security. There are additional issues of costs with some disagreement about how they should be allocated and thresholds of amounts providers and users are willing to pay.

At the same time, security demands must be reconciled with tourist convenience and comfort so that reassurance and safety are provided without provoking nervous agitation. Constant patrols of police or military personnel wielding machine guns may serve as an unpleasant reminder of terrorism while rigid and complicated immigration procedures can inhibit international tourism. More formidable defenses against terrorism should not spoil the visitor experience and securing a satisfactory compromise between security and other needs is an ongoing challenge for the tourism industry.

Summary and Conclusions

The presence and dread of terrorist activity thus represent a severe obstacle to tourism, impacting on both demand and supply. It is a source of crisis of differing degrees of intensity, sometimes of great magnitude, for all stakeholders and seems set to persist.

Analysts anticipate that tourists, destinations and transportation modes will be subject to more attacks. Certain nationalities will also be singled out and tourist attitudes and conduct alone may incite violence (Horner and Swarbrooke, 2004).

Nevertheless and as previously noted, the risk of terrorism must be placed in its proper perspective and not over-exaggerated. Leisure tourists in the past have proved willing to return to stricken locations as long as violence there is not endemic, using targeted modes of transport by choice or necessity. Other markets such as VFR (visiting friends and relatives) and business may be less vulnerable to the threat. Even in the case of 11 September 2001, regional and domestic tourism was resistant and benefited in some instances. Certain forms of special-interest tourism, where motivation to travel is very high, were also relatively unaffected (WTO, 2002). However, lessons can be learned from past experience in order to strengthen tourism's ability to survive terrorism and help in the struggle toward its eradication.

Case One: Bombings in Bali

The Bali bombings took place in October 2002 at two nightclubs in Kuta, a resort which is especially popular with young tourists. A total of 191 were killed and over 300 suffered injuries from the blast and fire which followed. Most of the casualties were Australian with Americans and Europeans also among the dead, as well as Balinese. An extensive area was laid waste and 450 buildings were damaged. Subsequent investigations revealed that the culprits were members of the JI group. Several governments, including those from principal source markets, issued advisories warning strongly against travel to Indonesia as a whole and recommended that any nationals there return home immediately.

The consequences were felt immediately with an exodus of tourists and prospective visitors, for both leisure and business purposes, canceled trips to destinations across Indonesia. Travel agents and tour operators in generating countries stopped selling Bali and made arrangements to repatriate any customers already there. All sectors of the industry were impacted, including the national carrier which cut the number of its flights due to lack of demand. Accommodation occupancy in Bali fell sharply and some hotels recorded rates of less than 10% compared with over 75% prior to the bombings. There was little business for the shops, attractions and food and beverage outlets which relied on tourism and the prospects of survival for smaller enterprises appeared bleak. Also at risk were the large number of hawkers who made up a substantial informal economy on the island and others such as self-employed tour guides and those engaged in arts and crafts.

The crisis was one for both Bali and Indonesia, the former accounting for over 40% of the country's foreign hotel guests in 2001. Officials initially reacted with expressions of sorrow and remorse and undertook a series of visits to countries which had lost the greatest number of citizens in order to convey these sentiments. There was an appreciation that marketing was a sensitive issue and that it would be difficult to erase the images of death and destruction which had circulated worldwide. However, there was also an awareness of the need to explain that Bali had not been fundamentally transformed and remained an appealing and welcoming destination. There was an effort to distribute accurate information about actual circumstances in Bali and stress that the terrorist threat was not confined to the island, but universal. Staying away would cause immense damage for an economy and society which was dependent on the income from tourists.

While marketing abroad was restrained, there was greater activity within Indonesia in an attempt to boost domestic tourism. Campaigns appealed to patriotic feelings and the importance of supporting recovery. Discounting was another central strategy and suppliers were urged to lower prices when selling at home and overseas. Officials from the public sector asked for support from private industry, emphasizing the importance of cooperation and solidarity. Appeals for sympathy and support from the international community were also made, including demands that travel warnings be lifted or lightened. There was discussion about the future and proposals for tighter controls over immigration and security in a bid to restrict terrorist movements. The crisis was also an opportunity to invest in infrastructure projects and entice investors through various incentives. However, such longer term action could not proceed without the involvement of the central authorities in the capital of Jakarta.

Balinese tourism showed some signs of recovery at the beginning of 2003, but the year was marked by unfavorable developments such as the onset of the war in Iraq and the SARS epidemic. There was also a further terrorist attack within Indonesia when the Marriott hotel in Jakarta was bombed in August 2003. Tourism in Bali had previously been protected from the adverse consequences of turmoil in other parts of Indonesia as the island had retained a distinct identity, but the Kuta bombs changed that situation. Arrivals into Bali dropped by 22.7% to under one million in 2003, although the figure increased again by 46.9% in 2004.

Sources: Bali Tourism Authority, 2005; BPS, 2005; Henderson, 2003a and 2003b.

Case Two: 11 September 2001

Using knives and boxcutters, five terrorists hijacked American Airlines Flight 11 with 92 passengers and deliberately piloted it into the North Tower of the World Trade Center in New York City at 0845 on 11 September 2001. United Airlines Flight 175 with 65 passengers was also hijacked and crashed into the South Tower at 0905. Both towers collapsed shortly after, killing about 3,000 people. Another group of terrorists hijacked American Airlines Flight 93 with 45 on board and headed it in the direction of Washington, DC, but passengers attempted to retake control and the plane crashed into the Pennsylvanian countryside. Finally, American Airlines Flight 77 with 64 passengers was flown into the west side of the Pentagon in the capital of Washington, DC, where 125 military and civilian personnel were killed. Al-Qaeda was later found to have organized the attacks.

These incidents had an immediate effect as airlines were grounded in North America and its airspace was shut down for two days. International and domestic flights were canceled and airports closed, affecting millions of passengers. Disruption continued after the two-day period, adding to the losses of the civil aviation industry. Meetings, conferences, events and sporting competitions were all abandoned or postponed alongside leisure and business travel in general.

Longer term outcomes included a drop in US outbound and inbound travel and in the rate of growth of global tourism. North American arrivals fell from 128.2 million in 2000 to 122.2 million in 2001 with a further decline to 116.6 million in 2002. World arrivals also contracted from 686 million in 2000 to 684 million in 2001, but recovered again to 703 million by 2002. Risk-averse markets such as the Japanese proved particularly sensitive, with a switch to domestic tourism, and there was an increase in intra-regional travel within the Muslim world. European centers, such as those in the UK, suffered financial losses due to the absence of American tourists. The day therefore had global ramifications, although the crisis was felt most intensely by the US tourism industry.

Transport, accommodation and catering, attractions and related services within the USA all lost business due to lack of demand. Cash flows and profits were damaged and jobs were lost. North American airlines were especially hard hit in a year when they had already been expected to lose more than US$1 billion due to difficult market conditions. Some were pushed nearer to bankruptcy and many employees were made redundant. Increased security measures were introduced and costs had largely to be met by the airlines which also had to pay much higher insurance premiums. There was a trend to postpone any planned investment. Overall, there was public anxiety and an erosion of confidence as travel became more stressful and subject to delays.

The severity of the situation demanded the intervention of government which responded by enhancing security, tightening law enforcement and providing assistance for enterprises threatened by the disaster. Modest and relatively inexpensive measures included tax allowances designed to ease cash-flow problems and boost business confidence. Compensation awards for airlines and installation of safety regimes were some of the more costly official actions.

Many private companies interrupted their marketing and there was uncertainty about the stance to adopt. Southwest Airlines, however, chose to deploy patriotic advertisements soon after the attacks and then introduced lower fares to stimulate demand. Most airlines waited and then launched advertising campaigns founded on emotional appeals which were felt to be in tune with the popular mood. Overcoming fears of flying and restoration of confidence were key objectives. United Airlines highlighted personal accounts by staff of their experiences since September 11, Continental drew attention to attributes of safety and reliability and American Airlines urged people to fly in order to enjoy visits with family and friends.

Hotels across the USA reacted in a variety of ways, with an emphasis on marketing and greater efficiency. Local and regional markets were believed to offer the best prospects in the short term and promotion was directed at these targets, accompanied by an increase in spending on advertising. There was also some price discounting to entice guests and attempts were made to maximize revenue through innovative use of space. Labor was regarded as a major area of cost cutting and staff hours were reduced and employees were requested to take vacation leave. Some properties took the opportunity to undertake repairs while others delayed these due to budgetary constraints.

The first priority for hotels in Washington, DC, immediately after the onslaught was to ensure that properties were safe. Information was then sought from official agencies about developments and instructions about how best to proceed. It was seen as important to avoid excessive price reductions and reopen closed airports and attractions as quickly as possible. Coordination was critical to recovery and there was widespread support for a later public relations campaign promoting the destination as a whole.

Sources: The Asian Wall Street Journal, 2001; Blake and Sinclair, 2003; Goodrich, 2002; Stafford et al., 2002; Taylor and Enz, 2002; WTO, 2005.

Concept Definitions

- Hijacking: The taking over by force of a conveyance, often with passengers on board, which is compelled to follow a route determined by the perpetrators in a bid to draw attention to their cause. The captured vehicle and occupants may be used as a bargaining tool in negotiations with officials related to the promotion of a particular political agenda.
- Hostage taking: The seizure by force and captivity of individuals and groups in order to draw attention to a cause and influence the decisions of governments.
- Security: The condition of being secure and free from anxieties, necessitating protection and defense which are the responsibility of the state in cases of national and international security.
- Suicide bombing: An attack in which the perpetrators are willing to give up their lives by deliberately crashing a vehicle containing explosives or detonating explosives, often in crowded areas to maximize damage, carried on their persons.
- Terrorism: The use of terror and violence by individuals or groups outside legitimate structures and processes to achieve desired ends which are usually political in nature.

Review Questions

1. Why has international terrorism become such a concern in recent years?
2. Is the terrorism threat exaggerated in general and with specific regard to tourism?
3. Why are tourists and tourism-related businesses popular terrorist targets?
4. What steps can destinations and businesses take to minimize the risk of a terrorist attack?

5. What strategies should an airline, hotel and destination marketing organization adopt in the immediate aftermath of a devastating terrorist attack and in the longer term?

6. Upon what factors does the severity of the impact of a terrorist attack on tourism depend?

7. Why should 11 September 2001 be considered such a significant occasion for global tourism?

8. Will Balinese tourism ever fully recover from the bombings in 2002?

Additional Readings

DFAT. (2006). Smartraveller. Australian Department of Foreign Affairs and Trade. Smartraveller website at http://www.smarttraveller.gov.au

Foreign and Commonwealth Office. (2006). Travel advice by country. Foreign and Commonwealth Office website at http://www.fco.gov.uk

US Department of State. (2006). International travel information. US Department of State website at http://www.travel.state.gov

References

Arthur Andersen. (2000). Tourism and terrorism: The road to recovery in Egypt. Hotel Online website at http://www.hotel-online.com, accessed 30 November 2004.

The Asian Wall Street Journal. (2001, 25 October). Airlines embrace emotion in new US ad campaigns.

Aziz, H. (1995). Understanding attacks on tourists in Egypt. *Tourism Management, 16*(2), 91–95.

Bali Tourism Authority. (2005). Statistics. Bali Tourism Authority website at http://www.balitourismauthority, accessed 5 June 2005.

BBC News. (2003). Heathrow tanks "deterred tourists." BBC News website at http://news.bbc.co.uk, accessed 3 December 2004.

Blake, A. and Sinclair, T. (2003). Tourism crisis management: US response to September 11. *Annals of Tourism Research, 30*(4), 813–832.

BPS. (2005). BPS Statistics Indonesia. BPS website at http://www.bps.go.id, accessed 5 June 2005.

CDI. (2002). *Terrorism project.* Washington: Center for Defense Information. CDI website at http://www.cdi.org, accessed 11 November 2002.

Desker, B. (2002). *Islam and society in Southeast Asia after September 11.* Working Paper 33. Singapore: Institute of Defence and Strategic Studies.

DFAT. (2005). Smartraveller. Australian Department of Foreign Affairs and Trade. Smartraveller website at http://www.smarttraveller.gov.au, accessed 1 December 2005.

Dimanche, F. (2004). The tourism sector. In G. Suder (Ed.), *Terrorism and the international business environment: The security-business nexus* (pp. 157–170). Cheltenham: Edward Elgar.

Foreign and Commonwealth Office. (2004). International terrorism. U.K. Foreign and Commonwealth Office website at http://www.fco.gov.uk, accessed 29 November 2004.

Goodrich, J.N. (2002). September 11, 2001 attack on America: A record of the immediate impacts and reactions in the USA travel and tourism industry. *Tourism Management*, *23*(6), 573–580.

Government of J & K. (2004). The official website of Jammu and Kashmir Government, India, at http://jammukashmir.nic.in, accessed 26 November 2004.

Hall, C.M. and O'Sullivan, V. (1996). Tourism, political stability and violence. In A. Pizam and Y. Mansfeld (Eds.), *Tourism, crime and international security issues* (pp. 77–93). Chichester: Wiley.

Henderson, H. (2004). *Global terrorism* (rev. ed.). New York: Facts on File.

Horner, S. and Swarbrooke, M. (2004). *International cases in tourism management*. Boston: Elsevier Butterworth-Heinemann.

Henderson, J.C. (2003a). Managing the aftermath of terrorism: The Bali bombings, travel advisories and Singapore. *International Journal of Hospitality and Tourism Administration*, *4*(2), 17–31.

Henderson, J.C. (2003b). Terrorism and tourism: Managing the consequences of the Bali bombings. *Journal of Travel and Tourism Marketing*, *15*(1), 41–58.

Hotels. (2003, October). Global update: Security challenge, 10–11.

Kemish, I. (2004, 14 August). Speech, The smart traveler. Delivered at the AFTA General Conference Sydney. Smartraveller website at http://www.smarttraveller.gov.au, accessed 14 November 2005.

Northern Ireland Tourist Board. (2004). Visits to NI and revenue generated. Northern Ireland Tourist Board website at http://www.ntb.com, accessed 2 December 2004.

Oshins, M. and Sonnabend, J. (1998, April). Sonesta International Hotels: Responding to a crisis. *Cornell Hotel and Restaurant Administration Quarterly*, 38–45.

PATA. (2005). Travel advisories: How to use them properly. Pacific Asia Travel Association website at http://www.travelwithpata.com/travel_advisories.html, accessed 14 November 2005.

Pizam, A. and Fleischer, A. (2002). Severity versus frequency of acts of terrorism: Which has a larger impact on tourism demand? *Journal of Travel Research*, *40*, 337–339.

Pizam, A. and Smith, G. (2000). Tourism and terrorism: A quantitative analysis of major terrorist acts and their impact on tourism destinations. *Tourism Economics*, *6*(2), 123–138.

Regester, M. and Larkin, J. (1998). *Risk issues and crisis management: A casebook of best practice*. London: Kogan Page.

Richter, L. (1999, August). After political turmoil: The lessons of rebuilding tourism in three Asian countries. *Journal of Travel Research*, *38*, 41–45.

Richter, L. and Waugh, W. (1986). Terrorism and tourism as logical companions. *Tourism Management*, *7*(4), 230–238.

Ryan, C. (1991, September). Tourism, terrorism and violence: The risks of wider world travel. *The Study of Conflict and Terrorism*, 1–30.

Santana, G. (2001). Globalisation, safety and national security. In S. Wahab and C. Cooper (Eds.), *Tourism in the age of globalisation* (pp. 213–241). London: Routledge.

Seddighi, H.R., Nuttall, M.W., and Theocharous, A.L. (2001). Does cultural background of tourists influence the destination choice? An empirical study with special reference to political instability. *Tourism Management, 22*, 181–191.

Sharpley, R., Sharpley, J., and Adams, J. (1996). Travel advice or trade embargo? The impacts and implications of official travel advice. *Tourism Management, 17*(1), 1–7.

Sonmez, S. (1998). Tourism, terrorism risk and political instability. *Annals of Tourism Research, 25*(2), 416–456.

Sonmez, S., Apostolopoulos, Y., and Tarlow, P. (1999, August). Tourism in crisis: Managing the effects of terrorism. *Journal of Travel Research, 38*, 13–18.

Sonmez, S. and Graefe, A. (1998). Influence of terrorism risk on foreign tourism decisions. *Annals of Tourism Research, 25*(1), 112–144.

Stafford, G., Yu, L., and Armoo, A. (2002, October). Crisis management and recovery: How Washington, DC hotels responded to terrorism. *Cornell Hotel and Restaurant Administration Quarterly*, 27–40.

The Straits Times. (2000, 17 September). Hostage crisis: Tourists still coming.

The Straits Times. (2002, 30 November). Tourism takes yet another hit.

Taylor, M. and Enz, C. (2002, February). GMs' responses to the events of September 11, 2001. *Cornell Hotel and Restaurant Administration Quarterly*, 7–20.

Thackrah, J.R. (2004). *Dictionary of terrorism* (2nd ed.). London and New York: Routledge.

Tourism Concern. (2004). Foreign and Commonwealth Office on travel advice. Tourism Concern website at http://www.tourismconcern.org.uk/campaigns/FCO-advisories.html, accessed 28 November 2004.

US Department of State. (2004). *Patterns of global terrorism 2003*. Washington, DC: US Department of State.

Weaver, D. and Lawton, L. (2002). *Tourism management*. Sydney and Melbourne: John Wiley.

Wikipedia. (2005). List of terrorist incidents. Wikipedia website at http://en.wikipedia.org, accessed 5 January 2005.

Witt, S.F. and Moore, S.A. (1992). Promoting tourism in the face of terrorism: The role of special events in Northern Ireland. *Journal of International Consumer Marketing, 4*(3), 63–75.

WTO. (1996). *Tourist safety and security: Practical measures for destinations*. Madrid: World Tourism Organization.

WTO. (2002). *Tourism after 11 September 2001: Analysis, remedial actions and prospects*. Madrid: World Tourism Organization.

WTO. (2005). *Tourism highlights. Edition 2004*. Madrid: World Tourism Organization.

5

Socio-Cultural Conflicts and Tourism

Learning Objectives

By the end of the chapter, the reader should be able to

- Identify the ways in which tourism can impact on the society and culture of destinations.
- Appreciate how such impacts may generate conflicts which can evolve into tourism crises.
- Understand that social and cultural conditions may impede the functioning of the tourism industry and threaten the well-being of tourists.
- Recognize the importance of managing the relationship between tourists and residents in order to minimize tensions and the possibility of crisis.
- Suggest strategies to protect tourists in the event of socio-cultural crises occurring, including those related to crime.

Introduction

Tourists and tourism development have the ability to induce change in the society and culture of destinations. These dynamics may generate tensions between visitors and residents, resulting in an industry crisis. Wider conditions can also be a barrier to public and private investment and a threat to tourist safety. Visitors may be caught up in outbreaks of civil unrest or become targets of crime and could be inconvenienced by modifications to travel itineraries and cancellations by tour operators due to disruption. The imposition of travel advisories by governments in response to uncertainty related to social disturbance is also likely to dampen demand and undermine industry confidence.

This chapter examines the above difficulties and proposes appropriate responses to the challenges posed by latent and actual tourism crises within a social and cultural context, whether internal or external in origin. The chapter case studies deal with crime in Florida and the Greek island of Rhodes, when tourists were victims and perpetrators of criminal acts, respectively, and attempts by the public and private sectors working independently and in alliance to defuse the crises.

Socio-Cultural Impacts of Tourism

Tourism brings together visitors and residents from different societies and cultures and, even if not directly involved in tourism, those living at popular tourist destinations are likely to be affected by the presence of visitors and a tourism industry. Factors such as warmth of welcome and friendliness of the population are valued by tourists and often promised by marketers, but subsequent studies confirm earlier findings (Butler, 1974; Doxey, 1975) that inhabitants of places which attract significant numbers of tourists display a range of attitudes from enthusiastic support to strong opposition. Various determinants are at work, but personal gain and inconvenience are key considerations. Most people probably incline toward the passivity which defines the silent majority, yet activists opposed to tourism in general or specific projects could create problems for the industry. There is a possibility of crises arising when hostility to tourism becomes intense and widespread.

Animosity may derive from the harmful social and cultural consequences of tourism and a distinction is sometimes made between the two fields. Social describes the way in which a society is structured and its attributes while cultural refers to aspects such as values, norms of behavior and heritage (Lea, 1988). However, they are frequently combined in tourism analysis and the phrase socio-cultural is used in this chapter to describe the features which characterize the multiple facets of the lives and beliefs of individuals and groups.

Such impacts are likely to be felt most acutely in Third World countries which host arrivals from developed nations whose personal circumstances and backgrounds contrast sharply with those of residents (UNESCO, 1976). Tourism's potential influence is perhaps greatest where the socio-cultural and economic distance between locals and visitors is widest. The relationship can become inequitable when the tourism industry and its customers assert authority and communities are marginalized, resulting in anger and resistance (Burns, 2001).

Causes of grievances are the displacement of local populations due to tourism-related development and movement away from traditional occupations such as farming and fishing. Tourism has a number of limitations as an employer and jobs on offer are frequently low skilled, inadequately paid, seasonal and without career prospects as noted in Chapter 2. Expatriates are seen to be favored regarding management positions, thereby disadvantaging locals (Kusluvan and Karamustafa, 2001). Migrants may be attracted and an influx of outsiders can lead to frictions among workers.

Tourism has been responsible for the degradation of various representations of culture and can overwhelm and destroy the indigenous, replacing it with the artificial and inauthentic (Robinson and Boniface, 1999). Acculturation occurs when two cultures meet and the weaker changes to accommodate the stronger; sometimes both may adapt to each other and permanent alterations are then passed down to the next generation. Alternatively, cultural drift takes place when the meeting of cultures results in temporary or seasonal adjustment with a reversion to original states after parting. Some modifications appear inevitable, however, including to mother tongues which are devalued because of demands that communications be in English or the tourist's native language (Mathieson and Wall, 1996). There can be a harmful demonstration effect whereby residents aspire to and seek to emulate the tourist lifestyle, abandoning established mores and customs. Envy of tourists and their material possessions and an appreciation that these are beyond reach may provoke feelings of resentment and enmity, perhaps encouraging crime, which is examined later.

Religion is another area of contention, especially when it is exploited for tourism purposes and those visiting important sites demonstrate a range of motivations and interest which may not be compatible. A lack of sensitivity on the part of tourists can undermine the sacredness of holy places and interfere with ceremonies and personal worship (Shackley, 2001). In Islamic states, non-Muslims may upset locals due to ignorance about or deliberate flaunting of the codes which dictate how daily life is conducted. Wearing scanty clothing, drinking alcohol, eating forbidden food and displaying physical affection to one of the opposite sex in public are all violations which may give offense when practiced openly by tourists (Din, 1989). Additional discontent about Westernization and the declining moral standards which are sometimes perceived to accompany tourism (Ap et al., 1991) have perhaps a wider applicability and are not confined to adherents of Islam.

Situations vary across the Muslim world and responses to international tourism are partly dependent on the degree of liberalism. Popular destinations like Egypt, the Gambia, Morocco and Turkey (WTO, 2004) appear willing to accommodate tourist differences and demands in return for the economic rewards they bring. However, the rise in Islamic extremism has been a source of new and potentially divisive socio-cultural forces which are evident in more moderate nations such as Malaysia (see Boxed Case One). Ideological dictates in combination with a desire to avoid social disturbance has led to some Middle Eastern governments discouraging visitors from the West, deeming their style of tourism inconsistent with Islam. Nevertheless, several are modifying this position as illustrated by the once-isolationist Iran and Saudi Arabia which are now seeking to develop their international tourism industry for reasons of economic diversification (Travel and Tourism Intelligence, 1998). Any such advances will have socio-cultural consequences which must be monitored and carefully managed to avoid the emergence of confrontation and crisis.

In contrast to developing countries, of whatever faith, developed states and their urban centers are perhaps more able to absorb tourists into societies which are already highly modernized, sophisticated, cosmopolitan and subject to constant cultural change. However, tourism still has the capacity to disturb resident populations and their everyday lives in such environments by inconveniencing them and exacerbating existing stresses. Tourism may thus be a source of discord in destina-

Boxed Case One: Islam and Tourism in Malaysia

Malay Muslims represent over 60% of Malaysia's population and Islam is a defining characteristic of the society. The country has, however, presented itself as a modern and progressive multicultural nation which is tolerant of other faiths. Such a stance has been challenged by a widening interest in a more conservative form of Islam, reflected in rising support for the Parti Islam SeMalaysia (PAS) in the late 1990s which committed itself to implementing full Islamic law.

PAS gained political control of the northerly state of Terengganu and introduced measures designed to ensure conformity with the more rigid strictures of Islam. They included shutting down karaoke premises and pubs and further restricting the sale of alcohol and issue of entertainment licenses. Attempts were made to ensure that men and women joined different lines when waiting in shops in addition to other steps affecting principally locals. It was announced that pictures of women were not to be used in tourism marketing materials and the possibility was raised of rules about attire incorporating the prohibition of clothing like two-piece swimsuits. Separating male and female swimming pool bathers and hotel staff in residence were also mentioned.

This policy was criticized by hotel managers and others in the tourism industry at home and overseas and led to confrontation with the federal authorities, which were anxious about the repercussions for perceptions of Malaysia abroad and tourist arrivals. In response, the state government claimed that its actions had been misrepresented and that matters were only at the discussion stage, stressing that tourists were still desired and would be warmly received.

Source: Henderson, 2003.

tions under pressure from rising numbers of visitors, irrespective of their overall development phase. Such sentiments can provoke an anti-tourism lobby which the public and private sectors must give due regard to in order to conciliate unfavorable opinion.

Socio-Cultural Conditions and Tourism Crises

As well as socio-cultural conflicts created by tourism itself, the nature of certain societies and cultures and events in these arenas can be a catalyst of crisis. Prevailing conditions and norms may frustrate the operation of the tourism industry and the promotion of the favorable destination images upon which tourism depends. This applies especially to locations which display long-term social instability, often rooted in political and economic systems, which are perceived as unattractive by visitors and investors and may be unsafe in reality. Realization of tourism's potential will therefore be hindered and the industry's performance will remain disappointing. Isolated upheavals also damage the tourism industry, although their repercussions will be more confined temporally and spatially.

Examples include parts of Central and South America, Africa and South East Asia. In the last region, Indonesia as a whole (with the exception of Bali) has struggled to secure growth in its visitor arrivals, despite a wealth of natural and cultural resources. This has been due to the chronic instability which has handicapped the nation in recent years (Prideaux et al., 2003). The collapse of the Suharto regime in the late 1990s ushered in a period of political and economic volatility which had social ramifications as unemployment and poverty levels rose. There was unrest in many areas involving looting and ethnic riots in which Chinese communities were targeted. Such a history and ongoing uncertainty inhibited tourism and its promotion, leading to an extended overall crisis for the industry. Particular incidents have precipitated smaller scale and localized crises, but their satisfactory resolution is impeded by doubts about the overall future stability of Indonesia (Henderson, 1999).

Certain forms of religious extremism may also discourage tourists and fierce disputes between rival faiths, sometimes linked to a political agenda, will alarm tourists and the tourism industry. Acrimony between Catholics and Protestants has had this effect in Northern Ireland and recurring violence between Muslims and Christians has been an additional obstacle to tourism in parts of Indonesia (see Boxed Case Two). More generally, tourism has been adversely affected by misunderstandings between

---

Boxed Case Two: Religious Violence in Lombok, Indonesia

The Indonesian island of Lombok, 40 kilometers east of Bali, experienced an outbreak of religious violence in early 2000 when gangs of Muslim youths attacked Christian homes, businesses and churches. They also attempted to block the capital's ferry terminal and threatened hotels. Police were ordered to shoot rioters on sight after three deaths and widespread damage to property. Similar incidents were occurring on the nearby island of Sulawesi and over 500 had already died since the beginning of the year across the Moluccas.

Officials claimed that the situation was under control and "harsh security measures" would be taken. Hotels and other enterprises displayed Islamic prayer mats and sacred texts to try to ensure immunity. Resident Christians and Hindus turned to the police and army for protection and many left, accompanied by tourists. One hotel sent its guests by ferry to Bali and flights were arranged by the government of Australia to repatriate its nationals. No tourists were harmed and the violence died down, although the image of Lombok and neighboring islands was sullied.

Source: BBC News, 2000.

Islamic and Western nations and mutual stereotyping. Relations have deteriorated since the incidents of 11 September 2001 and Islam is often seen as synonymous with antipathy toward Westerners, terrorist agitation, suppression and illiberality (Armstrong, 2001). At the same time, Western powers are viewed as neo-colonizers intent on asserting their superiority in every arena and in charge of immoral and godless societies (Said, 1979). These misconceptions shape attitudes and cultures in which religion plays a fundamentally different role may clash at destinations.

Crime and Tourism

Crime is one manifestation of socio-cultural dislocation connected to economics which has implications for tourism, although research reveals a lack of consensus about the relationship. Some commentators maintain that certain criminal actions are closely associated with tourism and increase alongside visitor numbers. Others argue than any linkages are more complex and that tourism does not inevitably lead to more crime which may be a consequence of related or unrelated sociological and economic factors (Pelfrey, 1998; Pizam, 1982).

Nevertheless, there is agreement that tourists as a whole are seen as relatively easy and appealing targets by some criminals because they are conspicuous and believed to be carrying substantial amounts of money as well as valuable personal possessions. They may also be less vigilant when away from home in strange surroundings and unfamiliar with areas which are best avoided (Ryan, 1993). Crimes committed against tourists range from petty thieving to more serious offenses of murder (Pizam, 1999) and are partly determined by the qualities of the destination (Prideaux, 1996). One theory explains how hot spots are centers full of establishments like bars and nightclubs which are magnets for both tourists and criminals (Crotts, 1996).

Such crimes and fears of them are features of many destinations and a topic which must be addressed by the tourism industry and local authorities. The potential for crisis is evidenced by parts of the Caribbean where there are high incidences of criminal activity, fueled by drug taking. Crime against tourists in Jamaica acquired prominence in the 1980s and was originally restricted to the main resorts, although international media stories suggested that it was rampant across the whole island. Isolated cases of murder attracted the greatest attention, inspiring formal government warnings in generating markets, and crime in general was a persistent problem throughout the 1990s (Albuquerque and McElroy, 1999).

Crime continued to mar Jamaica's reputation in the twenty-first century and there were riots in 1999 (BBC News, 1999) and gang warfare in the capital's streets in 2001 (BBC News, 2001a and 2001b). These outbreaks led to more official advisories and intervention by tour operators and travel agents to protect customers who were exposed to the violence. While arrivals remained steady, the country's Tourism Minister admitted in 2004 that crime statistics and negative publicity were still driving away tourists and investors from Jamaica (AP, 2004). A pattern of escalating tourist victimization has been repeated in other Caribbean islands and also threatened the industry in certain locations in North America, notably Florida in the early 1990s when there was a series of assaults on international tourists (see Case One).

Tourists too engage in criminal deeds from minor incidents of air rage to deadly drunken brawls and buying the services of child prostitutes. Anti-social behavior, showing disrespect for local inhabitants and their cultures as well as other tourists, may also border on criminality. While such acts are usually restricted in extent, they can be sufficiently serious to jeopardize the reputation of a resort and have commercial consequences for the industry. Loutish behavior and binge drinking by young British holidaymakers on the Greek island of Rhodes proved a mounting crisis for local businesses and authorities as well as tour operators in 2003 (see Case Two), symptomatic of a "lager lout" sub-culture in the UK spawned by social trends.

Resorts elsewhere in the Mediterranean have experienced these challenges and are searching for an appropriate strategy to curb the destructive self-indulgence displayed by sections of the youth market. In Australia, "Schoolies Week" celebrates the end of school for those finally leaving and has been condemned for excessive drinking and violence. Youths have traditionally congregated at Queensland's Gold Coast in an event which has become commercialized and is replicated at other locations. Although valued by some because of its contribution to local economies, the festival is not always welcomed by the police and local residents because of the unrestrained conduct of participants (ABC, 2003).

Managing Socio-Cultural Tourism Crises

Tourism crises may therefore be triggered by socio-cultural circumstances, usually at destinations rather than in generating countries, which are the result of tourism itself or the operation of unrelated factors. Internally induced difficulties in this sphere can also be reinforced by external troubles, compounding any crisis. Avoiding or minimizing the likelihood of socio-cultural clashes is therefore a key concern of the tourism industry, although this aim is easier to pursue when tourism is the principal cause of any such problems.

One tactic is to stress the positive impacts of tourism for local societies and cultures and work toward their realization. Programs of education can help to promote awareness of benefits and messages to communicate are that tourist interest and money can assist in a revival of local cultures and traditions and a resurgence of skills. It provides a rationale and funding for the conservation of heritage and has a function in the protection and assertion of national and cultural identities. Higher standards of living and improved public services are other gains to be emphasized and strived for.

The tourism industry must take into account conditions and socio-cultural sensitivities at destinations which tourists also need to be educated about. Knowledge and understanding of socio-cultural distinctiveness apply especially to the field of religion, not least with regard to Islam. Non-Muslim visitors to Muslim countries should be mindful of religious rules and those serving Muslims traveling overseas should seek to be similarly sympathetic to their special requirements (Syed, 2001).

Segregation of visitors and residents is one possible strategy, exemplified by the Maldives where certain of the numerous small islands are designated for the sole use of visitors and access to others that are inhabited is regulated (Ministry of Tourism, 2004). Such a policy is facilitated by the unique geography of the republic and is not always practical or possible. Enclave tourism, associated with integrated beach resorts, is also based on separation and means that local and tourist communities occupy their own clearly defined spaces and any interaction is minimal. However, such complexes often aggravate resentment of tourists and dissatisfaction on the part of visitors who wish to gain insights into a country's people and culture (Freitag, 1994). In most instances, contact between visitors and residents is desirable and inevitable so that attention must be given to reducing the chances of harm to both parties, one means being through careful planning.

Effectively dealing with tourism's damaging socio-cultural impacts and preventing their evolution into crisis are more likely to be achieved within a context of the planning of tourism as a whole. This allows destination authorities to exercise a degree of control over the pace of development and changes to the physical and cultural landscapes. King et al. (2000) described the merits of a societal marketing orientation which gives priority to the host community and resources, after which tourist needs are considered. A more equitable form of tourism thereby emerges, one element of which is satisfactory and rewarding relationships among all stakeholders.

While attainment of the more ambitious objectives of tourism plans sometimes seems elusive, practical steps at a micro level may be executed. This is evidenced by the Nusa Dua beach resort on the Indonesian island of Bali where early measures taken by the developers to appease locals and thwart any opposition encompassed socio-cultural issues. Few residents lived on the selected site which was largely unsuitable for farming, although fishermen were permitted to continue using parts of the beach and some public footpaths were installed. There were discussions with the community before work commenced and information about progress was conveyed regularly. Locals were given preference regarding jobs, being offered training at a new hotel school, and encouraged to set up their own businesses to take advantage of the tourism inflow. Farmers were advised to raise the quality of their output and sell it to hotels. The developers invested in infrastructure upgrading, leading to better communications and public amenities. Details about correct behavior and dress were distributed to tourists and celebrations of local culture were arranged (Inskeep, 1991).

Although appropriate and commendable, such initiatives require ongoing and heavy commitment and funding from business and government as well as support from tourists and residents if they are to succeed. The advantages of participatory planning in general are constantly hailed, but the concept may be unrealistic in countries which do not possess a tradition of popular political participation or the necessary facilitating structures. Even when these exist, there may be considerable apathy and a reluctance to take part. Nevertheless, officials and the industry both have responsibilities to seek to enter into a dialogue with locals and involve them in their decisions. Residents who are consulted and properly informed may be less antagonistic and the industry can stimulate goodwill by contributing to destination societies and cultures in meaningful ways. Such goals correspond to those which underpin the theory and practice of corporate social responsibility and sustainable development in general which have a particular relevance for the tourism industry because of its close linkages with local communities and economies (Hopkins, 1999; UNEP, 2005a and 2005b).

With regard to averting crime, the building of self-contained resorts became a marked trend in Jamaica in an attempt to insulate tourists from felony and harassment by traders and verbal insults. Barriers of fencing and security personnel were employed by many hotels and there were calls at the beginning of the 1990s from tour operators, hotels, officials and tourists for military surveillance. Patrols were eventually announced in 1999 and had the support of the Jamaican Hotel and Tourist Association. The move was, however, opposed by some politicians who argued that a greater number of tourists would be repelled than reassured. (Albuquerque and McElroy, 1999).

Writing about desired solutions within a Caribbean context, the authors proposed greater cooperation between the police and tourism industry. A stronger and more visible presence of police and official uniformed guards at major tourist centers was also urged. It appears that police often attribute any crime to tourist carelessness and such insensitive attitudes need to be revised. Information about risks can be circulated and residents should be consulted in tourism policy making, thereby preventing feelings of alienation and hostility which could find expression in oral and physical abuse of visitors. The authors asserted that action is imperative to ensure that other Caribbean islands do not duplicate the Jamaican model of growing violence directed at tourists.

In the instance of the assaults on tourists in Florida, the initial response was one of heightened police intervention and partnerships with industry. Public relations and marketing then concentrated on image enhancement and more conventional destination advertising as outlined in the case. The Miami experience was of interest to other American cities popular with tourists, but also threatened by crime like New York and San Francisco. Brunt et al. (2000) cited further examples of New Orleans in the USA and Kenya and South Africa where a similar approach to Miami's was followed and some successes were recorded. Commercial opportunities have also been acknowledged and one American company advertises tourist safety maps which show major attractions alongside safe and unsafe areas.

However, crime and deviancy and their fundamental causes have economic, social and political ramifications extending beyond the field of tourism. The tourism industry on its own cannot hope to achieve substantial progress in solving such dilemmas. It must therefore unite with the relevant authorities in crime prevention programs and the promotion of tourist safety (Pizam et al., 1997; Prideaux and Dunn, 1995).

Summary and Conclusions

Tourism affects and is affected by the social and cultural character of both tourists and destination residents. Its power to induce change is usually stronger among the latter because it is these populations which have to adapt to the influx of visitors and the creation of an infrastructure for them. The tourism development process may itself trigger crises due to socio-cultural conflicts between tourists and locals. While the industry is the author of such tensions, it is also the source of solutions to the underlying problems and can act to prevent potentially difficult situations from evolving or stop them deteriorating into crises.

In cases in which crises emerge from wider socio-cultural attributes and occurrences, the industry has much less authority. These crises may be severe and lengthy if instability is endemic or be of relatively short duration if the pivotal event is isolated and unlikely to be repeated. Whatever the scale, the industry has to work with external agencies in addressing and alleviating the root causes of local attitudes and behavior which threaten tourist safety and spoil destination images.

Case One: Crime Against Tourists in Florida

There was a 50% decline in British and German visitors to Florida after nine foreign tourists were murdered there within one year in the early 1990s. A number of the victims had hired vehicles for self-drive holidays, which were a popular choice among tourists. However, they were often unfamiliar with the American road network and it was easy for drivers to lose their way after departing from Miami International Airport. The incidents seemed to indicate a trend whereby youths with a criminal intent were picking on cars which were clearly marked as being rented.

The Greater Miami Convention and Visitors Bureau had anticipated a crisis after the earlier shooting of a British couple in 1991 and begun discussions with various agencies, leading to initiatives to improve safety among visitors by 1993. Components included better signage on highways near the airport and to beaches, the elimination of labels on cars which indicated they had been rented, distribution of safety literature, increased police patrols and presence at the airport and two new visitor desks there. The immediate aims were to convince the public that action was being taken and to improve Miami's battered image, helping to retain as many as possible of the large number of repeat visitors. Advertising for Florida was suspended at the height of the crisis when the subject of crime there received national and international publicity and a representative of the Convention and Visitors Bureau and its chief became the spokespersons throughout the crisis.

About 50 individuals from the public and private sectors set up a group dedicated to safe neighborhoods and lobbied state authorities to take a tougher stance against criminals. News stories began to circulate about these moves which presented a favorable picture of a commitment to eradicate crime. After an appropriate interval and taking advantage of a spell of exceptionally cold weather affecting much of the USA, a new advertising campaign for Miami was launched in 1994. Positive press releases also reported on the success of police campaigns, a decline in car rental theft and recovery and growth in international tourist arrivals.

Sources: Brayshaw, 1995; Greco, 1994; Pelfrey, 1998.

Case Two: Crime by Tourists in Rhodes, Greece

Faliraki, a former fishing village on the Dodecanese island of Rhodes, saw a rapid expansion in tourist arrivals between the 1970s and 1980s. It originally drew an assortment of types of tourists from countries across Europe, but was attracting large numbers of young people from the UK by the end of the century. They were lured by Faliraki's growing reputation as a place to drink and party to excess, encouraged by UK-based tour operators catering to the youth market which offered hedonistic promises in their marketing. Out of control drinking and lewd and offensive behavior, including street fighting, were commonplace in the town center and 34 reported rapes were perpetrated by tourists in 2002. The deteriorating situation was blamed on aggressive bar promotions by bar and club owners, pub crawls organized by representatives of tour operators with as many as 500 participants and inadequate policing.

Circumstances were largely tolerated until they reached a nadir when a British 17-year-old died in a bar brawl in 2003. The incident led to increased action by Greek authorities and police arresting more British tourists for drunkenness and disorderliness. There was consultation with police officers from the English seaside resort of Blackpool regarding their methods of curbing hooliganism and the mayor of the wider Faliraki district announced the introduction of the following measures:

- A new police station with 20 officers
- The police force to be supplemented by another 10 municipal officers
- Arranged bar crawls restricted to 50 participants, whose names would be submitted to the police, and a maximum of four bars
- Bars permitted to provide only one complimentary drink
- Stricter implementation of nightclub rules
- No music in bars after midnight

The mayor spoke about adopting a low-key approach and his desire that young people would continue to visit and enjoy themselves. Plans were also set out to showcase and draw tourist attention to the cultural, scenic, natural and culinary attractions of the area.

Both general and specialized tour operators in the UK faced difficulties in selling the destination which was already losing customers from the family and couples markets prior to 2003. According to operators, the youth market itself fell by an estimated 68% in the 2004 summer season due to adverse publicity. The managing director of one of the largest companies claimed that it would cooperate fully with the Greek authorities and anticipated that the decline in demand from the youth market would be offset by renewed interest from couples and families. Efforts would be made to restore Faliraki to the position of a resort for families, which it had been before the youth invasion. One of the more prominent youth market operators was reported to be "toning down" its program by canceling pub crawls and appealing to those who "crave a rest between the action."

Senior officials from the UK industry met with staff from the Greek National Tourism Organization and British Embassy in Athens in addition to public and private sector representatives in Faliraki to discuss the situation. They concluded that greater liaison with the police and enhanced policing and closer contact with local businesses were crucial to avoid another crisis on Rhodes and elsewhere in Greece. There were also demands that operators should revise the manner in which Greek destinations were presented in order to interest formerly untargeted groups.

Sources: BBC News, 2003a and 2003b; BBC News, 2004; Travel Weekly, 2003.

Concept Definitions

- Socio-cultural tourism impacts: Changes to societies and cultures at destinations as a result of tourism.
- Socio-cultural tourism crises: Crises for the tourism industry arising from social and cultural conditions and events which may or may not be directly related to tourism.
- Tourist victimization: A situation when tourists become targets of criminal acts ranging from minor misdemeanors to serious assault.
- Enclave tourism: A form of tourism in which tourists are segregated from residents, usually in developments designed for their exclusive use.

Review Questions

1. In what ways does tourism introduce change to destination societies and cultures and what does the degree of change depend on?
2. What action can destination authorities and the tourism industry take to try to prevent tourism's socio-cultural impacts from evolving into a crisis?

3. How might socio-cultural conditions unconnected to tourism lead to a crisis for the tourism industry and how much control can the industry exercise over such conditions?
4. What measures can be taken to protect tourists from becoming victims of crime?
5. How should tour operators react to an outbreak of civil disturbance at a location where their customers are staying?

Additional Readings

Mathieson, A. and Wall, G. (1996). *Tourism: Economic, physical and social impacts.* London: Longman.

Pizam, A. (1999). A comprehensive approach to classifying acts of crime and violence at tourist destinations. *Journal of Travel Research, 38*(1), 5–12.

Pizam, A., Tarlow, P., and Bloom, J. (1997, Summer). Making tourists feel safe: Whose responsibility is it? *Journal of Travel Research*, 23–28.

References

ABC. (2003). Schoolies festival: Learning from past mistakes. Australian Broadcasting Corporation website at http://www.abc.net.au, accessed 1 March 2005.

Albuquerque, K. and McElroy, J. (1999). Tourism and crime in the Caribbean. *Annals of Tourism Research, 26*(4), 968–984.

AP. (2004, 31 August). Minister: Jamaican crime hurting tourism. http://www.ttgapers.com, accessed 25 February 2005.

Ap, J., Var, T., and Din, K. (1991). Malaysian perceptions of tourism. *Annals of Tourism Research, 18*(2), 321–323.

Armstrong, K. (2001). *Islam: A short history.* London: Phoenix Press.

BBC News. (1999, 22 April). Riots trap British tourists. BBC News website at http://news.bbc.co.uk, accessed 25 February 2005.

BBC News. (2000, 19 January). Rioters to be shot on sight. BBC News website at http://news.bbc.co.uk, accessed 25 February 2005.

BBC News. (2001a, 11 July). Army quells Jamaican unrest. BBC News website at http://news.bbc.co.uk, accessed 25 February 2005.

BBC News. (2001b, 26 July). Five die in fresh Jamaica violence. BBC News website at http://news.bbc.co.uk, accessed 25 February 2005.

BBC News. (2003a, 29 August). Faliraki update. BBC News website at http://news.bbc.co.uk, accessed 25 February 2005.

BBC News. (2003b, 9 December). New rules for Faliraki revelers. BBC News website at http://news.bbc.co.uk, accessed 25 February 2005.

BBC News. (2004, 10 May). Youth moves on as Faliraki fades. BBC News website at http://news.bbc.co.uk, accessed 25 February 2005.

Brayshaw, D. (1995). Negative publicity about tourism destinations: A Florida case study. *Travel and Tourism Analyst, 5*, 62–71.

Brunt, P., Mawby, R., and Hambly, Z. (2000). Tourist victimization and the fear of crime on holiday. *Tourism Management, 21*, 417–424.

Burns, P. (2001). Brief encounters: Culture, tourism and the local-global nexus. In S. Wahab and C. Cooper (Eds.), *Tourism in the age of globalization* (pp. 290–305). London: Routledge.

Butler, R.W. (1974). Social implications of tourism development. *Annals of Tourism Research, 2*, 100–111.

Crotts, J. (1996). Theoretical perspectives on tourist criminal victimization. *Journal of Tourism Studies, 7*(1), 2–9.

Din, K. (1989). Islam and tourism: Patterns, issues and option. *Annals of Tourism Research, 16*, 542–563.

Doxey, G.V. (1975). When enough's enough: The natives are restless in Old Niagara. *Heritage Canada, 2*(2), 26–27.

Freitag, T. (1994). Enclave tourism: For whom the benefits roll? *Annals of Tourism Research, 21*(3), 538–554.

Greco, J. (1994, September). Miami manages a tourism crisis. *Hemisphere*, 26–29.

Henderson, J.C. (1999). Southeast Asian tourism and the financial crisis: Indonesia and Thailand compared. *Current Issues in Tourism, 2*(4), 294–303.

Henderson, J.C. (2003). Managing tourism and Islam in Peninsular Malaysia. *Tourism Management, 24*, 447–456.

Hopkins, M. (1999). *The planetary bargain: Corporate social responsibility comes of age.* London: Macmillan Press.

Inskeep, E. (1991). *Tourism planning: An integrated and sustainable development approach.* New York: Wiley.

King, B., McVey, M., and Simmons, D. (2000). A societal marketing approach to national tourism planning: Evidence from the South Pacific. *Tourism Management, 21*(4), 407–416.

Kusluvan, S. and Karamustafa, K. (2001). Multinational hotel development in developing countries: An exploratory analysis of critical policy issues. *International Journal of Tourism Research, 3*, 179–197.

Lea, J. (1988). *Tourism development in the Third World.* London: Routledge.

Mathieson, A. and Wall, G. (1996). *Tourism: Economic, physical and social impacts.* London: Longman.

Ministry of Tourism. (2004). Tourism Statistics 2004. Maldives Ministry of Tourism website at http://www.maldivestourism.gov.mv, accessed 19 July 2005.

Pelfrey, W. (1998). Tourism and crime: A preliminary assessment of the relationship of crime to the number of visitors at selected sites. *International Journal of Comparative and Applied Criminal Justice, 22*(2), 293–304.

Pizam, A. (1982). Tourism and crime. Is there a relationship? *Journal of Travel Research, 20*, 7–10.

Pizam, A. (1999). A comprehensive approach to classifying acts of crime and violence at tourism destinations. *Journal of Travel Research, 38*(1), 5–12.

Pizam, A., Tarlow, P.E., and Bloom, J. (1997, Summer). Making tourists feel safe: Whose responsibility is it? *Journal of Travel Research*, 23–28.

Prideaux, B. (1996). The tourism life-cycle: A beach destination study. In A. Pizam and Y. Mansfeld (Eds.), *Tourism, crime and international security issues* (pp. 59–76). Chichester: Wiley.

Prideaux, B. and Dunn, A. (1995). Tourism and crime: How can the tourism industry respond? *Australian Journal for Hospitality Management, 2*(1), 7–16.

Prideaux, B., Laws, E., and Faulkner, B. (2003). Events in Indonesia: Exploring the limits to formal tourism trends forecasting methods in complex crisis situations. *Tourism Management, 24,* 475–487.

Robinson, M. and Boniface, P. (1999). *Tourism and cultural conflicts.* New York: CABI Publishing.

Ryan, C. (1993). Crime, violence, terrorism and tourism: An accident or intrinsic relationship. *Tourism Management, 14*(3), 173–183.

Said, E.W. (1979). *Orientalism.* New York: Vintage Books.

Shackley, M. (2001). *Managing sacred sites: Service provision and visitor experience.* London and New York: Continuum.

Syed, O.A. (2001, 10–13 October). Catering to the needs of Muslim travellers. Paper presented at the Second Conference of Ministers from Muslim Countries, Tourism: Challenges and Opportunities, Kuala Lumpur.

Travel & Tourism Intelligence. (1998). *Iran country report.* London: Travel & Tourism Intelligence.

Travel Weekly. (2003, 26 September). Meeting finds Faliraki accord. Travel Weekly website at http://www.travelweekly.co.uk, accessed 28 February 2005.

UNEP. (2005a). *Integrating sustainability into business.* Paris: United Nations Environment Programme.

UNEP. (2005b). *Making tourism more sustainable: A guide for policy makers.* Paris: United Nations Environment Programme.

UNESCO. (1976). The effects of tourism on socio-cultural values. *Annals of Tourism Research, 4,* 74–105.

WTO (2004). *World tourism highlights 2001.* Madrid: World Tourism Organization.

6

Environmental Tourism Crises

Learning Objectives

By the end of the chapter, the reader should be able to

- Appreciate the role of natural resources as tourist attractions.
- Recognize the harmful impacts of tourism on natural environments and their potential to cause crisis.
- Understand how environmental changes unrelated to tourism may prove damaging to the tourism industry and threaten tourist safety.
- Identify strategies for averting environmental tourism crises and dealing with them when avoidance is not possible.

Introduction

The term environment can encompass all the surroundings of people, but this definition is rather too broad and the word is used here to describe the natural components of the physical environment such as climate, landforms, water, flora, fauna and ecological systems. Classifications of tourist attractions often distinguish between natural and man-made sites, but much of the earth has been subject to a degree of human interference and few pristine spaces remain. Nevertheless, many dimensions of the more natural environment are attractions for tourists; at the same time, the tourism industry makes use of these resources and tourism development alters the appearance and character of destination land and seascapes.

This chapter is devoted to the conflicts between tourism and the natural environment and the manner in which such tensions can evolve into tourism crises. In addition to crises caused by tourism itself, environmental problems which originate outside tourism and natural disasters are discussed. They are shown to disturb the operation of the industry, damage destinations and spoil the tourist experience to varying degrees. Chapter case studies are devoted to a particular instance of air pollution in South East Asia and the Indian Ocean tsunami in 2004. The latter was perhaps unprecedented in the magnitude of the event and its consequences, but both also illustrate how certain environmental issues transcend territorial boundaries to become international concerns!

Tourism and Environmental Damage

The relationship between tourism and the environment is potentially difficult (Hunter and Green, 1994) and there is now perhaps a greater awareness than ever before of tourism's negative environmental consequences (Gossling, 2002). Critics condemn the industry as an exploiter and consumer of nature and have become increasingly vociferous, arguing that the existing scenery of land and water has been obliterated in order to construct tourism amenities and infrastructure. Such restructuring increases the possibilities of erosion, flooding and landslides; in addition it destroys natural habitats. Untreated sewage and improperly disposed of waste pollute soils and surface and ground water. Excessive demand for water from tourists and its extravagant use in facilities such as golf courses may give rise to shortages. Tourist presence and activity upset delicate ecosystems which support a harmonious balance of animal and plant life, endangering biodiversity and native species of flora and fauna. Transport brings atmospheric, noise and visual pollution and general stresses are aggravated by seasonal peaking when destinations and sites may struggle to cope with an invasion of tourists. Coastal and marine locations, alpine areas and deserts are all especially vulnerable (APEC, 1996; GPA, 2005).

Tourist volumes, distribution, attitudes and actions help to determine the scale of development, intensity of land use and extent of impacts (Gunn, 1994). A place's special qualities must also be taken into account and some may suffer irreversible harm even if arrivals are low. This is evident in polar regions, which are host to a relatively small number of special-interest tourists, but the harsh environment is fragile and slow to recover from disturbance (Hall and Johnson, 1995). The extent and standard of planning are other important influences on the rate of change and its effective management, appropriate control measures being a means of averting an environmental tourism crisis (Inskeep, 1991).

Rapid development and an absence of planning can lead to conditions of crisis as shown by stretches of the Mediterranean coastline and resorts there which have seen a marked deterioration in environmental quality. Resorts combine elements of natural and purpose-built environments, but the former is a key aspect of their attraction. Torremolinos on Spain's Costa del Sol exemplifies a not untypical experience of sudden growth followed by physical decline, leading to a rise and fall in popularity (see Boxed Case One). Garcia et al. (2002, p. 472) described the overall situation in the south of Spain as one of "failures in the provision of promenades, means of access to beaches, proper traffic circulation and parking facilities, parks and garden facilities, and sewage systems." Such problems are now being addressed

---

Boxed Case One: Environmental Decline in Torremolinos

Torremolinos is a former fishing village in the south of Spain which was physically transformed by the boom in European package holiday tourism during the decades after the Second World War. It grew into a busy resort, characterized by high-rise hotels and apartment blocks and crowded beaches, which attracted mainly budget-conscious package tourists. There had been only limited planning and the town experienced severe congestion at the height of the tourist season, putting pressure on services and the infrastructure. Environmental degradation of the beach, sea water and inland area occurred as a result and Torremolinos came to symbolize the excesses of unplanned mass tourism. Overseas tourists were still visiting in the 1990s, encouraged by inexpensive prices, but this market was acknowledged to be low spending and there was also fierce competition from other established and up-and-coming centers.

Officials reacted to the problems and possibility of further decline by launching initiatives designed to upgrade the environment and rebuild certain areas. They were supported in these efforts by reforms aimed at making Spanish regional and national planning and coastal management more rigorous. The seafront was improved through steps such as the construction of a better promenade, stricter beach cleaning, new sewage systems and coastal protection measures. Promotion sought to convey images of a revitalized resort and entice higher spending tourists.

Sources: Barke and France, undated; Garcia et al., 2002; Pollard and Rodriguez, 1993.

---

and fading seaside resorts are looking to upgrade their environment and rejuvenate themselves, with mixed success (Amor et al., 1994).

In another illustration, Santana (2003) recounted how the needs of tourists, in combination with those of residents, and inadequate public services resulted in beach and water pollution in the Brazilian resort of Balneario Camboriu. Deficiencies were manifest in offensive odors, untreated sewage on the shore, contaminated tap and sea water and outbreaks of diarrhea and skin infections. Not surprisingly, arrivals dropped sharply. The initial reaction of the local government, in the face of national and international publicity, was to deny that there was anything amiss and refuse to talk to the media. The water supply infrastructure was subsequently renovated, but the crisis was only partially resolved because of official intransigence and a reluctance to return on the part of visitors.

Torremolinos and Balneario Camboriu serve as a warning about what can happen when coastal tourism is not properly managed. The pattern is observable elsewhere with signs of uncontrolled development and its costs in the Caribbean, Hawaii, Asia Pacific and Australia (Smith, 1992). Unless moves are made to reverse the process of environmental decay, centers can lose their appeal and acquire an unfavorable reputation. Such an outcome precipitates a crisis for all those involved in the tourism industry and has socio-economic and political ramifications.

Nevertheless, it must be acknowledged that tourism can assist in environmental protection, conservation and enhancement which lessen the likelihood of environmental tourism crises. Tourism's capacity to contribute positively to the environment is one dimension of sustainable tourism which seeks to establish more harmonious relations between tourism and the environment (UNEP, 2005b). Such an accord is, however, not easy to attain or maintain as reflected in the debate about the concept of ecotourism and the feasibility of putting it into practice (Weaver, 2001).

Other Causes of Environmental Crises and Tourism

Tourism is not the only industry and form of development which is detrimental to the environment and others may be equally or more destructive, with ramifications for tourism. The countryside is under great pressure from agriculture, mining, logging, industrialization and urbanization while cities are confronting unparalleled expansion, congestion and pollution. The United Nations estimates that 60% of the world's population will be urban dwellers by 2030 (UNEP, 2005a) and over 25% will be living in conurbations in excess of one million, one-third of these in slums and squatter camps in the developing world (BBC News, 2005a). This expansion will necessitate planning in all fields and questions of transport are especially acute, but there are already signs of inability to meet the challenges. The International Association of Public Transport (UITP, 2003) claimed that Asian metropolises like Bangkok, Jakarta and Manila have reached a stage of "general paralysis" regarding traffic for much of the day and that these conditions are set to worsen.

The ability of existing and emerging "megacities" to exercise their tourism functions as destinations and regional gateways and hubs will thus be impaired as physical movement becomes increasingly onerous (Page and Hall, 2003). Other factors of crime and poverty may make dense urban concentrations seem even more unattractive and unsafe to potential tourists. Planners have proposed transport solutions of restrictions on car ownership and usage, the application of technology to facilitate road traffic flows, integrated planning and greater investment in public transport. However, costs, lack of political will and popular resistance are all substantial barriers to implementation.

Vehicular traffic, together with industrial plants and power stations, generates atmospheric pollution, which is exacerbated by the lack of proper regulatory frameworks. Pollutants have combined in cities such as Athens, Hong Kong and Mexico City to produce an almost constant pall of haze and smoke which can curtail inbound tourism. Pollution does not respect administrative boundaries and the circumstances in Hong Kong are linked to its proximity to southern Chinese provinces which have a very poor environmental record (Sesser, 2004). This dilemma is further demonstrated by the photo-chemical smog which spread across much of South East Asia in 1997 due to deliberately lit forest fires in Indonesia (see Case One). The causes and ultimate solutions to such crises are clearly beyond the authority of industry practitioners and this frustrates their effective management by them.

Incidents at sea, whether accidental or because of human error, can result in water pollution and contamination of coastlines; this may be severe if oil tankers are involved in collisions or groundings (see Boxed Case Two). The coastal features on which tourism depends are marred by marine oil spillages, albeit in the short term, with the spoiling of beaches and killing of marine, plant and bird life. Shore amenities are damaged and opportunities to engage in recreational pursuits such as sun bathing, swimming, sailing and fishing are restricted. Enterprises such as hotels and restaurants, diving and fishing businesses and marinas will see a downturn in trade

---

Boxed Case Two: Oil Spillage Near the Galapagos Islands

The Galapagos National Park and Marine Reserve off the coast of Ecuador is a unique marine environment which is increasing in popularity as a destination, most visitors traveling there on cruises. The grounding of a supply tanker in 2001 near the islands and the discharge of between 180,000 and 240,000 gallons of fuel was thus an environmental and tourism crisis. The worst fears of environmentalists were not realized, however, and most of the oil eventually drifted out to the open sea where it either sank or evaporated. Nevertheless, some animals did perish and they included over 60% of marine iguanas on one of the islands. Oil had to be removed from a number of birds and animals and certain of the beaches accessible to tourists were closed temporarily. There were also concerns about the longer term effects of the oil and an appreciation that impacts would need to be closely monitored over an extended period.

There was a rapid response to the accident by officials from various agencies and representatives of the tourism industry. A spill management team was formed and technology was employed to track and anticipate the distribution of the oil. The news was of great interest globally and the world was informed that any damage was limited. Official websites were also used for fund raising to assist recovery efforts. Cruise companies took part in rescue operations and one vessel pumped fuel from the stricken tanker before it started leaking. The same business also allowed its yachts to be used by scientists working to clean up the site. Other enterprises provided funding, logistical help, materials and manpower. Their support was lauded by the Director of the Charles Darwin Research Station who maintained that the successful cooperation between the scientific and commercial communities demonstrated their common interest in and commitment to the conservation of the islands.

Sources: BBC News, 2005b; Clough, 2001; Galapagos News, 2001; MPA News, 2001.

which will not be restored until most traces of the oil have been removed (Reid, undated). The World Wildlife Fund (WWF) calculates that ecosystems and commerce take at least 10 years to recover from oil slicks, citing Galicia in northwest Spain which suffered five such accidents in 30 years (WWF, 2002).

Global warming is an exceptional environmental crisis of direct and indirect significance for tourism and emissions from tourist transportation contribute to the phenomenon. It might be considered a natural disaster by some, but the part played by industry and transport in the creation of carbon dioxide and other greenhouse gases means that it is also man-made. Although the crisis is evolving relatively slowly, it is a pressing issue for small island states like the Seychelles and Maldives. Climate change has implications for their very survival in addition to their tourism industries. Other destinations too are being affected by the melting of the polar ice caps and glaciers, rising sea levels, modifications to rainfall patterns and warmer seas. These will ultimately alter coastlines and threaten biodiversity; some corals, for example, are already dying because of higher water temperatures (Gossling, 2002).

Scientists have warned of an increase in air temperatures of over five degrees centigrade which would jeopardize ski resorts as snowlines recede, and research conducted by the United Nations concludes that 50% of Swiss resorts are facing economic hardship. Lower level resorts in other alpine countries will have to either relocate to higher ground or depend on snow-making technology which is not always friendly to the environment. American and Australian centers are similarly at risk, the latter perhaps losing its skiing industry by 2070. Scotland's ski resorts often now have insufficient snow cover, leading to a shifting focus in tourism promotion away from winter sports to summer pursuits (The Guardian, 2003).

Many environmental dilemmas capable of precipitating tourism crises are thus the result of broader and longer term trends and their satisfactory resolution depends on the commitment and actions of numerous public and private sector agencies over an extended period of time. Difficulties of securing agreement are indicated by the slow progress and limited scope of the Kyoto protocol, which aims to cut emissions of six greenhouse gases globally. It was signed by 84 countries in 1997 and had been ratified by 140 by the beginning of 2005 when it came into force, despite the refusal of the USA to participate (The Guardian, 2005; UNA-UK, 2005). Other environmental problems are more immediate and the outcome of accidents or specific instances of negligence which could have been avoided or contained. An important additional type of tourism crisis induced by nature is that of natural disasters which are considered below.

Natural Disasters and Tourism

The inherent geographical characteristics of destinations and the wider environment can both lure visitors and frighten them away (Murphy and Bayley, 1989). Even in the former cases of appealing coastal, riverside and mountainous locations, there are heightened chances of nature-related disturbances (WTO and WMO, 1998). Tourists and travelers may thus find themselves affected by numerous forms of natural disaster. The possibilities are indicated by a summary of events in the mid-1990s when "5,000 motorists were trapped by a Himalayan avalanche on the Jammu-Srinagar highway in India in 1995. In September of that same year, Hurricanes Luis and Marilyn, among the most powerful storms of the century, brutalized the Caribbean tourist resorts of Antigua, Dominica, Guadaloupe and Saint Thomas with 225 kilometer/hour winds. One year later, in August 1996, a camping site in Northern Spain was destroyed and over 70 killed by flash flooding of a mountain river" (UNOCHA, 2005).

As the number of tourists mount and their distribution expands to incorporate more remote parts of the world, the industry's exposure to the destructive power of nature, often associated with specific climatic zones, seems likely to intensify. Winter sports resorts rely upon snow, yet blizzards and avalanches are common on mountain slopes. Tropical weather also entices visitors with high temperatures and lush vegetation, but is associated with instability which can lead to deadly storms (Durocher, 1994; Pottorff and Neal, 1994). About 50 tropical storms develop into hurricanes every year, many centered on the Caribbean and therefore an anxiety for popular resorts on its shores (see Boxed Case Three).

Hurricanes usually give some advance notice of their arrival, permitting evacuation of people in their tracks, but volcanic eruptions and earthquakes are other natural hazards which cannot be so easily predicted. The risk from the former is, however, confined to areas near the world's 1,511 active volcanoes, over 50% of which are found in Pacific Rim countries. Seismic activity also usually occurs in identifiable locations lying on the fault lines where the adjacent tectonic plates making up the earth's surface meet (BBC News, 2005c). Nevertheless, it is not only tourism at the specific site which is interrupted by these events, but in the country as a whole if the devastation is on a large scale with heavy fatalities (Huang and Min, 2002).

Both earthquakes and volcanoes trigger tsunamis, waves which can be over 100 kilometers in length and move at 800 kilometers per hour. The waves increase in height to as much as 30 meters when they slow in shallow water, battering coastlines on reaching land. The strongest earthquake ever recorded, measuring 9.5 on the Richter scale, occurred off the Chilean coast in 1960 and led to deadly waves in Hawaii, the Philippines and Japan (BBC News, 2005c). However, the 2004 Indian Ocean tsunami, following an underwater earthquake near the Indonesian island of Sumatra, was exceptional with waves which struck the shores of 12 countries across two continents. It was perhaps one of the most serious natural disasters with which the world and its tourism industry have ever had to deal (see Case Two).

Other climatic phenomena of potential danger to tourists and tourist facilities are stormy weather and excessive rain in more temperate belts which may end in flooding, especially in the lower reaches of a river, and landslides (Faulkner and Vikulov, 2001). In contrast, an absence of rainfall can result in drought which undermines the attractiveness of stricken locations and poses practical difficulties regarding water supply.

Boxed Case Three: Caribbean Hurricanes

Florida was struck by four successive hurricanes over six weeks in late 2004 which caused death and disruption across the Caribbean region. Priority was given by the state to repairing the physical destruction and marketing activity. Focus group discussions were conducted by the Visit Florida marketing agency to gain an understanding of people's attitudes toward the state after the storms. There were talks involving the agency, the Florida Commission on Tourism and the state governor about possible strategies. Marketers anticipated that a great deal of effort and resources would have to be spent on promotion to offset all the negative publicity.

A US$30 million marketing plan was devised to remind audiences about the attractiveness of Florida. Slogans such as "Florida. We're Still Open" stressed that many areas had escaped the path of the hurricanes or sustained only minimal damage. Advertisements with these themes were to appear in the final months of 2004, followed by a return to normal content at the end of the year and thereafter when they would become more frequent and reach out to a wider audience. An assortment of print and electronic media was utilized with material directed at the domestic market and overseas visitors from Canada, Latin America and the UK. Regions within Florida were given assistance to run customized campaigns, reflecting variations in their exposure to the disaster. The main message again was that Florida was as attractive as ever and it was life and business as usual in most locations.

Sources: James, 2004; Owers, 2004; Stieghorst, 2004.

Looking to the future, some commentators predict that climatic change will accelerate the frequency of disasters connected to extreme weather with more storms, flooding and droughts. There is already evidence of such a trend and wind and rain, particularly American hurricanes and Japanese typhoons, were authors of unprecedented damage in 2004 when insured losses surpassed US$100 billion for the first time (McCarthy, 2004).

Responding to Environmental Tourism Crises

The capacity of tourism to induce harmful changes in the natural environment means that certain crises are of internal origin and can be overcome by private and public sector action. Acceptance of responsibilities and investment in appropriate services, facilities and conservation programs by industry sectors in both generating and host countries may all help in dealing with and recovering from such crises.

Effective management strategies, comprising both self-regulation and statutory imperatives, can also help to prevent the evolution of crisis if implemented at a sufficiently early stage in the development of tourism. This applies to urban and rural environments, including coastal resorts which can learn from the experience of Torremolinos. There are a variety of guidelines, codes of conduct and information about best practice now in the public domain and the range of materials is indicative of the growing literature on sustainable tourism (Godfrey and Clarke, 2000; Hall and Lew, 1998).

Crises which erupt from environmental disruption external to the industry are more difficult to plan for and manage because fundamental reasons and solutions are largely beyond its authority. Halting the deterioration in air quality in South East Asia, for example, was dependent on government enforcement, and tourism businesses and NTOs could only react to ensuing difficulties and lobby for official action. However, the transport industries can exercise some control over energy use and air pollution as they are calculated to account for 25% of the former and 22% of the carbon dioxide generated from fossil fuels (Penner, 1999).

Airlines in particular are responsible for a significant proportion of these figures (Gossling, 2002) and some carriers have acknowledged their obligations in environmental policies. British Airways publishes a social and environmental report (British Airways, 2004) which makes reference to corporate goals of greater fuel efficiency and a reduction in harmful releases. It also advocates emissions trading in a bid to constrain emissions of carbon dioxide from aviation sources and further research into the subject, especially the impact of other materials besides carbon dioxide in the upper atmosphere. While such moves are laudable, tackling global warming and other environmental menaces necessitates widespread collaboration among relevant parties. Resolution is long term, reflecting the character and dynamics of the crisis and perhaps can never be fully attained.

In environmental crises of narrower scope, the reaction of tour operators in the Galapagos suggests how the tourism industry can work in partnership in recovery efforts. This may be essential when the environment is central to the products being sold and commercial and conservation interests coincide. Marketing is vital when any immediate threat to tourist safety has receded and environmental revival is under way. Tourists and industry partners should be informed about measures taken and offered reassurance, while also being reminded about positive destination attributes. Campaigns should also be mindful of realities and not over-ambitious in what they promise.

With regard to natural disasters, those at work in the tourism industry can evaluate the likelihood of certain forms occurring and take practical steps accordingly. For example, specific sites which are prone to floods should be rejected for new projects and structures can be designed to resist damage from earthquakes in areas of seismic instability. Ski resorts can work with weather forecasting services and mountain rescue teams to safeguard visitors. Education also has an important role to play in advising tourists about dangers and recommending precautions (WTO and WMO, 1998).

Huan et al. (2004) acknowledged that publicizing contingency plans for emergencies may deter tourists by inspiring fears. On the other hand, customers could be relieved to know that there are procedures in place for their protection. The publicity given to visitor safety provision should therefore avoid alarming and aim for confidence building based upon local conditions, markets and risk assessment. Questions will inevitably be raised about the safety and security of a destination where natural hazards are known to exist and cannot be dismissed. Whether overt or covert, preparations for a natural disaster and its aftermath are essential if tourism is to be promoted and managed with assurance and integrity.

Strategies adopted in Florida after the hurricanes and in post-tsunami Thailand highlight the need for the communication of accurate and up-to-date facts to tourists and the tourism industry after a natural disaster. Information can be conveyed in regular announcements covering the state of communications and transport, accommodation, other facilities and services and the general environment. Conventional marketing is probably a waste of resources in the immediate aftermath of a catastrophe, but can recommence once the situation has stabilized and rehabilitation has reached a suitable phase (WTO and WMO, 1998).

Marketing communications is central, but should be accompanied by other actions. In its plan for tsunami-affected countries, the WTO also includes community relief, professional training, sustainable redevelopment and risk management (WTO, 2005). There are, however, contrasts in the ability of authorities and the industry to get ready for and respond to natural disasters and other environmental crises. These competences partly depend on financial resources and expertise which themselves are linked to stage of economic development.

Summary and Conclusions

A high-quality environment is a key component of tourism and certain natural features exercise strong appeal as attractions in themselves or settings for various activities. When these resources begin to deteriorate, sometimes posing a risk to personal health and safety, tourists may look elsewhere and substitute destinations which they perceive to be safer and more pleasant. Deterioration can be very sudden as in the case of a natural disaster or more gradual, illustrated by atmospheric pollution and weather patterns. Tourism development itself may be a cause and catalyst of environmental decline and crisis due to its many negative impacts. Recovery will be determined by the extent and duration of damage, alongside management responses.

Some forms of environmental tourism crises can be anticipated and planned for while others, especially those related to poor planning and management of the industry, can be avoided. Advances in settling some of the fundamental problems which underlie environmental threats to tourism are, however, not a matter for the tourism industry alone. They will require coordinated effort on a national and international level if the challenges presented by the crises which appear inevitable are to be surmounted.

Case One: Air Pollution in South East Asia

The clearance of forested areas through burning is well established, if technically illegal, in parts of South East Asia. However, the number of fires and weather conditions in late 1997 led to them burning out of control in Indonesia. In combination with other air pollutants, the smoke created a photo-chemical smog which was commonly described as "the haze." This haze extended across the region, although its density changed everyday and from place to place. Air quality sometimes reached dangerous levels and visibility was poor in Indonesia itself and neighboring Brunei, Malaysia and Singapore.

Stories about the situation were circulated in the media worldwide which transmitted pictures of towns and beaches blanketed in thick fog and residents wearing protective masks. Some airports were forced to close for safety reasons and a commercial plane crash was attributed to the smog. Governments in major markets such as Australia, Europe, Hong Kong and the USA warned their citizens to avoid affected locations. Tour operators and travel agents were also reluctant to send customers to parts of the region. Concerns were reflected in declining visitor arrivals as travelers shunned places which looked unattractive and where there was a threat to health, especially for those prone to respiratory illnesses.

The Singapore Tourism Board (STB) is the NTO in Singapore and it sought to communicate with tourists and the industry abroad through its network of offices. These offices were provided with up-to-date information on a daily basis and staff were asked to recommend that anxious tourists, particularly the elderly and those suffering from ailments like asthma, delay traveling. The NTOs of Association of South East Asian Nations (ASEAN) member states, which include Singapore, began to prepare and circulate common statements about circumstances. Regular reports on conditions in principal cities were sent to industry stakeholders and diplomatic staff around the world.

A plan titled "Operation Blue Skies" was produced by the STB for launching when the haze had finally dispersed. This involved intensified and aggressive marketing with special discount packages arranged in collaboration with tour operators. Media and industry representatives were also invited to join educational tours so they could see the return to normality firsthand. The worst of the smog had largely cleared by the end of the year, but the possibility of a recurrence remained as long as the practice of land clearance by fire was allowed to continue.

Source: Henderson, 1999.

Case Two: Thailand and the Indian Ocean Tsunami

It has been estimated that over 225,000 people died in the 2004 Boxing Day Indian Ocean tsunami and many of these were tourists. There was also extensive physical damage which was evident in some coastal resorts in Malaysia and India, but most severe in Thailand, Sri Lanka and the Maldives. More than 5,000 people lost their lives in Thailand, almost 2,000 of whom were tourists. Impacts were concentrated in six provinces, although there were marked variations. Almost all hotels in Khao Lak and Phi Phi Island, which had 6,000 and 4,000 hotel rooms, respectively, were lost. In contrast, less than 20% of Phuket's hotels were severely damaged and over 80% were open by the end of December.

The event attracted international media coverage which tended to emphasize the scale of the devastation as well as details of nationals of particular countries who were missing or injured, but many reports did note that most of Thailand had been spared. Officials spoke of differing rates of recovery from weeks to years, depending on the site. There was an exodus of tourists from the destinations which had been hit and mass cancellations by individuals and overseas operators and agents for travel to much of Thailand. However, several visitors chose to remain and others to go ahead with their vacation. UK newspapers printed pictures of tourists sunbathing on beaches the day following the waves as they were being cleared of debris.

The main initial task of resort businesses was to deal with any repairs and rebuilding, harder for many smaller units because of limited resources and a lack of insurance. Other urgent problems were those of generating some revenue in order to survive commercially and persuading tourists to come back. Unaffected hotels and those which had seen only minor disruption sought to explain the realities of the situation in press releases and advertising. Prices were discounted by both the accommodation and airline sectors and bargain packages were available. There was considerable flexibility over cancellations and postponements of bookings to accommodate nervous customers. Several companies donated to fund-raising schemes for tsunami victims or set up their own and asked for support. People were urged not to abandon the destinations as this would exacerbate the plight of local communities and economies, proceeding with visits being presented as a kind of charitable act.

The primary concern of the Tourism Authority of Thailand (TAT) at the beginning was tourist safety and it established three centers staffed by executives who cooperated with government officials and personnel from the tourism industry. These centers aimed to help tourists, some of whom had been left with nothing but the swimsuits they were wearing when the tsunami arrived. An emergency 24-hour telephone line was installed for use by worried friends and next of kin and the Communications Authority of Thailand permitted tourists to telephone overseas at no charge. Tracing missing tourists was a major exercise and Tourist Information Centers assisted in this process with updated bulletins distributed to TAT offices overseas. There was a need for translators to help with communications and tour guides and volunteer language students were called on to fill this role. The TAT headquarters in Bangkok created a Crisis Management Center which liaised with foreign embassies in Thailand and Thai diplomatic staff abroad.

Repatriation had to be arranged and Tourist Assistance Counters issued special Certificates of Identification which were a substitute for lost passports, thereby permitting overseas visitors to officially leave Thailand. These steps were taken in association with embassy staff from 30 countries who were deployed in the affected areas.

Thai aircraft evacuated the stranded and injured to Bangkok over a two-day period and foreign airlines organized flights to collect citizens and transport them back to their country of origin. Doctors and nurses were also on hand at the airports. The capital's hotels contributed by providing accommodation and the Association of Thai Travel Agents organized transportation to and within Bangkok, coordinated by the TAT.

Attention then moved to an assessment of the damage to land and marine environments. The TAT formed a survey group which reported its findings, of a positive nature overall, to both domestic and international audiences. Various media were employed to convey information in general, including a dedicated website. As well as advising about conditions in stricken locations, efforts were made to encourage visits to other areas in a bid to retain tourists and their expenditure which was critical to the national economy. Promotion focused on messages of reassurance and the restoration of confidence, in parallel with those conveyed in private sector initiatives. The argument was reiterated that staying at places hit by the tsunami was a way of expressing solidarity with residents and would accelerate the return to normality. Deciding to stay away meant further harm for communities which had already suffered enough.

Preparations were made for campaigns to re-launch specific areas and Thailand as a whole after final rehabilitation. The principal vehicle was television advertising which was chosen for reasons of speed and effectiveness, attributes compensating for its relatively high costs. Parties of travel agents and travel writers from key source markets of Europe and Japan were hosted so that they could personally observe and report on the progress that was being made. Marketing was directed at MICE customers and there was also a domestic campaign. Special deals were offered to Thai citizens and some trips promised the chance to take part in relief work.

The disaster was seen by some officials as an opportunity to revisit tourism development policy, taking into account former mistakes regarding hasty and unplanned growth. An upgraded environment and better quality resorts were envisaged, with proposals to reinvent somewhat tawdry centers like Phuket's Patong and turn them into "model beach cities." Finally, government at national and provincial level was involved in supplying emergency funding to avert business collapse. Compensation payments, loans and tax exemptions were also promised. There were international discussions, including inter-governmental talks about a tsunami early warning system for the Indian Ocean region, to try to prevent a repetition of the disaster. There was, however, some criticism of the formal stance and a feeling that tourist needs, rather than resident interests, were being given precedence in decision making.

Sources: EIU, 2005; Muqbil, 2004; TTG Daily News, 2005; Travel Newswire, 2005a and 2005b.

Concept Definitions

- Natural environment: Natural elements which collectively constitute the planet earth and its physical surroundings.

- Tourism environmental impacts: Changes to more natural environments as a result of the presence of tourists, the actions of the tourism industry and the tourism development process.
- Natural disaster: An event caused by forces of nature such as weather which leads to significant damage to the physical environment and may threaten human safety.
- Environmental tourism crisis: A crisis for the tourism industry originating in conditions in the natural environment.

Review Questions

1. What terms best describe the relationship between tourism and the environment?
2. How can tourism impacts on the environment evolve into crises?
3. In what ways can environmental changes unrelated to tourism disrupt the operation of the industry?
4. What types of natural disasters might tourists be exposed to?
5. What are the key components of a recovery strategy for a destination struck by a natural disaster?
6. Could more have been done in response to the tourism crisis arising from the haze in South East Asia?
7. Why was the tsunami an exceptional crisis for the TAT?

Additional Readings

Faulkner, B. and Vikulov, S. (2001). Katherine, washed out one day, back on track the next: A post-mortem of a tourism disaster. *Tourism Management, 22,* 331–344.

WTO. (2005). *Tsunami relief for the tourism sector: Phuket action plan.* Madrid: World Tourism Organization.

WTO and WMO. (1998). *Handbook on natural disaster reduction in tourist areas.* Madrid: World Tourism Organization.

References

Amor, F., Calabuig, C., Abellan, J., and Monfort, V. (1994). Barriers found in repositioning a Mediterranean "sun and beach" product: The Valencian case. In A.V. Seaton (Ed.), *Tourism: The state of the art* (pp. 428–435). Chichester: John Wiley.

APEC. (1996). *Environmentally sustainable tourism in APEC member economies.* APEC Tourism Working Group. Singapore: Asia-Pacific Economic Cooperation.

Barke, M. and France, L. (undated). *The development of Torremolinos as an international resort: Past, present and future.* Houghton-Le-Spring: The Centre for Travel and Tourism in association with Business Education Publishers.

BBC News. (2005a). Environment day spotlights cities. BBC News website at http://newsvote.bbc.co.uk, accessed 5 June 2005.

BBC News. (2005b). Oil tanker endangers eco-paradise. On this day. BBC News website at http://news.bbc.co.uk, accessed 2 February 2005.

BBC News. (2005c). Science and nature: Hot topics: natural disasters. BBC News website at http://www.bbc.co.uk, accessed 25 January 2005.

British Airways. (2004). *Social and environmental report 2003/4.* British Airways website at http://www.ba.com, accessed 12 June 2005.

Clough, J. (2001). Spills and thrills. Travel Telegraph website at http://travel.telegraph.co.uk, accessed 11 February 2005.

Durocher, J. (1994, April). Recovery marketing: What to do after a natural disaster. *The Cornell Hotel and Restaurant Administration Quarterly*, 66–71.

EIU. (2005). *Asia's tsunami: The impact. Special report.* London: The Economist Intelligence Unit.

Faulkner, B. and Vikulov, S. (2001). Katherine, washed out one day, back on track the next: A post-mortem of a tourism disaster. *Tourism Management, 22,* 331–344.

Galapagos News. (2001). The status of touristic resources. Galapagos News website at http://www.galapagosislands.com, accessed 11 February 2005.

Garcia, G.M., Pollard, J., and Hughes, R. (2002). Coastal zone management on the Costa del Sol: A small business perspective. *Journal of Coastal Research, Special Issue, 36,* 470–482.

Godfrey, K. and Clarke, J. (2000). *The tourism development handbook.* London: Thomson Learning.

Gossling, S. (2002). Global environmental consequences of tourism. *Global Environmental Change, 12,* 283–302.

GPA. (2005). Global tourism. Global Programme of Action for the Protection of the Marine Environment from Land-Based Activities website at http://padh.gpa.unep.org, accessed 9 June 2005.

The Guardian. (2003, 3 December). On the rocks: The grim forecast for winter sports as global warming increases. The Guardian website at http://travel.guardian.co.uk, accessed 3 December 2003.

The Guardian. (2005, 3 February). What is this Kyoto thing all about anyway? The Guardian website at http://www.guardian.co.uk, accessed 3 February 2005.

Gunn, C. (1994). *Tourism planning: Basics, concepts, cases.* (3rd ed.). Washington: Taylor and Francis.

Hall, C.M. and Johnson, M.E. (1995). *Polar tourism: Tourism in the Arctic and Antarctic regions.* Chichester: Wiley.

Hall, C.M. and Lew, A.A. (1998). *Sustainable tourism: A geographical perspective.* Harlow: Longman.

Henderson, J.C. (1999). Tourism management and the Southeast Asian economic and environmental crisis: A Singapore perspective. *Managing Leisure, 4,* 107–120.

Huan, T.C., Beaman, J., and Shelby, L. (2004). No-escape natural disaster: Mitigating impacts on tourism. *Annals of Tourism Research, 31*(2), 255–273.

Huang, J.H. and Min, J. (2002). Earthquake recovery and devastation in tourism: The Taiwan case. *Tourism Management, 23,* 145–154.

Hunter, C. and Green, H. (1995). *Tourism and the environment: A sustainable relationship?* London: Routledge.

Inskeep, E. (1991). *Tourism planning: An integrated and sustainable development approach*. New York: John Wiley.

James, C. (2004, 27 October). When Charley, Frances, Ivan and Jeanne came to visit. *Financial Times*, 6.

McCarthy, M. (2004, 27 December). The year of living dangerously. *The Independent*, 13.

MPA News. (2001). Case study of a spill response: How Galapagos managers handled Jessica spill. *MPA News*, 2(7). Florida Museum of Natural History website at http://www.flmnh.ufl.edu/fish, accessed 11 February 2005.

Muqbil, I. (2004). Crisis management by the Thai government and Tourism Authority of Thailand. Travel Newswire. Worldroom.com website at http://www.worldroom.com, accessed 15 February 2005.

Murphy, P. and Bayley, R. (1989). Tourism and disaster planning. *Geographical Review*, 79(1), 36–46.

Owers, P. (2004, 4 October). Tourism looks to revive. *The Palm Beach Post*.

Page, S. and Hall, C.M. (2003). *Managing urban tourism*. London: Prentice Hall.

Penner, J. (Ed.). (1999). *Aviation and the global atmosphere*. Cambridge: Cambridge University Press.

Pollard, J. and Rodriguez, R. (1993). Tourism and Torremolinos: Recession or reaction to environment? *Tourism Management*, 14(4), 247–258.

Pottorff, S.M. and Neal, D.M. (1994). Marketing implications for post-disaster tourism destinations. *Journal of Travel and Tourism Marketing*, 3(1), 115–122.

Reid, S. (undated). Environmental impacts of a major marine oil spill. Presentation by Environmental Emergency Planner, British Columbia Ministry of Water, Land and Air Protection. Ministry of Environment, Government of British Columbia website at http://www.env.gov.bc.ca, accessed 11 February 2005.

Santana, G. (2003). Crisis management and tourism: Beyond the rhetoric. *Journal of Travel and Tourism Marketing*, 15(4), 299–321.

Sesser, S. (2004, 19–21 November). Gray skies ahead. *The Asian Wall Street Journal*, 1.

Smith, R. (1992, July). Review of integrated beach resort development in Southeast Asia. *Land Use Policy*, 209–217.

Stieghorst, T. (2004, 26 September). Tourism ads aim to rebuild Florida's image. *South Florida Sun-Sentinel*.

Travel Newswire. (2005a). Crisis management by the Thai government and Tourism Authority of Thailand. Worldroom.com website at http://www.worldroom.com, accessed 15 February 2005.

Travel Newswire. (2005b). Summary of Thailand's response to the tsunami disaster. Worldroom.com website at http://www.worldroom.com, accessed 15 February 2005.

TTG Daily News. (2005). Assorted editions January–February.

UITP. (2003). Transport and quality of life. International Association of Public Transport website at http://www.uitp.com, accessed 20 January 2005.

UNA-UK. (2005). Kyoto: The beginning. 21st Century Vision. Website at http://mpwatch.blogs.com, accessed 9 June 2005.

UNEP. (2005a). *One planet many people: Atlas of our changing environment*. New York: United Nations Environment Programme.

UNEP. (2005b). Promoting sustainable tourism. United Nations Environment Programme website at www.uneptie.org/pc/tourism, accessed 9 June 2005.

UNOCHA. (2005). Tourism, natural disasters and safe destinations. United Nations Office for the Coordination of Humanitarian Affairs website at http://www.reliefweb.int/ocha, accessed 15 January 2005.

Weaver, D. (2001). *Ecotourism*. Sydney: John Wiley.

WTO. (2005). *Tsunami relief for the tourism sector: Phuket action plan*. Madrid: World Tourism Organization.

WTO and WMO. (1998). *Handbook on natural disaster reduction in tourist areas*. Madrid: World Tourism Organization.

WWF. (2002). Oil spill off Spain's NW coast. World Wildlife Fund website at http://www.panda.org/news, accessed 3 February 2005.

7

Tourism and Health Crises

Learning Objectives

By the end of the chapter, the reader should be able to

- Recognize some important health risks and concerns associated with tourism.
- Appreciate how matters of health can be a source of tourism crises.
- Suggest appropriate responses to tourism crises arising from health issues.
- Identify measures which can be taken to protect the health of tourists and avert health-related tourism crises.

Introduction

Health and tourism are connected in many ways and there are several distinct areas of study which include the physical and psychological benefits of vacation travel, the pursuit of improved health being a major motivator for tourism. However, there are dangers to health arising from participation in tourism and they can result in the emergence of tourism crises. Such situations and approaches to their resolution represent the subject of this chapter in which health risks when traveling and on arrival at destinations are considered, with a section devoted to infectious diseases affecting humans and animals and birds.

A distinction is made between involuntary and voluntary health threats, the latter illustrated by sexually transmitted illnesses and adventure tourism, which are also examined. Responses to these various types of tourism crises are then reviewed and detailed case studies of the 2003 outbreak of SARS and airline policy regarding deep-vein thrombosis (DVT) are presented at the end of the chapter. These examples afford insights into the impact of health-related tourism crises and their management at an international and national, and industry and corporate level, respectively.

Overview

Health is a major public and private concern in general and a key element in destination choice and visitor satisfaction, with individuals and the tourism industry likely to shun environments where there might be a risk to tourist well-being. While tourism's contribution to an enhanced state of mind and body is widely accepted, many health hazards confront overseas and domestic travelers (Clift and Grabowski, 1997; NCBI, 2003; WHO, 2002). These hazards have the potential to become crises for organizations and destinations when problems are severe and impact on a place's reputation and arrivals (Thompson et al., 2003).

Some studies have concluded that the health of as many as 50% of participants is impaired by the experience of international tourism (Dawood, 1989) and the rise in foreign travel has been accompanied by an increased incidence of disease, especially that of a tropical nature (Connor, 2005). An ageing population also means elderly travelers who are often more vulnerable to health risks. Tourism has additional repercussions for the health of destination residents (Rodriguez-Garcia, 2001) who tend to be neglected in any discussion (Bauer, 2003), but this theme is not explored here.

Government and commercial tourism agencies must therefore face the likelihood of health-related crises occurring and manage their consequences, as well as undertake preventive action where possible. Tourists themselves also have a part to play in terms of seeking information, taking precautions and behaving in an appropriate manner.

Risks to Health When Traveling

The act of travel poses dangers, detailed in the next chapter within the context of technological failure, and each mode is distinctive from flying to cycling (Nikolic et al., 2005). There may be accidents due to mechanical failures, human error and adverse weather either independently or in combination and public vehicles are popular targets for terrorist attack, crises which are examined more fully in other chapters. Air travel in particular has attracted considerable publicity with regard to both such events as well as its relationship with DVT and other medical conditions (see Case One).

It is not just tourists who are transported, but animal life which is a source of infection. The presence of rodents on planes, also a practical hazard, has been recorded as well as mosquitoes. Shipping ports and airports may be infested by rats and insects, with implications for the health of those exposed to them and inhabitants of countries where the diseases they carry are imported (Gratz, 2003).

Cruising is a means of transport, although ships can be seen as floating resorts, and outbreaks of gastrointestinal illnesses on cruise liners are regularly logged (CDC, 2003). Even the most luxurious cruises are not immune from health problems which are aggravated by the higher age profile of the cruise market, close proximity of passengers and the popularity of group activities. Norwalk-like viruses, with symptoms of diarrhea and vomiting, infected about 1,000 passengers and crew members on two Florida-based lines in late 2002. The operators abandoned voyages so that the ships could be thoroughly cleaned and disinfected. There was a similar instance the following year, although the cruise proceeded as scheduled (see Boxed Case One). Other reported maladies on board cruise ships are influenza, *E. coli* infections and shigellosis, which is a bacteria causing diarrhea (Schlagenhauf, 2004a).

Boxed Case One: On Board Viral Infection

The Aurora was on a 17-day Mediterranean cruise in 2000 when there was an outbreak of a very contagious Norwalk-like virus. There were 1,800 passengers on board, over 500 of whom fell ill with sickness and diarrhea alongside 29 of the 800 crew. The company maintained that everyone had recovered when the cruise ended at the British port of Southampton.

The virus is believed to be transmitted by personal contact and a "no touch" regime was imposed on the ship in a bid to contain its spread. Shared utensils and condiments were withdrawn from eating areas and furniture in public spaces was carefully cleaned after use. Passengers described how they had avoided touching surfaces like door handles. The usual medical complement of two doctors and four nurses was augmented by another doctor and nurse. The Greek authorities refused to let the ship into the port of Piraeus and Spain sealed its border with Gibraltar following its arrival there, despite official protests.

There were mixed reactions among the passengers on returning home about their experiences. Some expressed themselves satisfied with the vacation and the company's response to the problems on board, believing that fellow passengers were embellishing the situation with a view to obtaining compensation. Others were critical of the company for being slow to act in the initial stages of the outbreak and demanded refunds for expensive cruises which were priced between £1,000 and £5,000. The managing director accepted that the circumstances had been unparalleled and exceptionally demanding for the medical and other staff. With regard to the compensation issue, he said that all the relevant correspondence would have to be considered and each case would be assessed individually.

After docking and the disembarkation of passengers, the Aurora was thoroughly disinfected by cleaners who had donned face masks. It then sailed away for a short Channel Islands cruise, having been booked for a conference.

Source: The Guardian, 2003.

Health Risks at Destinations

Having survived the journey, tourists then face the possibilities of sickness and accidental injury on their arrival at destinations. The most prevalent forms of sickness resulting from tourism are often connected to standards of hygiene at destinations. Poor sanitation and inadequacies of water supply and sewage disposal may cause intestinal infections like gastroenteritis, with contaminated seafood another source. Diarrhea is a particular concern among travelers and one of the most common of travelers' complaints (Ericsson et al., 2003). These infections can strike and spread rapidly at venues where tourists gather such as hotels. Malaria, yellow fever, cholera and dengue are more serious and can have fatal consequences. There are also bites, stings and skin infections to contend with as well as unaccustomed sun and high or low temperatures (Keystone et al., 2004; Zuckerman, 2001).

The severity of health hazards and sensitivity to them partly depends on location, activity and the tourist's physical fitness. For example, those traveling off the beaten track in regions such as South East Asia, the South Pacific and Amazon Basin are in danger from endemic ailments (Rudkin and Hall, 1996; Shaw and Leggat, 2003). It seems probable that more tourists will succumb to both common and rarer diseases as peripheral areas of the world become accessible, a trend fueled by enthusiasm for ecotourism and other manifestations of alternative tourism in which travelers seek to escape the trappings of the mass industry. Articles in the *Journal of Travel Medicine* portray a rather alarming picture of medical perils awaiting visitors in remote places, although these perils also lurk in mainstream centers (Schlagenhauf, 2004b).

Cities too pose "myriad" threats which are especially acute in the developing world. They include "infectious diseases, trauma, air pollution, heat illness, crime and psychiatric illness" (Sanford, 2004, p. 314). The catalogue extends to "sexually transmitted diseases" and "recreational drug use" which perhaps belong to the category of volitional risk. These circumstances could be a principal or secondary cause of tourism crises and indicate how certain classes of tourism crisis overlap as environmental and socio-cultural factors are also at work.

Threats are not confined to developing countries or tropical climates and can be found in temperate zones in the developed world. Legionnaire's disease is contracted when mist is inhaled from tainted water sources such as air conditioning cooling towers, central plumbing machinery and whirlpool spas. It can therefore be caught within accommodation properties and conference centers and on cruise ships. There is a chance of tourists falling ill with respiratory viral infections like influenza, especially older people and those on organized group tour packages. Poor food hygiene gives rise to food poisoning, cholera, *E. coli* infections, hepatitis A and salmonellosis. Pathogens can be transmitted by food and ensuring food safety is an urgent task both currently and for the future (Kaferstein and Abdussalam, 1999).

Discussions about health and tourism tend to focus on sickness and disease, additionally, accidents must not be overlooked, although empirical data are limited (Page and Meyer, 1996). Health considerations at destinations thus extend to personal accident and injury, vulnerability to these is perhaps greater overseas when tourists find themselves in unknown environments. Those injured may also not have easy access to appropriate facilities and treatment, aggravating the damage and impeding their recovery. Unintentional injury is a universal health issue, but its prevalence can be partly explained by the extent of new travel opportunities in the current era when unprecedented numbers are on the move (McInnes et al., 2002).

Particular problems unrelated to tourist behavior and culpability are partly determined by the features of the destination. A BBC television program quoted by Page and Meyer (1996) examined some risks met by British holidaymakers in the Mediterranean. These risks were often due to building construction and maintenance faults like improperly serviced gas flues in self-catering accommodation units, unsatisfactory fire safety provision and swimming pool deficiencies. Any resulting crisis could therefore also be defined as technological in another example of crisis convergence. Engaging in new pastimes may be risky and even familiar pursuits like driving can be dangerous, with statistics dominated by motor accidents. Traffic accidents involving hired vehicles are routine occurrences and may not always be the fault of the driver. Resulting injuries and fatalities reflect badly on any commercial operators implicated and, should they recur, on the location which could be tainted by perceptions that it is unsafe and regulations are lax.

Infectious Diseases

Infectious or communicable diseases can be caught when traveling or after arrival and some have the ability to advance at great speed. Rapid diffusion is facilitated by modern travel patterns and is difficult to control. Containment is especially challenging for countries which lack resources, expertise and an adequate health-care infrastructure. Any epidemics are not just a crisis for tourism, but for society at large and can assume a global significance. Resultant fears among tourists may be magnified out of proportion, but the industry has to react to perceptions and not realities. Although few tourists were directly in danger, pneumonic plague in India in 1994 led to a "global alarm which escalated in meteoric fashion" (Clift and Page, 1996, p. 3). There was a 70% drop in arrivals and companies in overseas markets canceled their Indian tours.

Reference has already been made to established diseases, but there are new fears about those which are emerging such as West Nile fever and SARS. There have been outbreaks of the former in the USA and SARS had a devastating effect in 2003, severely damaging tourism in parts of Canada and across much of East Asia despite the relatively small numbers afflicted (see Case Two). The virus led to health warnings being published by governments and official bodies, the damaging influence of such advisories having already been discussed in Chapter 4, and their revocation was a major step on the road to recovery.

Questions of health may impact on tourism in a more indirect manner as evidenced by agriculture and food industry emergencies which influence the attractiveness of destinations and visitor volumes. One example is foot and mouth disease, which affects cloven-hoofed livestock and not humans, but can be carried on the soles of their shoes and vehicle wheels so that curbs on movement are a key instrument in fighting the disease.

There was a particularly severe and prolonged bout of foot and mouth in the UK in 2001 when it was also detected in some countries in Continental Europe (Horwath Consulting, 2001). News and photographs of the mass slaughter of herds of cattle and their incineration portrayed an unattractive picture of the British landscape, an official report condemning "sensationalist" and "hysterical" media reporting at home and overseas (UK Parliament, 2001). Restrictions imposed on access to farmland and misunderstanding about personal safety were other disadvantages with which the industry had to contend. Footpaths in rural areas and some roads in National Parks were closed, making it difficult to reach certain visitor attractions.

Fears that the UK was being depicted as a "disease-ridden hellhole" prompted a senior government official to promote inbound tourism at a meeting he was attending in New York, and there was a wider campaign to assure visitors that Britain was safe and "open for business." Tourism suffered, with estimated losses of about £6 billion (The Financial Times, 2003), but the effect was concentrated in the countryside. Hotels and attractions responded by intensified marketing, price discounting and cost cutting and several businesses demanded assistance from government to alleviate their financial plight.

The ramifications of foot and mouth were felt elsewhere due to anxieties about its being unwittingly exported. Busch Gardens in Tampa Bay, Florida, directed foreigners away from susceptible animals like giraffes and gazelles. Visitors with a history of travel to infected areas were requested to desist from joining the optional tours, the highlight of which was close proximity to wildlife, and offered alternatives such as half-price entry to the water park (The Business Journal, 2001). Immigration procedures were also modified in an attempt to prevent the disease invading countries such as the Irish Republic where livestock farming is a key economic sector. International arrivals were asked to complete declaration forms concerning their travels and walk across disinfected mats when entering countries.

Avian influenza or bird flu is a more serious illustration as humans can catch it from infected birds and now it appears endemic in parts of Asia. Cases in Hong Kong discouraged tourism in the late 1990s and have the potential to do so elsewhere. An especially virulent strain was discovered in several East and South East Asian countries in late 2003. Subsequent years saw further eruptions and its appearance in other continents, leading to the widespread culling of birds and attempts at immunization. There were also a number of human infections and several deaths.

Although most victims in Cambodia, China, Hong Kong, Indonesia, Thailand and Vietnam had been in contact with sick poultry, there are forecasts that it is only a matter of time before the potentially lethal virus mutates into a form which will allow human-to-human transmission among populations that have no immunity (WHO, 2005). This could trigger a global influenza pandemic with millions of casualties and is a subject of grave anxiety for both health and tourism authorities. Some countries have discussed closing their borders in a bid to protect nationals and it seems that international tourism would almost come to a halt and the international industry effectively cease to function if the worst scenarios were to be realized.

Risky Behavior

The above health threats are largely involuntary, although certain measures can be taken to reduce their magnitude and possibly avert a crisis. However, other types of risk can be classed as voluntary and tourists frequently engage in careless behavior which endangers their health. It has also been noted that individuals perceive risks differently depending on personality and social circumstances (Carter, 1998; Lepp and Gibson, 2003). Irresponsibility finds expression in several ways such as carelessness over food consumption, underestimation of dangers and a corresponding absence of preparedness and protection (Casteli, 2004).

Traffic accidents and drowning account form a significant proportion of deaths and injuries among international tourists (McInnes et al., 2002) and many cases are attributable to thoughtlessness. Drivers may be reckless, over-tired, insufficiently knowledgeable about local conditions, diverted by the passing sights, under the influence of alcohol and not using seat belts (Wilks et al., 1999). Sexual activity is one important high risk area described in the next section, followed by an account of adventure tourism which can also be seen as a type of willing engagement with danger.

Sex and Tourism

Some tourists may abandon their personal inhibitions when traveling and ignore norms to which they conform at home, thereby exposing themselves and those with whom they have contact to harm (Wickens, 2003). Such an attitude applies to sexual adventures with a heightened chance of catching or perhaps communicating a sexually transmitted disease, including HIV/AIDS, unless appropriate precautions are taken. The HIV/AIDS epidemic has been linked to international travel and sex tourism based on prostitution, trafficking in women and children and pornography is regarded as one vehicle for its spread. Cheaper air fares and the marketing of more Third World countries have favored sex tourism and the Internet has also created more opportunities for tourists in search of sexual gratification abroad, advertising adult and child pornography internationally. Such tourism is now a worldwide phenomenon which has benefited from inadequate laws in certain regions, especially regarding the welfare of minors.

Studies of sex tourism emphasize its complexity and variety (Bauer and McKercher, 2004; Clift and Carter, 2003), sex tourists shown to exhibit contrasting expectations from lonely individuals seeking a holiday "romance" to more commercial relationships (Oppermann, 1999). Provision also varies in terms of legality, official regulation and conditions and attitudes of sex workers. The morality of adult prostitution and its capacity to demean the sellers of services are topics for debate, although the view of prostitutes as naïve and innocent victims of more powerful tourists has been contested (Cohen, 1993; Ryan and Kinder, 1996). Nevertheless, all casual sex carries certain health risks for both parties.

The participation of children cannot be defended and has been widely condemned for the physical and emotional damage it inflicts. A Save the Children report maintained that about two million children aged between three and 17 in Africa, South East Asia, Latin America and Eastern Europe are being used for sex. Tourists come principally from France, Italy, Germany, Belgium and Spain and number about 3.5 million (The Lancet, 2004). It should, however, be remembered that customers are not confined to Western tourists and include Asians and local residents.

Opposition to such practices is intensifying and official organizations and pressure groups are trying to raise awareness and encourage action by the tourism industry and governments. Two examples are EPCAT (End Child Prostitution, Child Pornography and Trafficking of Children for Sexual Purposes) and UNESCAP (United Nations Economic and Social Commission for Asia and the Pacific). There have been some advances with signs of willingness in South East Asia to deal more rigorously with the sexual exploitation of children and pursue court convictions for organizers and offenders. In terms of demand, there have been endeavors in the UK to restrict overseas travel by certain groups of known sex offenders. Prosecutions can also now be conducted in the country of residence of the accused, not just where the alleged offences took place.

The negative connotations of sex tourism, particularly child prostitution, may discourage visits by many tourists to destinations where it is known to be rampant. Associated high rates of HIV/AIDS may also be a deterrent. Locations which have acquired a seedy and unsavory image could have difficulty promoting themselves to particular markets such as families, provoking a crisis for parts of the industry. One such example is Thailand. The TAT has been seeking to position the country as more exclusive with an emphasis on its natural and cultural heritage. At the same time, the authorities are faced with the realities of a thriving commercial sex sector in tourist hubs such as Bangkok, Pattaya, Koh Samui and Chiang Mai.

The TAT has tried to resolve this dilemma by publicly professing an abhorrence of sex tourism and its pursuit of the eradication of the worst excesses. It asks its overseas offices to report companies selling sex tours to Thailand and claims to be enforcing the country's anti-prostitution laws, together with the police. These laws impose penalties of fines and imprisonment on customers, procurers, brothel owners and those forcing children into prostitution who are sometimes parents (Tourism Authority of Thailand, 2001).

An end to illegal and unregulated sex tourism in Thailand and elsewhere is, however, problematic because of the economic rewards. It represents a major industry in some places and can be a vital source of income; for example, over 90% of young female Cambodian prostitutes may be the principal family breadwinner. Many commentators also question the commitment of officials to the drive against prostitution in general and involving children in particular. There is a lack of political will and changes will require immense effort. Campaigns do not always receive the full support of the local police and other bodies, corruption being a major obstacle. Sexual exploitation has socio-economic roots and is a product of poverty, lack of education and drug addiction. Until these issues are addressed, it seems that the more unacceptable manifestations of sex tourism in the developing world will continue to thrive (BBC News, 2000; UNESCAP, 2004).

Adventure Tourism

Adventure tourism is perhaps worthy of note as a kind of tourism in which participants deliberately search out danger, often taking part in what are described as "extreme sports." Such forms of tourism are popular in Australia, New Zealand and North America and have seen worldwide growth in recent years (Ryan, 1996). There are a variety of motives for taking part and the concept of adventure is subjective, reaching beyond specific recreational pursuits to encompass more passive groups taking part in overland tours (Weber, 2001). However, the term usually applies to physically demanding activities such as caving, white water rafting, canyoning (the entering of gorges and body surfing without a raft down the rapids and waterfalls which flow through them), climbing, sea kayaking and horse riding.

Participants thus expose themselves to accident and injury, although these are unlikely to be welcomed or desired. A degree of organization and commercialization is implied and operators are expected to protect their customers from undue risk with an assumption that they have given proper attention to safety matters (Bentley and Page, 2001; Hall, 1992).

It is impossible, however, to guarantee absolute safety and accidents do occur (see Boxed Case Two). Another tragedy happened in 1998 when two American divers died at sea after being mistakenly left behind on the Australian Great Barrier Reef (Wilks and Davis, 2000). The skipper of the vessel concerned was later charged with manslaughter on the basis of criminal negligence. It is not just the major catastrophes which are of relevance; minor incidents such as "slips, trips and falls" account for many injuries and insurance claims (Bentley et al., 2004). Again, events of this nature damage individual companies, the industry as a whole and possibly the destinations where they take place. Authorities in New Zealand have expressed concern over the number of adventure sports deaths there and the consequences they might have for tourist demand.

Responding to Health Concerns and Crises

There is thus great diversity in the characteristics and intensity of tourism crises arising from health and many cases of illness and personal accidents are limited in their scope and outcome. This makes any emergent crisis easier to manage, although

Boxed Case Two: Adventure Tourism Risks in Switzerland

A total of 21 people, 18 tourists and three guides, were killed in a flash flood in July 1999. The accident happened on a canyoning trip near Interlaken in central Switzerland which had been organized by a Swiss adventure company. The dead tourists, from 18 to 31 years of age, came from Australia, Britain, New Zealand, South Africa and Switzerland and belonged to a larger party of 45 tourists accompanied by eight guides. The guides failed to evacuate them from a gorge which filled with water during a flash flood and many were washed away.

The trial in 2001 lasted seven days and was attended by the families and friends of the deceased. Lawyers defending the company, which was then no longer in business, argued that the accident could not have been predicted and was the outcome of exceptional weather. Those who survived claimed that arrangements had been rushed and there were no clear explanations. The judge said in court that employees had not been appropriately trained and safety procedures were completely unsatisfactory. The fatal trip should have been canceled as there had been clear warnings of a storm, the progress of which could easily be seen. He ruled that six staff members had been guilty of negligent manslaughter and declared two junior guides innocent. The three directors were fined US$5,000 and received five-month suspended prison sentences while the three senior guides faced lower fines and reduced sentences.

There had been an earlier trial involving the same company in 2000 when two staff had also been convicted of negligent manslaughter and received suspended sentences of five months. The case related to the death of an American in his early 20s whose bungee jump cord was defective. The incident had contributed to the company's end. Partly in response to these events, Switzerland launched a code of conduct for extreme sports operators and introduced education programs for guides.

Source: BBC News, 2001b.

---

instances such as the death of airline passengers from DVT or adventure holiday could pose serious challenges to particular businesses and destinations. Other situations have the capacity to become major crises and this applies especially to disease which attracts intense media interest and may raise doubts about the competence of responsible authorities. Travel is an agent of globalization which can assist in the dissemination of communicable disease and many destinations are inadequately equipped to meet the ensuing demands on health services.

The tourism industry cannot ignore such developments as officials are predicting the recurrence and intensification of epidemic-prone viral and bacterial diseases which do not respect territorial boundaries. There have also been warnings about an increase in new infections and drug-resistant pathogens. In addition, there is the possibility of a coalescence of the threats to tourism from terrorists and ill health due to speculation that disaffected groups may gain samples of deadly viruses and toxic substances. These substances could then be employed as instruments of terror, perhaps specifically aimed at tourists, by such "bioterrorists."

Rampant infectious disease is not the only concern and there may be numerous other health risks at certain locations which are extremely attractive to tourists. Transportation and some leisure activities also have inherent dangers. Tourists and the industry will shun places where there is a known threat to visitor health, but may find themselves caught up in unexpected events. Coping with the worst of these situations is a daunting exercise for the tourism industry, but readiness is essential in view of the inevitability of health-related tourism crises.

Preventive steps can help to avert the evolution of a full-scale tourism crisis, but the industry has sometimes shown itself reluctant to deliver appropriate health warnings because of fears about scaring customers away and losing business (Lawton and Page, 1997; Stears, 1996). Analysis of Australian travel brochures (Bauer, 2002) and international commercial travel websites (Horvath et al., 2003) reveals that little useful information is provided and that which is available is insufficient.

Authors of these studies advise that customers should be fully informed about problems and advised to take precautions and purchase travel insurance. Destinations could also be classified on the basis of risk and overall awareness promoted through education. There are opportunities for greater collaboration between medical workers, health educators and the travel trade with advice and guidelines channeled by way of travel agents. Specific information about sexually transmitted diseases can be distributed to tourists before departure, counseling about safe sex and condom use.

In terms of child prostitution, the abuse of minors represents a crisis of ethics for the industry, which must acknowledge and act upon its responsibilities regarding the transgressions of customers. There has been some progress in this direction and EPCAT has cooperated with the French hotel group Accor in an initiative against child prostitution in Asia. It is also liaising with the WTO to promote acceptance of a code of conduct among industry members (EPCAT, 2003), although campaigners argue that much more needs to be done.

With regard to accidents, travel health professionals can again try to educate the traveling public through material covering active and passive protection (Hartgarten, 1994). The industry has ethical obligations regarding the safety of its customers and there are additional legal reasons for giving due regard to health and safety matters. The European Commission Directive on Package Travel, for example, insists that travel organizers and agents must provide health and safety details for their clients and may be liable for any harm they suffer.

Some initiatives to minimize unnecessary dangers and avoid serious injuries in the field of adventure tourism are operator accreditation schemes, strict health and safety rules, codes of conduct, staff training and the education and prior assessment of participants (Bentley and Page, 2001). Risk management is also critical (Wilks and Davis, 2000). Such moves are still voluntary in most countries and statutory regulation might be deemed imperative, extending to other areas such as general road safety. It is unfortunate that tragic loss of life, such as that in Switzerland, is often the catalyst for long-overdue reforms. Promoting a culture of safety would also reduce the number of more common minor incidents (Bentley et al., 2004) which collectively constitute a crisis.

The industry can also cooperate with destination authorities in upgrading utilities and public services for the benefit of the whole community. Investment in water supply and sewage disposal facilities would alleviate sickness arising from poor hygiene and training in food handling and regular inspection and monitoring of premises could be introduced. Many countries lack basic health-care provision and priority should be allocated to improving the lives and health of residents as well as to meeting tourist needs, an approach in correspondence with the philosophy of sustainable tourism development. Such displays of corporate social responsibility will assist in reducing the likelihood of another type of crisis, those derived from resentment toward tourists among residents when the former are believed to be receiving preferential treatment.

Action is thus required at a company and industry level, with governments and tourists also having a vital contribution to make. The WTO has stressed the significance of health as an aspect of tourist safety and proposes that member states pursue the following program to enhance their capabilities in dealing with difficulties (WTO, 1991):

- Identification of risks to tourists related to particular activities, locations and sites.
- Introduction and strict enforcement of safety standards and practices at facilities and venues.
- Establishment and distribution of operator guidelines.
- Provision of information to the public about possible health hazards, protective steps and sources of assistance.
- Proper staff education and training.
- Clarification of liability issues and formulation of rules and regulations.
- Development of national tourism health policies, including systems of reporting to inform the international community.

At a Caribbean Tourism Organization seminar (CTO, 2003), a WTO representative cited four critical considerations pertaining to the effective handling of health crises. They were the allocation and acceptance of responsibilities, transparency, assistance mechanisms and management of fear. The tourism sector was urged to improve its responses by being more proactive and there were calls for greater global cooperation. Eradication or minimization of both health and safety risks at resorts is a collective effort involving stakeholders of owners, operators, staff, visitors, officials and medical experts (Phillip and Hodgkinson, 1994).

However, some damage to tourism is to be expected even when such systems are in place. SARS, and to a lesser extent foot and mouth, overwhelmed the industry, which had little scope to react or room for maneuver. Tourism was at the mercy of the epidemic dynamics and initiatives to generate business were thus constrained. It was only when the health crisis abated that advertising campaigns and product development started to yield significant results, although discounting and a focus on domestic markets did generate some revenue prior to the onset of recovery.

Summary and Conclusions

Questions of health therefore represent a potential source of tourism crises, although their severity varies considerably. The magnitude of any crisis will depend partly upon the numbers involved and whether there are any fatalities, dimensions which determine the amount of publicity generated. Media coverage is a critical influence on popular opinion and handling external communications is a core element of crisis management.

The examples cited in the chapter suggest that prompt efforts to enhance safety and security systems following a critical incident are essential to demonstrate a commitment to safeguard tourists and inspire confidence that the event will not be repeated. Matters of compensation also need to be resolved in a fair manner and this is related to questions of liability and obligations to next of kin when there have been fatalities. Negligence must be seen to be punished and companies to make amends for their shortcomings if an organization and its reputation are to survive the crisis. These issues are returned to in Chapter 8, which deals with transport accidents as an illustration of technological failure.

Health is perhaps an arena of crisis which is more amenable to avoidance than some others. While certain contagious diseases and their progress are unpredictable and uncontrollable, the likelihood of other illnesses and accidents occurring may be minimized by increased awareness, changed behavior and better hygiene and safety standards. These goals are easier to achieve within controlled environments such as cruise ships, individual hotels, attraction sites and aircraft cabins, but are more formidable and costly tasks for destinations. The latter cannot be left to the tourism industry alone, but demands intervention by governments and relevant international agencies as well as responsible behavior from tourists themselves.

Case One: Airlines and DVT

Medical reports indicate that as many as 10% of long-haul flyers could be at risk from DVT, or so-called "economy class syndrome." Some experts believe that sitting for long periods in the cramped seating of an aircraft cabin encourages the formation of blood clots in the legs which can break away and travel to the lungs, leading to potentially deadly pulmonary embolism. There may also be a relationship between reduced cabin air pressure and blood oxygen which could promote dizziness, nausea and fainting on long-haul flights.

Several victims of DVT and their families have sued airlines, contending that air travel caused the malady. American Airlines, United Airlines, Delta, Northwest, Japan Airlines, Qantas, Singapore Airlines, British Airways, KLM and Virgin Air were among a total of 27 carriers named in a 2001 lawsuit. A London court concluded that blood clots were a "serious personal injury" and could not be defined as an "accident" under the Warsaw Convention; the 1929 treaty recognizes that airline liability regarding damages applies only to the latter. The Supreme Court in the Australian state of Victoria, however, decided in favor of the plaintiffs in a parallel case, permitting a landmark lawsuit to proceed. American Airlines, the world's largest carrier, reportedly reached an out-of-court settlement in a blood clot dispute at the end of 2002. Analysts were watching for any court judgment in the United States where the award of damages would probably be very high and perhaps set a precedent.

Following the London ruling, British Airways said that it sympathized with DVT sufferers. However, it also stated its belief that any link with air travel was uncertain and this would inform its position on other claims. It had, nevertheless, introduced a new Manual of Inflight Medical Care in late 2001 to assist crew in looking after passengers who became ill during flights. The manual provided instructions on dealing with many scenarios and was complemented by staff training and a CD-ROM version, the company's intranet used for additional training purposes. These materials are supplemented by a telephone link to a 24-hour advice center on the ground. Other measures to minimize the risks of DVT had been in operation for some time. Sources of information and advice included the corporate website, phone lines, in-flight videos and magazines and ticket wallets. A Healthy Journey leaflet recommended that passengers drink plenty of fluids, eat moderately and limit their intake of alcohol and caffeine. They were also advised not to remain seated for the whole of a long-haul flight and appropriate exercises were suggested.

It was announced in early 2002 that British Airways would be cooperating with the medical school of Birmingham University in a study of DVT. Travelers drawn from a sample of about 1,000 members of its frequent flyer loyalty program were to be surveyed. Respondents would be asked about any precautions they took regarding DVT, attitudes toward the disease and extent of alarm. It was considered a significant step, being the first occasion that a British airline had been willing to participate directly in such a research project.

The company's support for the research study was welcomed, especially as there had been reports that a similar World Health Organization (WHO) project was facing funding problems. Critics and campaigners had been arguing that the industry was refusing to acknowledge DVT risks and evading its responsibilities regarding informing passengers. Reporters suggested that Britain's airline industry was anxious to avoid any further damaging news stories about deaths resulting from flying in the aftermath of 11 September.

Sources: BBC News, 2001a; The Observer, 2002; One News, 2002; Travel Telegraph, 2003.

Case Two: The 2003 SARS Epidemic

A new virus which initially surfaced in the south of China in 2002 was given the name of Severe Acute Respiratory Syndrome (SARS). It is a type of pneumonia which seems to be transmitted by vapor droplets and close personal contact, although little was known about its characteristics in the early months. While knowledge has subsequently increased, there is still no vaccine or cure and control depends upon the rapid identification of sufferers and their isolation. Any people they have been in association with also need to be quarantined in order to interrupt transmission.

Authorities in China were caught by surprise and slow to inform the international community about the disease so that preventive measures were not taken immediately. Infected travelers were thus free to carry the virus abroad to locations such as Toronto in Canada, Hong Kong, Singapore, Taiwan and Vietnam. These locations recorded the highest numbers, but there were isolated cases found elsewhere in 29 countries altogether. Despite fears of a global pandemic, the virus proved less contagious and fatal than originally feared and the outbreak had essentially ended by mid-2003. There had been a total of 8,096 infections and 774 deaths, the majority of these in Asia.

Initial ignorance and the speed at which SARS was advancing created great anxiety and a degree of panic among resident populations and tourists. Governments and international agencies such as the WHO identified places affected by SARS and advised against visits to where it was spreading in the community due to risks of contraction. The WHO intervention was unprecedented and its pronouncements carried considerable authority. Officials were concerned about the importation of the disease and inbound arrivals from SARS states were monitored. The WHO also recommended certain procedures for airlines and airports to follow and SARS came to be associated with air travel, with some airline crew donning face masks. The virus dominated the headlines in much of Asia and received extensive publicity around the world. The media broadcast disturbing accounts of a mysterious deadly illness on the rampage and pictures of deserted streets and locals wearing masks.

Tourism was immediately affected as people were unwilling to travel, especially by plane, for fear of catching SARS. The worst hit areas were shunned by inbound tourists and outbound travelers faced various restrictions. Countries saw falls of over 70% in arrivals during the worst months and there was also a slump in domestic tourism and consumer spending in general. The transport, accommodation, attraction and retail sectors all lost business and the survival of some companies was threatened.

Recovery was dictated by the progress of the epidemic and the lifting of the WHO travel advisories was a major turning point for individual countries. Nevertheless, worries about a return of the virus persisted and figures for the year were depressed with declines of 10.4% for China, 6.2% for Hong Kong, 24.5% for Taiwan and 18.5% for Singapore. The WTTC estimated that the industry's contribution to GDP would drop by 24.5% in China, 41.1% in Hong Kong and 43% in Singapore. Vietnam had only 40 cases and five SARS deaths, all confined to a Hanoi hospital, but tourism there too was forecast to be worth 14.5% less in terms of its GDP contribution. The reverberations were felt in countries where there were very few or no cases of SARS such as Thailand and the contraction in travel throughout the Asia Pacific region of 9.3% in 2003 was attributed to the outbreak. Outside Asia, Toronto was estimated to be losing C$5 every day in April due to the cancellation of major conventions.

There was a common pattern of reaction among official institutions and private enterprises which included the gathering and communication of information, marketing aimed at reassurance, efforts to sell to domestic markets, price cutting, a search for cost savings and greater efficiency, rationalization, capacity reduction and staff redundancies. A great deal of attention was also given to the devising and implementation of health and safety regimes designed to convince customers that the industry was prepared and particular sites were safe. Governments were also active in support of tourism businesses and in initiatives to enhance standards of public hygiene. It proved very difficult to combat the adverse impacts of SARS when it was still spreading and even after it had been contained, but marketing efforts were intensified when places had been formally declared free of SARS. The WHO announcement was the occasion for re-launching affected destinations such as Hong Kong and Singapore in a bid to generate maximum publicity.

Sources: Euromonitor, 2004; Henderson, 2003; McKercher and Chon, 2004; WHO, 2003; WTO, 2004; WTTC, 2003.

Concept Definitions

- Adventure tourism: A form of tourism involving participation in physically demanding activities which expose the tourist to risks of injury.
- Economy class syndrome: Another name for DVT (deep-vein thrombosis), potentially lethal blood clots which may be caused by seating conditions in commercial passenger aircraft.
- Sex tourism: Tourism in which the primary motivation is the satisfaction of sexual needs, often met by prostitutes and seen as a source of sexually transmitted disease.
- Tourist health risks: Factors and forces which threaten the physical and psychological well-being of tourists.

Review Questions

1. In what ways are issues of health a major concern for the tourism industry?
2. What are the principal types of health-related crises that accommodation, transport and attraction operators are likely to encounter?
3. How do health questions impact on the work of destination marketing organizations?

4. What preventive strategies can be employed by the tourism industry regarding the contracting of illness and disease by tourists and what will their success depend on?
5. Have airlines responded appropriately to the risks of DVT among passengers?
6. Was there an over-reaction to the threat of SARS by tourists and the tourism industry in generating countries and could this have been avoided?

Additional Readings

Castelli, F. (2004). Human mobility and disease: A global challenge. *Journal of Travel Medicine, 11*(1), 1–2.

CDC. (2003). Vessel sanitation program. Centers for Disease Control and Prevention. website at http://www.cdc.gov, accessed 7 November 2003.

Clift, S. and Grabowski, P. (Eds.). (1997). *Tourism and health: Risks, research and responses.* London: Pinter.

CTO. (2003). Tourism sector responsiveness to health crises. Caribbean Tourist Organization website at http://www.onecaribbean.org, accessed 7 November 2003.

WHO. (2002). *International travel and health.* Geneva: World Health Organization.

References

Bauer, I.L. (2002). Health advice in Australian travel brochures. *Journal of Travel Medicine, 9*(5), 263–266.

Bauer, I.L. (2003). The health of host communities: Missing from printed travel health advice. *Journal of Travel Medicine, 10*(6), 350–352.

Bauer, T. and McKercher, B. (Eds.). (2004). *Sex and tourism: Journeys of romance, love and lust.* New York: Haworth.

BBC News. (2000). Asia's child sex tourism rising. BBC News website at http://news.bbc.co.uk, accessed 7 December 2004.

BBC News. (2001a, 29 October). Airlines face legal action over DVT. BBC News website at http://news.bbc.co.uk, accessed 17 October 2003.

BBC News. (2001b, 11 December). Six guilty in Swiss canyoning trial. BBC News website at http://news.bbc.co.uk, accessed 30 November 2003.

Bentley, T.A. and Page, S.J. (2001). Scoping the extent of adventure tourism accidents. *Annals of Tourism Research, 28*(3), 705–726.

Bentley, T.A., Page, S., and Walker, L. (2004). The safety experience of New Zealand adventure tour operators. *Journal of Travel Medicine, 11*, 280–286.

The Business Journal. (2001, 29 April). Disease daunts tourism. The Business Journal website at http://www. bizjournals.com/tampabay, accessed 26 November 2005.

Carter, S. (1998). Tourists' and travellers' social construction of Africa and Asia as risky locations. *Tourism Management, 19*(4), 349–358.

Castelli, F. (2004). Human mobility and disease: A global challenge. *Journal of Travel Medicine, 11*(1), 1–2.

CDC. (2003). Vessel sanitation program. Centers for Disease Control and Prevention. website at http://www.cdc.gov, accessed 7 November 2003.

Clift, S. and Carter, S. (Eds.). (2003). *Tourism and sex: Culture, commerce and coercion*. London: Pinter.

Clift, S. and Grabowski, P. (Eds.). (1997). *Tourism and health: Risks, research and responses*. London: Pinter.

Clift, S. and Page, S.J. (Eds.). (1996). *Health and the international tourist*. London and New York: Routledge.

Cohen, E. (1993). Open-ended prostitution as a skillful game of luck: Opportunities, risk and security amongst tourist-oriented prostitutes in Bangkok. In M. Hitchcok, V.T. King, and M.J. Parnwell (Eds.), *Tourism in South East Asia* (pp. 155–178). London: Routledge.

Connor, B.A. (2005). Trends in travelers. *Journal of Travel Medicine*, *12*(S1), S1–S2.

CTO. (2003). Tourism sector responsiveness to health crises. Caribbean Tourist Organization website at http://www.onecaribbean.org, accessed 7 November 2003.

Dawood, R. (1989, December). Tourists' health: Could the travel industry do more? *Tourism Management*, 285–287.

EPCAT. (2003). *Annual report*. Bangkok: EPCAT.

Ericsson, C.D., DuPont, H.L., and Steffen, R. (Eds.). (2003). *Travelers' diarrhea*. Hamilton: Becker.

Euromonitor. (2004). *Travel and tourism in Canada*. London: Euromonitor International.

The Financial Times. (2003, 12 October). UK tourism 2001: Open for business. FT.com special report.

Gratz, N. (2003). Disease vectors and international transport. *Journal of Travel Medicine*, *10*, 202.

The Guardian. (2003, 7 November). Cruise ship health alert exaggerated, say passengers. The Guardian website at http://www.guardian.co.UK, accessed 26 November 2003.

Hall, C.M. (1992). Adventure, sport and health tourism. In C.M. Hall and B. Weiler (Eds.), *Special interest tourism* (pp. 147–158). London: Belhaven Press.

Hartgarten, S. (1994). Injury prevention: A crucial aspect of travel medicine. *Journal of Travel Medicine*, *1*(1), 48–50.

Henderson, J.C. (2003). Managing a health-related crisis: SARS in Singapore. *Journal of Vacation Marketing*, *10*(1), 67–78.

Horvath, L.L., Murray, C.K., and DuPont, H.L. (2003). Travel health information at commercial travel websites. *Journal of Travel Medicine*, *10*(5), 272–279.

Horwath Consulting. (2001, 6 April). Foot and mouth crisis hits hotels in the Veluwe. Press Release.

Kaferstein, F. and Abdussalam, M. (1999). Food safety in the 21st century. *Bulletin of the World Health Organization*, *77*(4), 347–351.

Keystone, J.S., Kozarsky, P., Nothdurft, H.D., Freedman, D.O., and Connor, B. (Eds.). (2004). *Travel medicine*. London: Mosby.

The Lancet. (2004, 14 February). Spain makes plan to combat sex tourism. *The Lancet, 363*, 542.

Lawton, G. and Page, S.J. (1997). Evaluating travel agents' provision of health advice to travellers. *Tourism Management, 18*(2), 89–104.

Lepp, A. and Gibson, H. (2003). Tourist roles, perceived risk and international tourism. *Annals of Tourism Research, 30*(3), 606–624.

McInnes, R.J., Williamson, L.M., and Morrison, A. (2002). Unintentional injury during foreign travel: A review. *Journal of Travel Medicine, 9*(6), 297–307.

McKercher, B. and Chon, K. (2004). The over-reaction to SARS and the collapse of Asian tourism. *Annals of Tourism Research, 31*(3), 716–719.

NCBI. (2003). PubMed. National Center for Biotechnology Information. National Library of Medicine website at http://www.ncbi.nlm.nih.go, accessed 7 November 2003.

Nikolic, N., Missoni, E., and Medved, G. (2005). Medical problems in cycling tourism. *Journal of Travel Medicine, 12*(1), 53–54.

The Observer. (2002, 14 April). BA hauls in flyers to check DVT risk. Aviation Health website at http://www.aviation.health.org, accessed 17 October 2003.

One News. (2002, 20 December). UK court blocks DVT bid. One News website at http: onenews.nzoom.com/onenews, accessed 17 October 2003.

Oppermann, M. (1999). Sex tourism. *Annals of Tourism Research, 26*(2), 251–266.

Page, S.J. and Meyer, D. (1996). Tourist accidents: An exploratory analysis. *Annals of Tourism Research, 23*(3), 666–690.

Phillip, R. and Hodgkinson, G. (1994). The management of health and safety hazards in tourist resorts. World Tourism Organization. *International Journal of Occupational Medicine and Environmental Health, 7*(3), 207–219.

Rodriguez-Garcia, R. (2001). The health-development link: Travel as a public health issue. *Journal of Community Health, 26*(2), 93–112.

Rudkin, B. and Hall, C.M. (1996). Off the beaten track: The health implications of the development of special interest tourism activities in South East Asia and the South Pacific. In S. Clift and S.J. Page (Eds.), *Health and the international tourist* (pp. 89–107). London and New York: Routledge.

Ryan, C. (1996). Linkages between holiday taking travel risk and insurance claims: Evidence from New Zealand. *Tourism Management, 17*(8), 593–601.

Ryan, C. and Kinder, R. (1996). Sex, tourism and sex tourism: Fulfilling similar needs? *Tourism Management, 17*(7), 507–518.

Sanford, C. (2004). Urban medicine: Threats to health of travelers to developing world cities. *Journal of Travel Medicine, 11*(5), 313–327.

Schlagenhauf, P. (2004a). Focus on cruise ship travel. *Journal of Travel Medicine, 11*, 191.

Schlagenhauf, P. (2004b). Travel-associated infectious diseases. *Journal of Travel Medicine, 11*, 265–266.

Shaw, M.T. and Leggat, P. (2003). Life and death on the Amazon: Illness and injury to travelers on a South American expedition. *Journal of Travel Medicine, 10*, 268–271.

Stears, D. (1996). Travel health promotion: Advances and alliances. In S. Clift and S.J. Page (Eds.), *Health and the international tourist* (pp. 215–234). London and New York: Routledge.

Thompson, D.T., Ashley, D.V., Dockery-Brown, C.A., Binns, A., Jolly, C.M., and Jolly, P.E. (2003). Incidence of health crises in tourists visiting Jamaica, West Indies, 1998–2000. *Journal of Travel Medicine*, *10*(2), 79–86.

Tourism Authority of Thailand. (2001). TAT supports fight against child prostitution. TAT website at http://www.tourismthailand.org, accessed 27 November 2003.

Travel Telegraph. (2003). BA gets serious about health risks. Travel Telegraph website at http://www.telegraph, accessed 17 October 2003.

UK Parliament. (2001). Select Committee on Culture, Media and Sport. *Tourism—the hidden giant—and foot and mouth. Fourth Report.* London: The UK Parliament.

UNESCAP. (2004). Sexual exploitation in Asia and the Pacific. United Nations Economic and Social Commission for Asia and the Pacific website at http://www.unescap.org, accessed 7 December 2004.

Weber, K. (2001). Outdoor adventure tourism: A review of research approaches. *Annals of Tourism Research*, *28*(2), 360–377.

Wickens, E. (2003). Health risk-taking and tourism. *ASEAN Journal on Hospitality and Tourism*, *2*(2), 160–170.

Wilks, J. and Davis, R.J. (2000). Risk management for scuba diving operators on Australia's Great Barrier Reef. *Tourism Management*, *21*, 591–599.

Wilks, J., Watson, B., and Faulks, I.J. (1999). International tourists and road safety in Australia: Developing a national research and management programme. *Tourism Management*, *20*, 645–654.

WHO. (2002). *International travel and health*. Geneva: World Health Organization.

WHO. (2003). World Health Organization SARS website at http://www.who.int/csr/sars, accessed 6 June 2003.

WHO. (2005). Avian influenza. World Health Organization website at http://www.who.int, accessed 30 April 2005.

WTO. (1991). Recommended measures for tourism safety. World Tourism Organisation website at http://www.world-tourism.org, accessed 7 November 2004.

WTO. (2004). *World tourism barometer*, *2*(2). Madrid: World Tourism Organization.

WTTC. (2003). WTTC special reports on the impact of SARS. World Travel and Tourism Council website at http://www.wttc.org, accessed 6 December 2004.

Zuckerman, J.N. (Ed.). (2001). *Principles and practice of travel medicine.* Chichester and New York: Wiley.

8

Technological Failure and Tourism

Learning Objectives

By the end of the chapter, the reader should be able to

- Understand how various types of technological failure and deficiency can have consequences for tourism.
- Appreciate the particular significance of transport accidents as a form of tourism crisis.
- Identify appropriate actions which can assist in containing tourism crises resulting from technological failures and deficiencies.
- Recognize that crises can be an opportunity to review and upgrade safety standards in the tourism industry.

Introduction

Tourism employs technology in an assortment of forms which has allowed the industry to improve products and their delivery to customers. Modern technology also offers advantages of greater efficiency and cost savings. Sophisticated information technology systems allow the rapid communication of information and the building of strong relationships among suppliers, distributors and markets. Advances in transport technology have facilitated the development of modern mass tourism, allowing more people to travel further than ever before, and many leisure attractions are technology based. Building technology has also allowed the construction of impressive new amenities to serve tourists and the industry.

While facilities and services have been enhanced as a result, technology may cause problems when it fails totally or does not perform in the manner expected. It can be a source of serious crisis, especially when customers and staff are injured or killed. This chapter is concerned with incidents of technological failure and focuses on transport accidents, aspects of which have already been discussed with reference to voluntary and involuntary health risks in Chapter 7. Accidents are frequently a result of both mechanical and non-mechanical factors and case studies of a ferry sinking and air crash at the end of the chapter illustrate how these can combine to create fatal disasters and tourism industry organizational crises.

Fire hazards, information technology disruption and certain other examples of technology-related crises are also examined. The potential for crisis when technology lets the industry and tourists down is revealed, although human error is often a key element in emergencies connected to technology. It is not the technology alone which is at fault, but those using it and making decisions about its application.

Transport Accidents and Tourism

There are no comprehensive global statistics on transport safety and international comparisons are complicated by national differences in definitions and data collection and analysis. It seems probable that there will be considerable variations around the world depending on circumstances locally and nationally, the extent of regulation and stage of economic development. Figures available also do not allow comment on the proportions of victims who are tourists compared to excursionists and residents. Nevertheless, all tourists are exposed to risks when traveling by public or private transport and some of these were described in Chapter 7.

Within the more advanced Organization of Economic Cooperation and Development (OECD) countries, the percentage of accidental deaths linked to transport averaged 24% in 1999. The figure ranged from 13% in Finland and Sweden to 35% in New Zealand and Portugal, 39% in Spain and 50% in Greece. Vehicle traffic accidents accounted for over 90% of deaths in half of the OECD countries in the 1980s and 1990s. Deaths caused by railway and water transport accidents averaged between 1% and 3% and 2% to 4%, respectively, rarely exceeding 5% in any one year. Air transport, including balloons, hang gliders and ultra light planes, was responsible for 2% to 3% of all accidental deaths in most countries (ATSB, 2004). Perceptions of the comparative safety of alternative modes do not therefore always correspond with empirical evidence as suggested by the prevalence of anxiety about flying.

Although relatively rare, there is a possibility of tourists being hurt or killed by chance in public transport accidents and a greater likelihood of them experiencing travel disruption due to a host of operational reasons. Hazards may be intensified by deficiencies in safety standards and regulations, especially in developing nations which are popular destinations. Crashes and collisions are usually the outcome of mechanical and engineering faults in association with other forces such as human mistakes, terrorist acts and severe weather. They are a subject of popular and media interest and test the capabilities and competences of companies and staff, often necessitating immediate decisions from management taken in the public spotlight. Governments may also be called on to act because of their responsibilities as regulators and action demanded from the tourism industry sector as a whole.

These observations apply especially to the civil aviation business due to the higher chance of fatalities should there be a mishap, although surface transport accidents are also a challenge for commercial enterprises and official agencies. Such situations are considered in the following sections after an account of the perils of traveling by private car and implications for the tourism industry.

The Private Car

Private road transport appears to be the most dangerous way to travel within OECD member states and a similar pattern emerges in Europe, where approximately 120,000 die and 2.5 million are injured in traffic accidents annually, almost one-third of fatalities being under 25 years of age (WHO, 2004). In the case of the UK, people in cars are nine times more likely to be killed than rail passengers and there are about 3,500 road deaths every year. Those on planes face a slightly higher risk than rail travelers and buses, coaches and boats are safer than rail (RSSB, 2004). US statistics correspond to these trends and more than 90% of transport fatalities in the USA are linked to motor vehicles, deaths reaching 42,643 in 2003 (NHTSA, 2004).

Car ownership is lower in less-developed countries, but mortality statistics seem disproportionate in magnitude. The Asian Development Bank (ADB) reports that 44% of road deaths occur in the Asia Pacific region even though it has only 14% of the world's vehicles (ADB, 2004), although this includes motorcycles which are a more affordable choice of motorized transport in the developing world.

The private car has an important role in the tourism industry in terms of car hire operators at destinations and fly-drive vacation packages, as well as the use of personally owned vehicles for touring purposes. Cars offer freedom and flexibility and permit easy access to more isolated attraction and accommodation sites. High accident rates are therefore a cause of concern to tourists, service providers and destination authorities.

Vehicles have been shown to be a major cause of accidents among international tourists. A sizeable percentage of injuries and fatalities among American visitors to Mexico in the period 1975–1984 were due to crashes (Guptill et al., 1991) and Canadians, Australians and Europeans abroad are also at risk (Macpherson et al., 2000; McInnes et al., 2002). Tourists hurt in car accidents on the Mediterranean island of Crete were more likely to be accustomed to driving on the other side of the road (Petridou et al., 1997); this and driving under the influence of alcohol (Colon, 1985) are widespread problems. Each country has its own constraints and distances in Australia, leading to excessively long journey times and driver fatigue, and roadside encounters with wildlife such as kangaroos can precipitate accidents there in addition to catalysts which prevail elsewhere (Wilks et al., 1999).

Tragedies involving private vehicles driven by and carrying tourists can affect the image of a place if sufficiently numerous and create a perception that it is generally unsafe. Commentators suggest that tourists driving are advised to exercise extreme caution and be mindful of local conditions. Possible accident prevention measures include the provision of areas where drivers can stop for a rest, stricter regulations against drink driving, enactment of compulsory seat belt legislation and better information targeted at tourists and commercial suppliers (Wilks, 1999; Wilks et al., 1999). Additional strategies are the encouragement of responsible actions by tourists to protect themselves and ensuring that hired cars have superior safety features (Hartgarten, 1994; Page and Meyer, 1996).

Car hire companies do appear to have made some attempt to improve the safety of their vehicles and address the overall security concerns of customers (Paternie, 2004). These companies incorporate special programs with an emphasis on informing drivers about distinctive destination circumstances and reassurance for female customers. Other measures introduced in Florida to protect tourists in hired vehicles from criminal attack were noted in Chapter 5.

Bus and Coach, Rail and Sea Travel

Public and private bus and coach road accidents are uncommon, representing 0.3% to 0.5% of traffic deaths in Europe (Albertsson and Falkmer, 2005). Nevertheless, they are a crisis for operators implicated which have to contend with media coverage, official enquiries, falls in demand and compensation issues. Trips overseas by UK schools were in the news at the beginning of the decade after coach crashes in which schoolchildren and teachers died (BBC News, 2002). Safety regulations can save lives if they exist and are adhered to, but cannot stop certain tragedies. They include situations when coach drivers are negligent and such events can jeopardize the survival of small coach businesses which find it difficult to recover from the adverse publicity. Geography is a relevant consideration in risk and some adventure tours explore difficult terrain like the Australian outback (Bauer, 2002) which requires suitable vehicles appropriately equipped if they are to cope with the physically demanding routes.

Railways are considered one of the safest, as well as least environmentally damaging, forms of transport. There have, however, been several rail disasters of human and mechanical origin either separately or in alliance. The Eschede disaster in 1998 was the worst in German history when 101 died after the derailment of an ICE high-speed train, moving at over 200 km/hour, because of a broken wheel. Railways in Britain have also seen several fatal incidents, eroding confidence in an industry which was privatized in the 1980s. For example, a collision between two trains at a busy rail junction in London due to confusion over the signals led to 31 dead and over 200 injured in 1999. Many rail services are patronized largely by residents, but travelers in funicular railways and cable cars are likely to be predominantly visitors. Cable cars especially are common features in winter sports resorts where there have been deadly accidents as a result of entangled and broken cables, the detachment of cars from cables and cutting of cables by low-flying aircraft (Browne, 2000).

Although sea travel as a means of transport has declined with the expansion in civil aviation, ferry services and cruising are key components of the tourism industry. Here too, there are operational dangers with questions about the seaworthiness of ferries in some parts of the world. Accidents may be limited in number, but they do occur regularly and afford insights into the technical and other shortcomings which threaten the safety of passengers and crew.

As ferries have become larger, the potential scale of accidents has grown. The 1994 sinking of the MS Estonia, a car and passenger ferry, was Europe's gravest maritime disaster since the Second World War. The ship was sailing in the Baltic Sea in very poor sea and weather conditions when it sank with 950 on board, 852 of whom died. A report published in 1997 concluded that the accident had been due to the incompetence of the crew and design faults in the ferry's front doors which broke under pressure from the waves. There had also been insufficient public warnings and doubts about rescue arrangements (Joint Accident Investigation Commission, 1997). Another commission, established by the shipyard which built the vessel, claimed that the causes were inadequate maintenance and undue speed. The International Maritime Organization conducted its own study of safety aspects of this type of ro-ro (roll on, roll off) ferry and new regulations were developed as a consequence (CNN Interactive, 1997).

It seemed that lessons had not been learned from the capsizing of the MS Herald of Free Enterprise in 1987 which was also a ro-ro ferry (see Case One). The death toll of 193 was the highest in the UK since the Titanic. The operator, Townsend Thoresen, was described as having "clammed up" (Regester and Larkin, 1998, p. 185) and its approach was compared to that of Stena Line, one of whose ferries was grounded on a sandbank off the French coast in 1995. Then, information was provided quickly with stress on positive news about the passengers and the situation on board. Individual ferry captains were able to activate a crisis management program, alerting head office and technical and public relations teams which were ready to act (Simms, 1998). Comparisons can be misleading, however, and the accident was perhaps more easily managed because of the absence of casualties. Some observers also judged Stena to have been slow in providing satisfactory reasons for the grounding and explaining its decision not to immediately evacuate the ship (Mott, 1995).

In another example of poor media management, the managing director of Da-No line was criticized for his handling of a fatal fire on its Scandinavian Star ferry in 1990 when 139 people lost their lives. His statements diverged from those of survivors and he declined to answer questions about the alarm system and the reactions of the crew. There was no corporate response to accusations about incompetence, further undermining trust in the company (Eales, 1990). Uncertainty about the exact circumstances persisted after 12 years with demands to reopen the formal investigation which had blamed an arson attack and ended with the captain and two company officials being sentenced to six months' probation.

Cruising is a growing market with projections of 17 million passengers by 2006, mainly sailing on large ships. These ships can accommodate more than 1,500, sometimes in excess of 3,000, making them floating destinations where those on board are exposed to the illnesses detailed in the preceding chapter. While having an excellent safety record overall (Cartwright and Baird, 1999), other risks can arise relating principally to fire, collision and grounding. Lois et al. (2004) listed 16 serious accidents between 1992 and 2001 resulting from grounding (five cases), fire (four cases), collision (three cases), the striking of a submerged vessel, a botched refit, electrical power failure and holed on a shoal (one case of each). The damage was mainly to the ships' hulls and there were fatalities only on the two ships which sunk. Three died and six were classed as missing on the Royal Pacific in 1992 and 100 died on the Cebucity in 1999.

The same study (Lois et al., 2004) identified the principal operational stages of a cruise as passenger embarkation, getting under way, the cruise itself, docking and disembarkation and identified the hazards which can arise. They are reproduced in Table 8.1 and can be extended to ferry activities, although there are additional steps in the latter of loading and off-loading freight and passenger vehicles.

The authors proposed a framework for the advance recognition of risks and rating of their probability, the intention being to avert the onset of undesirable developments or at least contain any damage should these happen. They concluded that there is room for improvement among cruise companies in the areas of human relations and resources, particularly with regard to communicating with and managing passengers and crew (who could speak an assortment of languages) and the collection and distribution of information. Greater attention should also be given to staff education and training and practical matters of fire fighting.

Civil Aviation

Civil aviation disasters generate global publicity and the world's worst took place in Tenerife in the Canary Islands in 1977 when Boeing 747s flown by KLM and Pan Am collided on the runway (see Case Two), but it should be remembered that crashes in the air and on the ground are extremely rare. There were only 92 accidents in 2003; of these, 32 led to 947 fatalities with most jets lost in Africa. Air accident rates are falling and there was a decline from 1.19 per million departures in 1994 to 0.68 in 2003. According to IATA (IATA, 2004, p. 28), this improvement has been due to preventive strategies founded on "technology, human factors and risk management, safety management systems, change management, engineering reliability and maintainability." However, the possibility of an accident is always present and airlines are expected to be in a constant state of readiness (IATA, 1998).

Practical matters have to be dealt with subsequent to a crash, but the importance of communications during the crisis should not be forgotten (Strategic Direction, 2000). Airlines have a range of options regarding the position they assume such as the denial or evasion of responsibility, ingratiation, seeking to make amends and soliciting sympathy (Ray, 1999). Immediate acceptance of responsibility is another and appropriate choice when there is no doubt of company blame. This is illustrated by the crash of a Japanese aircraft in 1985 when 520 died and the airline, JAL, pursued an "elaborate protocol to atone." The company president personally apologized for the accident and proffered his resignation and the head of maintenance

Table 8.1: **Cruise hazards**

Operation phases	Possible hazardous events
Passenger embarkation	Passenger and crew injuries while alongside
	Passenger violence
	Fire/explosion in terminal
	Noise
	Overloading gangway/collapse
	Injuries to unattended children
	Lifting injuries when loading wheelchairs
Getting under way	Fall in water/man overboard
	Collision with another vessel
	Loss of control (ice, wind, restricted visibility)
	Slips, falls at gangway
	Fire during fueling
Cruise	Injuries due to machinery failure
	High-speed collision, grounding
	Situational management (loss of awareness, distraction, multiple events)
	Electric shock
	Exposure to elements
	Medical emergency/evacuation
	Vessel fire
	Engine failure
	Noise due to conflicting groups
Docking	Squish injury
	Dock fire
	Contact with unknown/hidden objects
	Complacency (hard docking)
Disembarkation	Sewage spills
	Injuries due to overloaded gangway
	Slips and falls while disembarking
	Careless attendance to handicapped passengers

Sources: Reprinted from *Tourism Management*, *24*(1), Lois, P., Wang, J., Wall, A., and Ruxton, T. Formal safety assessment of cruise ships, p. 104. Copyright (2004), with permission from Elsevier.

killed himself (Regester and Larkin, 1998, p. 146). Memorial services were organized, relatives were given monetary aid and staff were deployed to support next of kin. These moves were seen as proper by the Japanese market and made it possible for JAL to survive the crisis with its reputation almost intact.

A similar approach was adopted by Singapore Airlines after one of its flights crashed when taking off from the wrong runway in Taiwan in 2002, killing 82 people. It was soon apparent that the pilots had made mistakes, although there was some criticism about airport facilities and air traffic control. The company quickly moved to recognize its obligations, display penitence and offer reassurances about safety. Such actions helped to confine the damage to an airline which had previously prided itself on an unblemished safety record (Henderson, 2003). The chairman of British Midland Airways was also praised for his attitude and demeanor in media interviews following a crash in the English Midlands, enhancing his own stature and that of the airline despite 47 deaths (Regester and Larkin, 1998).

In contrast, two Asian airlines were criticized in the aftermath of accidents. Four planes of Taiwan's China Airlines crashed between 1994 and 2001 and Korean Air also saw a spate of emergencies in the 1990s. The chairman and seven board members of the former offered to resign and the head and founder of Korean Air actually did so, but this was insufficient to appease public anger. There was much debate about flight safety (BBC News, 1999; CNN.com, 2001) and the media in Taiwan gave prominence to the outrage felt by relatives of the deceased. Pan Am's ill-considered attempts to distance itself from the Lockerbie tragedy also had a negative outcome for the organization as related in Chapter 4.

The onerous task of rebuilding a company's good name after an accident is demonstrated by the ValuJet crash in the Florida Everglades in 1996 which killed all 110 people on board. An inquiry that year concluded that this could have been the result of maintenance and operating faults and weaknesses in the airline's policies and procedures were uncovered. The airline was grounded for a period by the authorities and later taken over, indicating the financial repercussions of severe safety failures. The case also raised wider issues about whether budget carriers were compromising on safety with a view to saving money, enabling them to maintain low fares (Buckingham and Harper, 1997). Such questions continue to be relevant in the twenty-first century when low-cost airlines are carrying greater volumes of passengers and establishing themselves in other regions of the world outside North America and Europe.

Fire Hazards

Deficiencies in technology can result in fires which affect transport and accommodation units as well as attraction venues. Even when causes are unrelated to technological issues, an absence of technological expertise and resources for fighting fires may augment harm and compound the ensuing crisis. Many hotel fires, for example, are made worse by safety systems which are out of date or inadequately maintained. The crisis is most acute when lives are lost, but there are also economic implications concerning damage to property and equipment and lost business (Davies and Walters, 1998).

The fire in the rail tunnel under the English Channel in 1996 disrupted operations and called into question the standing of the company running the venture which was already under commercial pressure (see Boxed Case One). More recently, a funicular train in the Austrian ski resort of Kaprun caught fire in a tunnel in 2000. The fire was blamed on a faulty heater which created a "fire storm," flames being fanned by air from both ends of the tunnel. The situation was aggravated because

131

Boxed Case One: Eurotunnel Fire

Eurotunnel is the company in charge of the rail tunnel under the English Channel which connects the UK and France. It also operates the shuttle services which carry freight and private vehicles on separate trains. There are two main rail tunnels and a third tunnel between them which is used for maintenance purposes and serves as an escape route. Fire broke out in the main tunnel on a November evening in 1996 and reached temperatures of 1,000 degrees centigrade. It appeared to start on one of the trucks being transported and a subsequent enquiry concluded that this had been deliberately set alight. Although there were no deaths or injuries, the blaze caused sufficient damage to close freight operations for six months. There were reports that Eurotunnel was losing £1 million daily at a time when it was already heavily debt-laden. The fire was also the subject of widespread publicity and placed managers under close scrutiny.

An official report found that there were "fundamental weaknesses" in safety management and that "emergency procedures were too complex and demanding and staff on duty had not been adequately trained to carry them out." Eurotunnel committed itself to remedy these deficiencies and completed the necessary rebuilding while continuing passenger rail services. Transport through the tunnel was back to normal by mid-May 1997 and the company eventually recovered £180 million in an insurance claim. The newly appointed chief financial officer took the opportunity to reorganize and restructure parts of the business with a view to long-term cost savings. It was later claimed that tunnel security had been considerably enhanced by the improved safety regime.

Sources: BBC News, 2004c; Department of Transport, 1997; Holmes, 2001; Simpson and Noulton, 1998.

---

there were no lights in the tunnel, only a single service staircase and the train doors could not be opened internally. Most of the 155 passengers were skiers of eight nationalities and only 12 of those on board survived. A total of 16 individuals representing train operators, suppliers and inspectors were tried by an Austrian court, but acquitted in 2004 because of insufficient evidence (BBC News, 2004a).

Fire is a notable hazard in hotels because of their structural characteristics and the presence of potential danger zones such as kitchens, electrical equipment, boilers and stored goods. They are usually sited on lower levels with guest rooms on the floors above, complicating escape should a fire break out. Both staff and guests may be careless and many fires begin when the latter fall asleep smoking in bed. Large numbers of people are gathered in confined spaces and several will be new to the hotel and have trouble finding their way around, especially in the panic of an emergency. There could be language problems in directing overseas visitors and guests may be sleeping when fire breaks out, making evacuation even more difficult (Roberts and Chan, 2000). The potential for loss of life is thus considerable and increases with the size of the hotel (Chow and Kot, 1989).

There is a history of hotel fires around the world and death tolls were exceptionally high in the cases of those in Atlanta in 1946 (119 deaths), Seoul in 1971 (166 deaths), Belgium in 1977 (302 deaths) and Puerto Rico in 1986 (96 deaths). In addition to fatalities, many were injured in these and other fires (Emergency Management, 2005). It was estimated in the early 1980s that there were between 4,000 and 8,000 hotel fires annually with thousands of deaths (Slough, 1984) and it seems likely that these figures will have risen in the intervening years.

Complete sets of national data are not always available, but the annual average for structure fires in hotels and motels in the USA was 4,900 from 1994 through 1998. The main causes were cooking equipment; appliances, tools or air conditioning and deliberate and fires mainly started in kitchens, bedrooms and laundry rooms (Ahrens, 2003). These statistics reveal an improvement after a series of major incidents in the 1980s, one of which was the 1980 MGM Grand Hotel fire in Las Vegas (see Boxed Case Two), when the lack of smoke alarms and sprinklers contributed to casualty rates.

Due to greater vigilance and despite a substantial growth in hotels, the volume of American hotel fires has fallen by almost 66% in the past two decades. The National Fire Protection Association has devised codes and standards, often in association with the hotel industry, which inform most corporate fire safety procedures and a majority of hotels now have sprinklers. These measures have also been introduced in properties overseas, although this is not an easy exercise in some older and historic hotels where the fabric and appearance of the building must be respected and preserved (Touger, 2001).

However, regulation and enforcement are lax in many countries, especially in the developing world. Fire at the Manor Hotel in the Philippine capital of Manila in 2001 killed 70 and injured 100, making it the country's deadliest. The trigger appeared to be an electrical fault and it was later found that smoke alarms were not functioning, fire exits were either locked or blocked, there was no emergency lighting or sprinklers and many windows had metal bars. There were suggestions that many hotels were in breach of formal fire regulations, but these were overlooked by corrupt officials who were reluctant to prosecute known offenders (Roberts, 2001). Similar circumstances were observed in Thailand after the 1997 Resort Hotel fire in Pattaya in which 90 died. The fire alarm and sprinkler systems did not work, fire doors were locked and an engineer could not be found. A subsequent report concluded that 200 other high-rise buildings in Pattaya did not conform to safety standards (Leggatt and Leggatt, 2003).

Hotel fires are a crisis which can be avoided or at least made less deadly by various measures. A study identifies eight prerequisites of structural fire protection, escape routes, smoke control, ventilation, automatic sprinklers, fire detection systems, fire hydrants and hose reels and careful storage of dangerous and

---

Boxed Case Two: Las Vegas MGM Grand Fire

The fire at the MGM Grand Hotel was the outcome of an electrical fault in a café on the first floor where extended refrigeration wires were not insulated and subject to friction due to vibrations from the unit. The flames reached the air conditioning system above the casino, consuming an assortment of flammable materials, and burned for a number of hours without being detected. They then erupted at about 7 a.m., moving almost six meters every second to engulf the casino. There were approximately 5,000 people in the 26-story complex at this time and many were trapped by the fire in their rooms, corridors and stairwells. Most of the fatalities (85) occurred at the hotel or in nearby hospitals and a few died from connected causes within one year, the numbers making it the second deadliest hotel fire in the USA. A further 700 were injured.

The investigation revealed several reasons for the scale of the fire connected to design shortcomings as well as inspection failures. There had been no fire alarm, important escape routes were obscured by smoke and there were weaknesses in the heating, ventilation and air conditioning systems which facilitated the spread of the flames. It was reported that earlier advice to install sprinklers had been ignored because of the US$192,000 costs. The hotel had to make legal payments of US$223 million and is now known as Bally's Las Vegas Hilton Casino Resort. The incident led to a review of safety in Nevada and encouraged the adoption of smoke detectors and sprinklers in the state's principal hotels.

Source: NFPA®, 2001.

---

combustible materials. Guests and staff can be properly informed to raise awareness, minimizing the chances of fire through inappropriate behavior, and a tighter security regime can lessen opportunities for arson. Staff also need to be taught how to deal with fires and organize orderly evacuations, working with fire officials to achieve these ends (Chow and Kot, 1989, pp. 273–274). This is an example of the partnership with external agencies on which successful tourism crisis planning and management depends.

Information Technology Failure

The Internet and other forms of information technology have transformed the way in which the tourism industry does business. They have become vital tools in commercial transactions and the distribution of products, creating new sales and marketing opportunities. Tourists have also gained access to unprecedented amounts of information about destinations around the world and can book a host of services directly and instantly on personal computers in the comfort of their own homes. However, there are some limitations to the modern state of growing dependence on information technology with possibilities of uncertainty and crisis when this goes wrong. For example, air traffic control computer collapses can prevent aircraft from taking off and landing and upset schedules for an extended period even if the computer is out of action for only a short time.

The millennium bug (Y2K) is an interesting case of a widely predicted technology crisis that did not materialize. There had been forecasts of disruption of operational systems as well as damage to databases and administrative programs as the world entered the twenty-first century. These were expected to affect essential services such as transport, telecommunications and power and water supplies and perhaps cause chaos for travelers. In the UK, the government and private sector as a whole spent about £430 and £20 billion, respectively, in efforts to battle the bug and avert the worst scenarios (The Guardian, 2000).

Tourism companies recognized the threat and sought to prepare. Galileo, one of the world's major airline booking networks, began a scheme in 1995 which cost over US$20 million. British tour operators tried to avoid compensation claims by adding exemption clauses in their brochures relating to customer difficulties because of Y2K. Several circulated a comprehensive checklist of necessary steps to ensure year 2000 compliance to their hotel partners, some even advising clients to avoid travel over Christmas and New Year. Liability remained unclear and insurance companies were unwilling to give 100% coverage to businesses or travelers for losses related to the bug. Luckily, the hypothetical case of a customer delayed for hours at the airport who found the hotel had no record of his reservation and was trapped in the lift because of a power failure and then could not find a working automated cash machine was never tested (Travel Weekly, 2004).

Other Types of Technological Failure

Other technological defects arising within the tourism industry which may impact adversely on its operation include poor architectural design and workmanship and mechanical faults. It has already been suggested how the former can contribute to fire hazards in hotels, but there are also possibilities of maintenance problems and even structural implosion due to construction errors. Many striking new buildings appear to sacrifice functionality and practicality for form and this applies to some ambitious airport projects. For example, part of a passenger terminal at Charles de Gaulle Airport in Paris collapsed in 2004, less than a year after its opening, killing four people and closing the terminal until the end of the year. The building was noted for its futuristic shape with a self-supporting curved glass and concrete roof.

French officials pledged that those responsible would be suitably punished and ordered an immediate probe into the accident, promising an interim report within a month. The architect and others were also subject to separate criminal investigations. Preliminary conclusions indicated that structural weaknesses were to blame.

Various repair strategies were examined, but it was decided in 2005 to demolish and rebuild the roof at a cost of €100 million. The new terminal is expected to be operational by 2007 and the events were a severe setback to visions of the airport as a global civil aviation hub (Associated Press, 2005; BBC News, 2004b).

Interruption of air conditioning, central heating or water supply in transport terminals and hospitality enterprises represents a crisis due to mechanical breakdown; tourist attractions are also venues where this can occur. Cases involving theme park rides, which are becoming increasingly sophisticated and reliant on technology to provide more thrills to attract visitors, may put customers in danger. Operators are in competition to build higher and faster roller coasters and other rides, but there are anxieties about safety as reported injuries are on the rise (Braksiek and Roberts, 2002). Such accidents, especially when children are hurt, are often headline news and put organizations on the defensive.

An American review indicated that the principal mechanical problems were defective or missing parts, exposed electrical wires, inadequate safety restraints and improper detachment (Bestwire, 1999). Inherent design faults have also been discovered, although mistakes by staff operating rides and visitors play a part. There is obviously a need for constant vigilance to ward off a crisis associated with ride accidents which management tend to respond to with expressions of sympathy to families of casualties, a commitment to cooperate fully with investigating authorities and emphasis on their dedication to safety and previous safety records. The International Association of Amusement Parks and Attractions (IAAPA) has developed safety standards related to design and manufacture, testing, operation, maintenance and inspection (IAAPA, 2003), but there are no international codes of conduct and practice.

Technological difficulties in the external environment must also be recognized as a source of tourism crisis and electricity blackouts can lead to complete confusion. Power failures in Italy and North America in 2003 affected almost 100 million people and posed serious difficulties for hoteliers. Elevators or lifts are a major worry because occupants might be trapped and experts are required to deal with their rescue. The Director of Risk Management at The Peninsula in New York, commenting on the 2003 emergency, writes about the significance of communications within the hotel and with outside parties and the need to account for guests. A blackout can also be a business opportunity when people are stranded in the city, especially if hotels are well stocked and have their own generators which permit emergency lighting and air conditioning (Chin, 2003).

Responses to Technological Failure

This chapter has concentrated on crises originating in technological failure which result in fatalities, particularly transport accidents and hotel fires. The former are distinguished by the pace with which they progress and crashes constitute an immediate crisis when there may be no chance of escape. Underlying causes such as particular types of mechanical faults and human blunders cannot be anticipated so that risks are constant. Transport companies are therefore always on the point of crisis and the pursuit of maximum levels of safety and security should be standard industry practice, reinforced by official regulations which are strictly enforced.

Transport crises might lead to death, injury and physical and emotional suffering which adds to their gravity. Fatal accidents of a certain scale attract widespread media interest and reporters thus exercise considerable influence. Organizations may try to convey positive images, but they will also be exposed to searching examination in a situation of often great uncertainty. Excluding the media or refusing to cooperate with them can arouse suspicion and criticism, communicated in damaging publicity. It is also advisable to identify an appropriate person or persons who can speak with one voice on behalf of the organization so that any statements are neither conflicting nor contradictory. Such public pronouncements must be delivered with care, particularly on the subject of disputed questions like those of responsibility.

The cases cited in the chapter suggest the importance of providing a swift and concise explanation of events surrounding any accident and the setting up of an internal enquiry, as well as willing participation in any formal investigations. Delay in reporting findings should be minimized and guilty parties should be seen to be brought to justice, although this may not be easy and depends upon legislative procedures. In the UK, for example, it has proved difficult to secure convictions for corporate manslaughter in several transport disasters and there have been calls for legal reforms to facilitate this process (McLean and Johnes, 2000). Compensation is another issue to be resolved as quickly as possible in acknowledgement of obligations to the well-being of victims and their next of kin. Protracted lawsuits mean that the company and the original incident remain in the public eye and this can impede resolution.

Finally, action must be taken at both a company and industry level to improve safety based on lessons learned from the experience of critical incidents. News about the introduction of such measures should be conveyed to all parties with an interest to assuage anxieties and restore confidence. Nevertheless, it must be appreciated that absolute safety cannot be guaranteed and there is perhaps a threshold regarding the price both businesses and tourists are prepared to pay for safety enhancements.

Not all technologically initiated tourism crises involve death and destruction. Other illustrations of computer viruses or the temporary unavailability of air conditioning in a tropical city hotel are less serious. These crises too still have to be managed to minimize customer inconvenience and safeguard the good name of the company.

Summary and Conclusions

There are many different classes of technology such as those related to transport, building, computers and public utilities which are all relevant to tourism. Overall, technology is of vital importance to the modern tourism industry and it occupies a central role in the creation and delivery of tourism services. It is relied upon by many businesses and has enhanced the tourist experience of transport, accommodation and attractions. However, technology may also be a catalyst of crisis when it breaks down completely or displays serious inadequacies in performance. Resulting crises range in severity from the multiple deaths of customers to the comparatively minor disturbance of malfunctioning power supplies.

Precautionary measures can be taken and regimes of vigilance, inspection and regulation will reduce risks of even the worst scenarios being realized. Crises are often the outcome of collective forces and defy precise categorization with overlapping causes. Human error may underlie technological failure and staff training and education of both staff and customers are also core components of safety and security policies. Technological problems require technological solutions and investment in systems and staff to ensure efficiency in operations and the prompt identification and speedy repair of faults before they evolve into major crises.

Case One: MS Herald of Free Enterprise

The Herald of Free Enterprise, carrying 459 passengers and 80 crew, had left the Belgian port of Zeebrugge in early March 1987 with its bow doors open and ballast which should have been pumped out still in the tanks. It rolled over shortly after leaving the harbor and remained half submerged until it was refloated almost two months later, a visible reminder of the company (Townsend Thoresen, part of the P&O Group) and tragedy. Human errors included the following:

- The assistant bosun who was directly responsible for closing the doors was asleep in his cabin, having just been relieved from maintenance and cleaning duties.
- The bosun noticed that the bow doors were still open, but did not close them as he did not see that as part of his duties.
- It seems that the captain was to assume that the doors were safely closed unless told otherwise, but it was nobody's particular duty to tell him.
- The chief officer, responsible for ensuring door closure, testified that he thought he saw the assistant bosun going to close the door. The chief officer also had to be on the bridge 15 minutes before sailing time.

The official report commented "at first sight, the faults which led to this disaster were the aforesaid errors of omission on the part of the master, the chief officer and the assistant bosun, and also the failure by Captain Kirk to issue and enforce clear orders. But . . . the underlying or cardinal faults lay higher up in the company. The Board of Directors . . . did not apply their minds to the question: What orders should be given to the safety of our ships? . . . From top to bottom the body corporate was infected with the disease of sloppiness . . . The failure on the part of the shore management to give proper and clear directions was a contributory cause of the disaster." The top-heavy design of roll on, roll off ships in this class was also deemed inherently unsafe.

As an example of "sloppiness," there was no information display to tell the captain if the bow doors were open. Two years earlier, the captain of a vessel owned by the same company had requested that a warning light should be installed, following a similar incident when he had gone to sea with his bow doors open. Company management had treated the request without seriousness. Following the loss of the Herald, bow door warning lights were made mandatory on roll on, roll off car ferries.

Overall, it was concluded that a combination of errors relating to management, design and individuals had resulted in the disaster. A coroner's inquest in the UK recorded a verdict of unlawful killing and attempts to secure convictions of corporate manslaughter failed.

In April 1997, new international maritime safety regulations were agreed upon. The regulations target the latent design errors and are intended to ensure that a roll on, roll off ship can maintain stability with the car deck flooded to a depth of 50.8 cm (20 inches). This involves installing internal partitions (bulkheads) or additional flotation devices within the hull. The aim is to prevent disasters such as the Herald of Free Enterprise and the Estonia by making the ships safe enough for the orderly evacuation of passengers. Standard cruise ships are expected to stay afloat for at least half an hour after being irreparably holed.

Source: Safety Line Institute, 2000.

Case Two: Boeing 747s' Collision in Tenerife

Pan Am Flight 1736 had been diverted to Tenerife in the Canary Islands in March 1977 because the major airport at Las Palmas had been closed due to a terrorist bomb attack by Canary Island separatists. The airport at Tenerife, which was notorious for fog and did not have runway radar, was therefore exceptionally busy. The Pan Am flight landed safely and was waiting to leave, having been held up by KLM Flight 4805 which was being refueled. The aircraft and fuel trucks were blocking the taxiway.

There was some confusion about the instructions given to both cockpits and misunderstandings between the crew and Tenerife air traffic control which could not see the planes due to dense fog. The KLM captain assumed that he had been given clearance to take off, but the Pan Am plane was actually taxiing on the runway ahead, having missed the exit it was instructed to use because of the fog. The two collided as the KLM plane was leaving the ground and caught fire. Everyone aboard the KLM flight was killed, but 61 Pan Am passengers and crew survived, including the captain, although most of them were injured. A total of 583 died.

The accident has been explained in terms of "hurry-up syndrome" defined as "any situation where a pilot's human performance is degraded by a perceived or actual need to hurry or rush tasks or duties for any reason" (McElhatton and Drew, 1993). An Air Line Pilots Association (ALPA) investigation found that the KLM crew was worried about returning to Amsterdam in order to remain within its duty time regulations. The Pan Am crew was also concerned about being delayed.

Other investigations involved 70 Spanish, Dutch and American experts and representatives from the two airlines. The accident was blamed on poor communications between the pilots and control tower which had led to misunderstanding and misinterpretation. Reforms introduced as a result included the rule that standardized phrases in the English language had to be used by all parties and aircraft manufacturers started to install equipment which improved visibility in foggy conditions. Changes were made to cockpit procedures with less stress on hierarchal authority and more on mutual decision making, partly because the KLM captain had overruled the first engineer who had expressed concern about the Pan Am plane's position. Another airport was also built in the south of the island which was less prone to fog.

Sources: BBC, 2005; McElhatton and Drew, 1993; Pan Am, 2004; Wikipedia, 2004.

Concept Definitions

- Corporate communications strategies: Approaches adopted by companies to the establishment and maintenance of contact with external groups.
- Human error: A failure by staff to fully complete tasks or make serious mistakes in the execution of such tasks.
- Technological failure: The inability of technology to function effectively and in the manner expected.
- Technological tourism crises: Crises for the tourism industry and tourists which are caused by assorted technological forces.

Review Questions

1. What forms of technological failure have the potential to precipitate tourism crises?
2. Why is an airline crash a particularly demanding type of tourism crisis to manage?
3. What are some of the principal causes of transport accidents?
4. How can the risk of a hotel fire and resultant damage be minimized?
5. Has the tourism industry become over-reliant on information technology systems?
6. What lessons can be learned from the Herald of Free Enterprise and Boeing 747 disasters?

Additional Readings

Henderson, J.C. (2003). Communicating in a crisis: Flight SQ 006. *Tourism Management, 24,* 279–287.

Lois, P., Wang, J., Wall, A., and Ruxton, T. (2004). Formal safety assessment of cruise ships. *Tourism Management*, *25*, 93–109.

Regester, M. and Larkin, J. (1998). *Risk issues and crisis management: A casebook of best practice*. London: Kogan Page.

WHO. (2004). Accidents, transport and health. World Health Organization website at http://www.euro.who.int/transport, accessed 11 December 2004.

References

ADB. (2004, 22 November). Road crashes costing Southeast Asian countries US$15 billion per year, ADB studies say. Asia Development Bank News Release, 155/04.

Ahrens, M. (2003). *Selections from the U.S. fire problem overview report: Leading causes and other patterns and trends: Hotels and motels*. Quincy, MA: National Fire Protection Association.

Albertsson, P. and Falkmer, T. (2005). Is there a pattern in European bus and coach incidents? A literature analysis with special focus on injury causation and injury mechanisms. *Accident Analysis and Prevention*, *37*(2), 225–233.

Associated Press. (2005, 18 March). Paris to rebuild terminal. *The Straits Times*.

ATSB. (2004). Road safety statistics. Transport accident fatalities: Australia compared with other OECD countries 1980–1999. Australian Transport Safety Board. Australian Government website at http://www.atsb.gov.au/road/stats/oecd.cfm, accessed 11 December 2004.

Bauer, I. (2002). Health advice in Australian travel brochures. *Journal of Travel Medicine*, *9*(5), 263–266.

BBC News. (1999, 2 December). Korean Air safety concerns grow. BBC News website at http://news.bbc.co.uk, accessed 24 July 2002.

BBC News. (2002). School coach trips: The regulations. BBC News website at http://newsvote.bbc.co.uk, accessed 13 December 2004.

BBC News. (2004a, 19 February). Austria clears ski blaze suspects. BBC News website at http://newsvote.bbc.co.uk, accessed 12 December 2004.

BBC News. (2004b, 24 May). Probe into Paris airport collapse. BBC News website at http://newsvote.bbc.co.uk, accessed 12 December 2004.

BBC News. (2004c, 28 June). Tunnel "safer" after blaze. BBC News website at http://newsvote.bbc.co.uk, accessed 26 November 2005.

BBC News. (2005). On this day. 1977: Runway collision kills 560. BBC News website at http://newsvote.bbc.co.uk, accessed 26 November 2005.

Bestwire. (1999, 30 August). Insuring thrill seekers: Most accidents are not equipment related.

Braksiek, R.J. and Roberts, D.J. (2002). Amusement park injuries and death. *Annals of Emergency Medicine*, *39*(1), 65–72.

Browne, A. (2000, 12 November). Safety fears as list of tragic accidents grows. The Observer website at http://observer.guardian.co.uk, accessed 26 November 2005.

Buckingham, L. and Harper, K. (1997, 27 September). What price safe transport? *The Guardian*, 26.

Cartwright, R. and Baird, C. (1999). *The development and growth of the cruise industry.* Oxford: Butterworth-Heinemann.

Chin, J. (2003, November). Reacting to power failures. *Hotels*, 18.

Chow, W.K. and Kot, H.T. (1989). Hotel fires in Hong Kong. *International Journal of Hospitality Management*, 8(4), 271–281.

CNN.com. (2001, 31 May). China Airlines bosses offer to quit. CNN website at http://cnn.worldnews, accessed 23 July 2002.

CNN Interactive. (1997, 3 December). Report: Design flaw led to Estonia ferry sinking. CNN website at http://www.cnn.com, accessed 1 December 2003.

Colon, I. (1985). The role of tourism in alcohol-related highway fatalities. *International Journal of Addiction*, 20(4), 577–582.

Davies, H. and Walters, M. (1998). Do all crises have to become disasters? Risk and risk mitigation. *Disaster Prevention and Management*, 7(5), 396–400.

Department of Transport. (1997). *Channel Tunnel Safety Authority report into channel tunnel fire.* London: The Stationery Office.

Eales, R. (1990, 15 April). Honesty is better for company image than criticizing journalists. *The Independent on Sunday*, 28.

Emergency Management. (2005). Hotel fires. Emergency Management website at http://www.emergency-management.net, accessed 12 June 2006.

The Guardian. (2000, 4 January). Millennium bug fails to bite. The Guardian website at http://www.guardian.co.uk, accessed 15 December 2004.

Guptill, K.S., Hargarten, S.W., and Baker, T.D. (1991). American travel deaths in Mexico: Causes and prevention strategies. *West Journal of Medicine*, 154, 169–171.

Hartgarten S. (1994). Injury prevention: A crucial aspect of travel medicine. *Journal of Travel Medicine*, 1(1), 48–50.

Henderson, J.C. (2003). Communicating in a crisis: Flight SQ 006. *Tourism Management*, 24, 279–287.

Holmes, L. (2001). Richard Shirrefs. CFO Europe.com.website at http://www.cfoeurope.com, accessed 15 December 2004.

IAAPA. (2003, 21 January). Statement of IAAPA President Clark Robinson re two scientific studies released by Six Flags.

IATA. (1998). *Crisis communication manual.* Montreal: International Air Transport Association.

IATA. (2004). *World air transport statistics.* Montreal: International Air Transport Association.

Joint Accident Investigation Commission. (1997). *Final report on the capsizing on 28 September 1994 in the Baltic Sea of the ro-ro passenger vessel MV Estonia.* Helsinki: Edita.

Leggatt, P.A. and Leggatt, F.W. (2003). Reported fatal and non-fatal incidents involving tourists in Thailand July 1997–June 1999. *Travel Medicine and Infectious Disease*, 1, 107–113.

Lois, P., Wang, J., Wall, A., and Ruxton, T. (2004). Formal safety assessment of cruise ships. *Tourism Management, 25*, 93–109.

Macpherson, D.W., Gurillot, F., Steiner, D.L., Ahmed, K., Gushulak, B.D., and Pardy, G. (2000). Death and dying abroad: The Canadian experience. *Journal of Travel Medicine, 7*(5), 227–233.

McElhatton, J. and Drew, C. (1993, March). Hurry-up syndrome. ASRS directline, the Aviation Safety Reporting System (ASRS), 5. ASRS website at http://asrs.arc.nasa. gov/directline, accessed 2 December 2004.

McInnes, R.J., Williamson, L.M., and Morrison, A. (2002). Unintentional injury during foreign travel: A review. *Journal of Travel Medicine, 9*(6), 297–307.

McLean, I. and Johnes, M. (2000). *Aberfan: Governments and disasters*. Cardiff: Welsh Academic Press.

Mott, D. (1995, 21 September). Calais ferry grounding heightens safety fears. *Lloyds List International*.

NFPA. (2001, March/April). NFPA remembers the 1980 MGM Grand fire in Las Vegas. *National Fire Protection Association Journal*®. NFPA website at http://www.nfpa. org, accessed 13 June 2005.

NHTSA. (2004). *Traffic safety facts 2003*. National Highway Traffic Safety Administration. US Department of Transport. Washington: National Center for Statistics & Analysis.

Page, S. and Meyer, D. (1996). Tourist accidents: An exploratory analysis. *Annals of Tourism Research, 23*(3), 666–690.

Pan Am. (2004). Accidents site at http://www.panamair.org/Accidents/tenerife.htm, accessed 11 December 2004.

Paternie, P.P. (2004). Making a rental car work for you: Not against you. Road and Travel Magazine website at http://www.roadandtravel.com/safetyandsecurity/ ts_rentals.html, accessed 25 November 2005.

Petridou, E., Askitopoulou, H., Voirvahakis, D., Skalkidis, Y., and Trichopoulos, D. (1997). Epidemiology of road traffic accidents during pleasure travelling: Evidence from the island of Crete. *Accident Analysis and Prevention, 29*(5), 687–693.

Ray, S. (1999). *Strategic communication in crisis management: Lessons from the airline industry*. Westport: Quorum Books.

Regester, M. and Larkin, J. (1998). *Risk issues and crisis management: A casebook of best practice*. London: Kogan Page.

Roberts, D. and Chan, D. (2000). Fires in hotel rooms and scenario predictions. *International Journal of Contemporary Hospitality Management, 12*(1), 37–44.

Roberts, J. (2001). Philippines hotel fire reveals neglect of safety standards. World Socialist website at http://www.wsws.org, accessed 12 June 2005.

RSSB. (2004). *Rail Safety and Standards Board Annual Report 2003–2004*. London: Rail Safety and Standards Board.

Safety Line Institute. (2000). Herald of Free Enterprise sinking. Safety Line Information Service website at www.worksafe.wa.gov.au/institute/, accessed 13 December 2004.

Simms, J. (1998). The Stena Challenger grounding. In M. Bland (Ed.), *Communicating out of a crisis* (pp. 181–192). Basingstoke: Macmillan Business.

Simpson, L. and Noulton, J.D. (1998). The Eurotunnel fire. In M. Bland (Ed.), *Communicating out of a crisis* (pp. 223–231). Basingstoke: Macmillan Business.

Slough, D. (1984, September). How to survive a hotel fire. *Security and Fire News Asia.*

Strategic Direction. (2002). Crisis management. There is a right way and a wrong way. *Strategic Direction, 18*(2), 17–19.

Touger, H.E. (2001, March/April). Top-to-bottom hotel fire safety. *National Fire Protection Association Journal.* NFPA website at http://www.nfpa.org, accessed 12 June 2005.

Travel Weekly. (2004). Operators sharpen their clause against the bug. Archived article. Travel Weekly website at http://www.travelweekly.co.uk, accessed 15 December 2004.

WHO. (2004). Accidents, transport and health. World Health Organization website at http://www.euro.who.int/transport, accessed 11 December 2004.

Wikipedia. (2004). Accidents and incidents on commercial airlines: Tenerife disaster. Wikipedia website at http://en.wikipedia.org/wiki/Tenerife_disaster, accessed 11 December 2004.

Wilks, J. (1999). International tourists, motor vehicles and road safety: A review of the literature leading up to the Sydney 2000 Olympics. *Journal of Travel Medicine, 6*(2), 115–121.

Wilks, J., Watson, B., and Faulks, I.J. (1999). International road safety in Australia: Developing a national research and management programme. *Tourism Management, 20,* 645–654.

9

Commercial Crises

Learning Objectives

By the end of the chapter, the reader should be able to

- Appreciate how the primary causes of some tourism crises may be inherent within the tourism industry and business organizations.
- Recognize the different types of commercial crises which can strike tourism enterprises.
- Acknowledge the complexity of certain tourism industry organizational crises which result from internal and external factors in combination.
- Identify approaches to the resolution of different forms of tourism commercial crises and assess their merits.
- Understand some of the differences between large businesses and smaller scale ventures of relevance to the development and management of tourism crises.

Introduction

Previous chapters have discussed causes of crisis external to tourism businesses; the focus of this chapter is on commercial crises, defined as those which are rooted in industry and organizational features and deficiencies. Instances from the various sectors of the tourism industry are discussed and ways in which selected aspects of industry operations can be sources of crises are examined. A crisis triggered from outside may be exacerbated by internal conditions and exogenous pressures reveal indigenous stresses, thereby compounding commercial crises which can seriously damage the industry as a whole and individual companies if sufficiently severe. This coincidence of forces is evident in crises of financial weakness which are initiated and aggravated by developments in the wider environment. A final section at the end of the chapter makes reference to the smaller enterprises which have an important role in the tourism industry, but are distinctive with regard to exposure to crises and their management. The chapter case studies describe the opening of Hong Kong Disneyland and the experience of low-cost airlines in Singapore which illustrate a major crisis of finance and a lesser one of public relations, respectively.

Forms of Commercial Crises

Key characteristics of corporate crises were outlined in the opening chapter and can be summarized as rapidly unfolding events with an apparent momentum of their own, limited information and control and a need for decisions which sometimes have to be taken in the spotlight of media and public attention. As previously noted, there have been numerous studies of organizational crises in general which reveal an assortment of causes. Mitroff (1988) identified almost 20 possibilities which include defective products, sabotage and boycotts. Other types are related to finance, human resources, regulatory regimes and demand (Evans and Elphick, 2005; Meyers, 1986). Such crises can harm operational structures and processes, profitability, company and brand reputations and staff morale and may even lead to collapse.

Management decision and policy making may be a prime or secondary reason for commercial crises. Judgments made by senior managers, their choice of organizational systems and styles of corporate cultures fostered by them can predispose companies to crises in assorted ways. For example, rigidity can inhibit responsiveness and strategic errors may be expensive and inspire a loss of confidence among employees and investors. Corruption and fraudulent practices are also not unknown in the corporate world, leading to crisis when uncovered. Insufficient attention to crisis management planning may prove an additional shortcoming. The existence of plans will not prevent crises, but can ensure a level of preparedness and assist companies in coping.

Such generic problems and the risk of crises which accompany them are applicable to the tourism industry, although some modifications are necessary to terminology more suited to manufacturing. Tourism's particular attributes must be taken into account because they affect the features of the commercial crisis and may add to the difficulties of its management. The distinctive qualities of tourism demand and supply were explained in Chapter 1, which described a large and powerful industry concentrated in the major generating markets of the developed world, with an influence extending to remote and less-developed regions. It sells multifaceted products of experiences which rely on a collection of parties and display the characteristics of all services, with the attendant challenges. The scope of operations, frequently within the international arena, and sensitivity to events in the wider environment heighten propensity to crisis. Leiper (2004) recounted the cases of a South Pacific island resort hotel, Ansett Airlines and the Big Banana attraction in Australia to illustrate tourism industry failures which could be interpreted as the worst outcome of the crises which tourism is prone to.

The many tourism crises considered throughout the book have all had commercial impacts, but this chapter concentrates on more industry-specific questions of changing markets, internationalization, competition, finance and staffing. These appear to be common causes of crisis at industry, sector and organization level and there is some overlap, with a distinction to be made between single cause and more complex crises. Companies also exhibit their own strengths and weaknesses regarding vulnerability to crisis and competence in dealing with any threats and it should be remembered that every crisis is unique and generalizations must be qualified accordingly.

Changing Demand

Crisis is a consequence of change and it has already been demonstrated how tourism is sensitive to alteration and upheaval in a series of domains. The industry itself is also constantly changing and this is reflected in product development and a search for untapped markets. While having an influence over demand, companies must be alert to new developments and aim to anticipate and accommodate emerging trends. Those which fail to do so could face a decline in business; this danger has been evident among large-scale tour operator and travel agency groups in the UK, one of the world's major generators of international tourists, in recent years.

Tour operators have always had to contend with evolving tourist tastes and behavior, but the pace of these movements seems to be accelerating. The burgeoning of budget airlines and use of the Internet for travel bookings, associated with more independent and adventurous tourists, have had repercussions across Europe. In the UK, more people are making their own arrangements online and this has affected purchases of conventional package tours organized by tour operators and sold through traditional retail agents. British package holiday tourism has traditionally centered on the Mediterranean and been led by a small number of very large companies, but this dominance has been undermined by the new trading environment and type of tourist. Questions have thus emerged about the future form and existence of some of the leading firms (BBC News, 2004d; The Sunday Times, 2005).

For example, the large and well-known MyTravel faced debts of £800 million in 2004 because of a failed expansion policy, accountancy mistakes and unresponsiveness to tourist needs (BBC News, 2004c). This placed it at risk of losing the official license awarded only to tour operators which conform to certain financial standards. Although the company reacted with a restructuring program of capacity cuts, product enhancement, cost controls and recapitalization measures (MyTravel, 2005), its plight attracted considerable publicity in the general and financial media (BBC News, 2004c; The Scotsman, 2004), perhaps undermining the confidence of investors and actual and potential customers.

In an interesting contrast, one of its competitors named First Choice Holidays had sought to take advantage of new travel demands by directing its business away from short-haul beach tourism to longer haul destinations and special-interest and activity vacations. Its objective was to acquire a series of smaller niche operators in these areas which would generate 60% of profits within three years (The Sunday Times, 2005), approval of the plan reflected in the company's rising share price.

Despite the innovative approach adopted by First Choice, there was a more common pattern of cutting costs and trying to improve productivity within existing organizational frameworks. This was practiced by the sector overall, including Europe's biggest travel companies such as TUI and Thomas Cook, whose predicament was made worse by difficult years since 2001 and events such as the SARS epidemic and Iraq war (BBC News, 2004b and 2004d). Whether these steps are effective remains to be seen and more radical strategies may be necessary which could include fundamental structural reforms, the sale of main units and mergers with rivals if the slowdown in demand for traditional organized holidays continues.

Internationalization

Another potential cause of crisis among the largest tour operator and travel agency groups is that of expansion beyond their country of origin, with the giants having a presence in many states and others aspiring to follow. Enterprises, however, may grow too large too quickly and pan-continental activity may not be sustainable if a company has insufficient reserves and expertise. Internationalization, which occurs when companies enlarge their scope and move into markets outside their home base, may thus give rise to difficulties which result in a crisis. When companies operate globally, risks from internal and external forces at home increase. Unfamiliarity with local practices and circumstances and inappropriate policies and decisions could be detrimental, ways of doing business needing to be reviewed in the context of unfamiliar societies.

Even if they are flexible and technically competent, cultural ignorance and an inability to communicate in the local language could undermine management effectiveness and the respect in which individuals, and indirectly their employers, are held. Conditions in China afford insights into the pitfalls of entering unknown and alien markets and some companies have been frustrated in the realization of ambitious plans there. While the Chinese tourism boom has drawn much commercial interest, especially among hotel chains in search of growth outside saturated markets of Europe and North America, there are also significant hurdles to overcome. These hurdles incorporate matters of economics and politics, regulations about hotel ownership and operation, relations between Chinese and non-Chinese firms and management capability and resources (Pine and Qi, 2004). Wide gaps are found not only between the corporate worlds of East and West, but misunderstandings can occur among management and staff within both regions.

The troubled history of Euro Disney, the name of the holding company for the theme park which now trades as Disneyland Paris, and its search for profitability can be partly attributed to the management assumption that the American formula could be replicated in Europe with few modifications. There was little appreciation of the differences among European markets and the vital task of devising a formula to entice French visitors was neglected (Mills et al., 1994). This injured attendances and revenue from the beginning, although there were subsequent attempts to rectify the problem (The Manager, 1996), and the long-standing heavy debt burden is attributable to a variety of considerations. Hong Kong Disneyland, which opened in 2005, was perhaps an opportunity to apply some of the lessons learned in France, yet efforts at cultural sensitivity seemed to backfire. Indeed, the new park saw a succession of public relations embarrassments which collectively represented a minor crisis and detracted from positive news about its launch, with company representatives placed on the defensive and having to justify their actions (see Case One).

As well as confirming the importance of media relations and a good communications strategy, the experience of Disney overseas suggests that leisure products cannot always be transplanted from one country to another in their entirety and may require reassessment and revision. Consumers in an era of globalization share some attributes, but are also divided by their respective socio-cultural, economic and political backgrounds. It is therefore imperative for management to undertake thorough research, demonstrate a sympathetic understanding of national distinctions and be willing to adapt to them. Such observations apply to the tourism industry as a whole and are not restricted to theme parks.

Competition

Internationalization can be regarded as a manifestation of competition as companies search for routes to grow and win market share from rivals at home and abroad. Competitive pressures are strong across the tourism industry and they can be interpreted as a sign of its good health, from which customers and other stakeholders benefit. However, they may prove damaging and destructive, acting independently or in combination with other agents, and become a catalyst of crisis.

Competition as a source of commercial crisis is illustrated by the historic example of Laker Airways which was set up in 1966 with the intention of providing low-cost air travel for British holidaymakers within Europe. The company then sought a license which would allow it to offer transatlantic services, proposing to undercut existing prices by as much as two-thirds as a result of cost savings. Its submission met opposition from the few airlines already flying across the Atlantic, but a license was awarded in 1977 and flights commenced to New York and Los Angeles. The founder had plans to extend the route network which were turned down by the British authorities, leading to the possibility of an anti-competitive practices legal case coming before European courts.

However, Laker Airways was declared bankrupt in 1982 when over 6,000 of its customers stranded abroad had to be brought home by other airlines. Debts exceeded £250 million and were explained by the unfavorable economy and over-hasty expansion, but fierce competition from established airlines which engaged in heavy discounting was a crucial issue. It was subsequently reported that there had been illegal attempts to try to ruin the company and a number of lawsuits followed. British Airways and 11 other airlines were accused of conspiring against Laker and the matter was settled privately in 1985 (BBC News, 2002; Chronicle of Aviation 1966–1985; Wikipedia, 2005).

Despite the company's failure, the concept of the budget or low-cost airline which it pioneered in the UK later flourished to become a powerful force in Europe and North America (Donne, 2000; Lawton, 2002). These airlines are a serious competitive threat for previously dominant full-service carriers and have heightened the financial difficulties of the latter which are outlined in the next section. They are being compelled to revise modes of operation in response and some are adopting certain of the techniques of their low-cost rivals. There is a degree of convergence as all airlines vigorously pursue greater efficiencies (Franke, 2004) and the civil aviation industry is being transformed, creating some uncertainty and instability.

Although the low-cost segment has prospered, many individual carriers have struggled. Principal difficulties are the volume and strength of competitors as well as regulatory barriers (Francis et al., 2006), with a tendency for customers to seek out the cheapest price and abandon any brand loyalty (Gillen and Morrison, 2003). The constant danger of losing business to airlines which match or beat prices, coupled with the demands of maintaining low costs, appear to be ingredients for a financial crisis and failure is common, including of subsidiaries formed by so-called legacy carriers (Strategic Direction, 2003). The success of the model is now being tested in Asia, where an estimated 16 low-cost airlines have started flying since mid-2003 (Fullbrook, 2005). There is, however, a feeling that the number is too high and a degree of consolidation will ensue (Dow Jones, 2005), as happened in Singapore (see Case Two). There are also wider concerns about the consequences of a preoccupation with costs for safety (The Independent, 2005) which were mentioned in Chapter 8.

Questions of Finance

All businesses are expected to generate revenue and profits and those in the tourism industry are no exception. Inability to do so, for whatever reason, raises doubts about the caliber of management and the organization's future and could provoke a fundamental crisis if not reversed.

The commercial crises discussed so far have all had a financial component and a financial crisis may evolve from one of different origin and become the dominant theme, although resolution will depend on addressing and overcoming the root causes. Financial repercussions are also a measure of the gravity of the crisis and their relationship with other influences confirms how crises exhibit a scale of complexity, from compound crises of multiple causes to more straightforward, single issue, crises.

While every tourism industry sector has recorded financial casualties, the situation of full-service airlines has received particular attention as many have been seen to be battling to secure profitability. The opening years of the current century were a period of falling demand and revenues and rising costs due to a sluggish economy, terrorism, the Iraq war, SARS, unprecedented oil prices and the incursions of low-cost operators (IATA, 2004). Analysts argued that the crisis conditions were inevitable and that events had accelerated existing trends which were pushing several weaker companies close to bankruptcy. Nevertheless, the urgency of the situation had not been anticipated and airlines fought to contain damage and, in certain cases, prevent collapse.

In one example of cost cutting, British Airways introduced a program titled "Future Size and Shape." As many as 13,000 jobs were axed in stages and under-performing routes were withdrawn. Some of these steps were resisted by the unions and anxieties were expressed about staff morale and deteriorating relations between management and staff (BBC News, 2004a; BBC News, 2005d). Drastic measures were also adopted by Aer Lingus, the national carrier of Ireland, whose Survival Plan aimed to restore the company's viability (Department of Transport, 2004). Key elements were job cuts of over 30% and 16% cost savings. Cheaper fares were offered and capacity realigned with demand, new services being added to promising locations in expectation of immediate returns. The company concentrated on Internet sales, lowered agency commissions and maximized plane usage (Unisys, 2003). Essentially, it remade itself into a low-cost airline with a superior quality of service.

Progress in implementing the strategy was indicated by reports of an expected profit of €100 million in 2004, compared to a loss of €140 million in 2001. Much of the credit for this achievement was given to the chief executive who was appointed in 2001, but the importance of the partnership between the government, unions and management was also recognized. The company then agreed on another three-year plan designed to complete the process, but there were still hurdles to overcome regarding fuel prices, greater competition from low-cost carrier Ryanair and union support. The chief executive also left unexpectedly in a decision which was believed to be connected to a takeover bid by senior managers which had been rejected by the government and opposed by staff (The Wall Street Journal Europe, 2004). He later joined British Airways and in an interesting development, the merits of which divided analysts due to its severity, announced plans in late 2005 to cut the number of executives by half and middle managers by one-third in a phased initiative designed to save £150 million (The International Herald Tribune, 2005).

The accommodation business too was not immune from the slowdown in international tourism following 11 September 2001, although the effects again often served to reinforce longer standing adverse tendencies. The hotel chain of Le Meridien saw debts climb to over US$2 billion, leading to complicated negotiations about rescue packages (Caterer-Online, 2005; Hotel Online, 2004). Such discussions give rise to insecurity and may tarnish corporate brands which are assets of great potential value (Balmer and Gray, 2003).

Staffing Issues

Commercial crises can derive from aspects of human resources issues such as the size and skills of the workforce. Tourism is a service industry and depends on the ability of employees to deliver an appropriate quality of service and good relationships between front-line staff and customers. However, tourism employment is frequently perceived to possess limitations referred to in Chapter 2 of unsatisfactory working conditions, below-average wages and a lack of prospects. These factors can discourage suitable individuals from entering the industry or remaining in it. Problems of recruitment and retention, high turnover and inexperienced and inadequately trained personnel may lead to a crisis due to the disruption of operations, inefficiencies and dissatisfied customers. The ageing of the world's population also means fewer young people entering the labor market, intensifying existing shortages. For example, the UK hospitality business already has insufficient staff and estimates that an additional 100,000 will be necessary by 2012 (RSA Migration Commission, 2005).

Tourism businesses may look overseas to fill vacancies, but this is potentially contentious. There are claims that it harms local employment opportunities and subjects expatriate workers to abuse and exploitation. Certain states have imposed quotas whereby economic migrants take second place to nationals (OECD, 1998), although the European Commission promulgates the unimpeded circulation of labor within its borders (EUROPA, 2004). Irrespective of any barriers, employers may still find it easier to recruit or choose to hire foreigners who are satisfied with lower earnings and accept jobs dismissed as demeaning and taxing by locals. Some hospitality firms in the USA are heavily dependent on foreign workers and this engendered a crisis in 2004 in a selection of popular centers because of restrictions on particular classes of visas which had been increased due to security fears. There were calls for relaxation of strict rules, but debate too about the importance of making a career in hospitality more attractive and remunerative (Sadi and Henderson, 2005).

Some developing countries also seek to limit expatriate management employment in an effort to ensure that their citizens occupy a proportion of more senior positions. However, most multinational corporations, like hotel chains, display an ethnocentric orientation regarding such posts and conflicts can occur between local and expatriate managers (Go and Pine, 1995). Companies need to be aware of government employment policies and stances on job localization and align their own positions accordingly. In addition, resources should be invested in management training and education to promote local capabilities and establish an acceptable local and non-local manager mix.

Industrial Action

Irrespective of the criticisms of tourism as an employer, industrial action is comparatively rare and the industry is not highly unionized. There are exceptions, one of these being documented in Chapter 2 with regard to dissatisfaction amongst hotel workers, and airlines occasionally have to deal with formal and informal strikes. It has already been seen how British Airways' efficiency drive met with hostility from staff which had been displayed in an earlier incident in 2003 when about 500 employees at London's Heathrow Airport walked out in protest over an automated clocking on system. This resulted in over 500 flights being canceled and almost 100,000 passengers stranded at the airport before its settlement after discussions with the unions (BBC, 2003; ST Interactive, 2003).

The airline was expected to lose between £30 and £40 million because of the events which also impacted on advanced reservations and earnings forecasts for the third quarter of the year. Compensation was arranged, but the chaos and media coverage harmed British Airways' reputation, which it recognized would need to be repaired. One other outcome was unexpected gains for its rivals with budget carriers Easyjet and Ryanair carrying 6,000 and 7,000 more passengers, respectively (ST Interactive, 2003), indicative of how one company's crisis can be another's opportunity.

In an example from the USA, the strike over pay by Northwest Airline pilots in 1998 grounded all its flights for over two weeks. However, the company had actively prepared for the eventuality and possessed a crisis management plan which established a crisis command center headed by the chief financial officer. It gave priority to the dissemination of information to the media and public in advance and emphasis was placed on customer service and the protection of corporate image following the onset of the strike. Nevertheless, costs were high at an estimated US$630 million and the money and loss of customer goodwill were not easily or quickly recovered (PATA, 1999).

Discontent may prevail for much longer periods and Hong Kong's Cathay Pacific was consistently troubled by disagreements with its pilots throughout the latter years of the 1990s. Lengthy talks between management and unions did not make headway and relations worsened in 2001 before 11 September. A campaign of industrial action was launched, leading to flight cancellations and the chartering of planes from other airlines. Similar to the case of Northwest, importance was attached to establishing and maintaining contact with different stakeholders during the crisis, informing them of developments. The media were also used to communicate the management's position and express its regret for the inconvenience to customers. The points of contention were still not fully resolved by 2002 and monetary and less tangible costs were again considerable and hard to recoup (Henderson, 2002).

Unhappy staff and incidents of withdrawal of labor inevitably affect service delivery and company earnings. An airline seen to have poor industrial relations, with the possibility of disruption to the traveling public, risks permanent damage to its reputation and turnover. It also has to meet the immediate financial burden of practical arrangements covering delays and cancellations. It is difficult to maintain customer loyalty and attract new passengers if these uncertainties are prolonged, representing additional lost revenue. The new realities of the twenty-first century have perhaps made civil aviation union leaders and staff more amenable to measures dedicated to corporate survival, but there has been a reluctance to implement certain radical plans. The cases cited suggest the potential for havoc and heavy expenses regarding economics and corporate image of comparatively minor disputes. Airlines and other tourism businesses can ill afford such losses and the maintenance of harmonious labor relations is central to the avoidance of certain types of crises and the management of others.

Smaller Enterprises and Commercial Crises

The book has concentrated on major crises affecting large companies and destinations, but medium and small enterprises and the additional crises of lesser magnitude which threaten them should not be forgotten. Such enterprises are usually defined in terms of the workforce with commentators proposing a range of upper limits from 10 to 50, units of no more than four described as "micro businesses" (Getz and Carlsen, 2005). Revenue is another criterion, although again amounts vary. It is frequently stated that a majority of the world's tourism is conducted by these ventures, often family owned and operated (Morrison and Teixeira, 2004; Page et al., 1999), but comprehensive data to verify this do not yet exist. However, national statistics support the conclusion and 95% of UK hotels, for instance, are in the hands of smaller businesses (RSA Migration Commission, 2005). The segment is also acknowledged to make a significant contribution to rural economies and communities and destination development (Tinsley and Lynch, 2001).

Small tourism businesses are characterized by limited resources of manpower and finance and the studies quoted above which deal mainly with Europe, North America and Australia and New Zealand have discovered strengths and weaknesses. The latter include management (in)capability, irregular cash flow, uncertain profitability, an absence of influence and vulnerability to external forces. Seasonality is a basic problem in many locations and small businesses often turn to official agencies for advice and possibly financial assistance, especially in rural areas where such schemes are frequently available. There are low barriers to entry, encouraging new start-ups, but failure rates are also high.

Unlike big business, income and profit generation may not be the primary goal or measure of success. Shaw and Williams (1998) wrote about different degrees of entrepreneurship. One group is attracted by the lifestyle attached to running certain types of tourism enterprises in attractive environments with possibilities of pursuing personal interests (Getz and Petersen, 2005). Family needs may also take precedence in any business decisions and premises may be the family home. At the same time, not all owner operators are casually indulging in a hobby and some may be financially dependent on a business in which they have invested their savings (Page et al., 1999).

There are obvious contrasts with corporations which have a sizeable labor force, a complex structure, substantial resources, generous marketing budgets, a management team directed by a strategic plan, global reach and power in the marketplace. The smallest of businesses are less formal with a simplified organization, are more personal in their dealings with customers and suppliers, may have difficulty accessing financial and other resources and may be at the mercy of events (Page et al.,

1999). They therefore possess some advantages regarding flexibility and an ability to move rapidly in response to an impending crisis without any worries about internal communications, but cannot engage in expensive and sophisticated risk assessment and damage limitation exercises. Restricted reserves of cash undermine the capacity to react to and survive prolonged loss of business and failure could be a personal tragedy.

The human cost of small business crises and collapse is especially pertinent in places which are heavily reliant on tourism whether in developed or developing countries (Cushnahan, 2003; Dahles and Bras, 1999). There are also one-man businesses of individual vendors and street and beach hawkers, who comprise a substantial informal economy in many such Third World destinations, to take into account (Timothy and Wall, 1997). They too are exposed to numerous crises which can result in lost livelihoods, with social and economic repercussions, and may be ill prepared to handle resolution. Asia-Pacific Economic Cooperation (APEC) recognizes the particular needs of smaller businesses in member states and highlights the importance of "human resource development, access to finance, market access and development, technology and technology sharing and access to information" (Gammack et al., 2003, p. x). Difficulties in these areas impede the functioning of this tier of the industry and may contribute to the emergence of crises.

In addition to internal deficiencies, smaller businesses may have little protection against harmful outside occurrences. The 2004 Indian Ocean tsunami caused economic and human devastation and the PATA and WTO have been concerned about small business recovery in its aftermath. A report observes that establishments like food and beverage outlets, boat hirers and craft workers cannot obtain recovery funding as readily as large companies and many traders lost relatives who were also workers (WTO, 2005). The tsunami was a commercial crisis for all levels of the industry, but the most modest ventures and individuals are in danger from changing circumstances which would not register on the corporate scale of risk. Crisis management and planning therefore have to be re-conceptualized to suit this particular type of business and the overall subject of crises and tourism small enterprises is perhaps one for another book.

Summary and Conclusions

The defining characteristics of the tourism industry create a dynamic of continuous change among tourists and suppliers which may favor the evolution of crises. Features of a company such as its management composition and style, policies, structure and financing can also be a generator of crisis. An inappropriate style, unfavorable corporate culture, mistaken strategies, inflexibility and financial insecurity may themselves create internal stresses which evolve into crises. Pressures imposed on companies by external agents are also a test of management and organizational capability and responsiveness. If these are lacking, the crisis will be more severe and indigenous and exogenous forces in combination could cause permanent damage and perhaps destroy the company. Good corporate governance and sound management are thus as important in tourism as any other economic sector, although the industry also includes smaller enterprises which have distinct challenges arising from their particular operating environment.

Case One: Disney in Hong Kong

Hong Kong Disneyland is a joint venture between the government of Hong Kong and Walt Disney Company, the former investing heavily in the US$1.8 billion project in anticipation of economic returns from the projected rise in tourism due to the new attraction. The park opened in September 2005, but the event was partly eclipsed by a series of media stories in the preceding weeks which were largely negative in tone and content.

These stories began with a controversy about shark's fin soup, a traditional Chinese delicacy regarded as fitting for special occasions. The fact that some of the park's hotel restaurants would be offering the soup on their banquet menus outraged animal welfare groups opposed to the way in which fins are removed by fishermen before throwing the sharks back into the sea to die a painful death. The topic drew worldwide publicity and led to various protest campaigns. The company's initial reaction was to stand by its decision because of the soup's cultural significance, but it then promised that it would ensure that the shark fins were purchased from responsible fisheries. Customers choosing the dish would be given leaflets informing them about the objections of environmentalists. It was subsequently announced that the dish would not be available because of the problem of guaranteeing the environmental credentials of suppliers.

This controversy was followed by reports of the culling of about 40 stray dogs on the park site which were described as threatening staff safety, an assertion disputed by some locals and comparisons were made between these actions and the portrayal of cartoon characters like Pluto. One week before opening, the media featured articles about disgruntled staff who had been complaining of regulations at work which were stricter than those in force in the USA. These regulations related to questions of breaks, drinking water on duty and personal appearance. Trade union representatives said that they would distribute information to staff at the park, urging them to form their own union, a move which did take place after the park opened. The company stated that it valued all its "cast members," respected their rights and did not see the need for a union.

Again close to the official opening, there were complaints that health inspectors investigating three suspected food poisoning cases had been asked to conceal their badges of identity to avoid alarming guests at one of the open days. This resulted in more publicity, locally and internationally, and comments by politicians that Disney was not "above the law." There was an apology from the company which pledged that it was committed to abide by the law and such a situation would not recur. Other incidents included Hong Kong pop stars upset by officials when filming in the park, a sacked worker who threatened to commit suicide by jumping from the Space Mountain ride and overcrowding and long queues during pre-opening rehearsal days. At the same time, and sometimes indirectly linked to the park by reporters, there were accusations that Walt Disney was using mainland Chinese factories to manufacture some of its goods where the staff were working very long hours for extremely low wages. The company said that it would be investigating the allegations.

Sources: AFP, 2005; BBC News 2005a, 2005b, 2005c and 2005e; The Daily Telegraph, 2005; USA Today, 2005.

Case Two: Singapore's Low-cost Airlines

Singapore authorities granted approval for three low-cost airlines which commenced operations in 2004, but were to have a somewhat turbulent first year ending in the merger of two. Valuair was the first low-cost airline to start flying in May and was headed by a CEO with senior management experience at Singapore Airlines (SIA), the national carrier. It was financed mainly by local businessmen and initially raised US$19.4 million, undergoing a second round of financing in late 2004 in order to double its capital. It positioned itself as distinct, claiming on its website that "there are full service airlines, budget airlines and then there is Valuair. We challenge the norm."

One means of differentiation was to highlight the service and selling points were a 32-inch seat pitch (compared to the usual 29 inch on low-cost carriers), 20-kg cabin baggage allowance, allocated seats and free refreshments. The airline had a new fleet of four Airbus A320s and was serving the six destinations of Bangkok, Chengdu and Xiamen in China, Hong Kong, Jakarta and Perth in Australia by mid-2005. The Chinese and Australian routes meant that the company was working beyond a five-hour radius of Singapore and it had designs to continue flying such distances to locations in Eastern Australia and North East Asia, aiming to acquire wide-bodied aircraft.

However, Valuair lost heavily in its first seven months of flying and there were reports that it was seeking fresh cash injections and "close to running out of funds." A newspaper article in May wrote about difficulties of constantly escalating fuel costs, high ticket prices in relation to both low-cost and full-service competitors, fare cutting by the latter and 60% load factors. The CEO had resigned in April and the company was unable to predict when it would break even.

Jetstar Asia was Singapore's third low-cost airline and began operations in late 2004 with a CEO from Qantas. Qantas had a share of 49%, Temasek Holdings (a government investment group) held 19% and the remaining 32% was in the hands of two local businessmen. The airline originally concentrated on routes of up to five hours flight time and announced it would be traveling to the seven destinations of

Hong Kong, Jakarta and Surabaya in Indonesia, Manila, Pattaya in Thailand, Shanghai, and Taipei. It had four new Airbus A320s and ambitions to expand its fleet to 20 aircraft after three years. Passengers were allocated seats and allowed 20 kg of cabin baggage, but refreshments had to be purchased and in-flight entertainment equipment hired on longer flights.

In March 2005, the company announced that it had given up its plan of flying eight aircraft by the end of the year due to a failure to secure landing rights at preferred cities, particularly in China and Indonesia. Flights to Pattaya ceased after two months and it was flying to Bangkok, Hong Kong, Manila and Taipei in July 2005. It too was making heavy losses in its first seven months.

The difficulties experienced by Jetstar Asia and Valuair led to their merger in July 2005 under a holding company titled "Orange Star." The two airlines were to continue to function separately, with few immediate major changes, but there would be some rationalization and management spoke of a "single model" in the future.

Sources: The Edge, 2004; The Financial Times, 2005; Jetstar Asia, 2005; The Straits Times, 2005a, 2005b and 2005c; Valuair, 2005.

Concept Definitions

- **Commercial crisis:** A crisis with its roots in the industry or a business organization or which is exacerbated by the prevailing culture, conditions and management.
- **Corporate brand:** The name of the company which carries associations about the perceived quality of its products and services and which can be enhanced or damaged by the handling of a crisis.
- **Internationalization:** The extension of a company's business beyond its country of origin, closely linked to the concept of globalization.
- **Small business tourism:** Tourism services sold by enterprises which employ only a few staff and have a comparatively low turnover. Many are family owned and operated.

Review Questions

1. Why are some tourism businesses more prone to commercial crises than others?
2. What are some of the principal reasons for internal tourism commercial crises?
3. How can external events trigger commercial crises within the tourism industry?
4. What role does investor confidence play in the evolution of tourism commercial crises of a financial nature?
5. To what extent do the media influence the progress and outcome of a labor-related tourism commercial crisis?
6. How might socio-cultural misunderstandings precipitate a crisis for a tourism company expanding overseas and can such situations be averted?

7. Why were some sections of the media apparently hostile to the opening of Hong Kong Disneyland and how could this have been countered?

8. What type of crisis did Singapore's low-cost airlines face and why did it occur so soon after they entered the market?

Additional Readings

News about topical events and issues in the tourism industry, including both positive developments and actual or potential crises, is available from an assortment of specialized print media. A selection is listed below:

Travel Business Analyst. Asia Pacific and Europe monthly newsletters

Travel Daily News. Available online at http://www.traveldailynews.com

Travel Trade Gazette. Available online at http://www.ttglive.com

References

AFP. (2005, 9 September). Hong Kong Disney staff protest hair-dye, water ban: union.

Balmer, J.M. and Gray, E.R. (2003). Corporate brands: What are they? What of them? *European Journal of Marketing*, 37(7/8), 972–997.

BBC News. (2002, 26 September). That was then: Sir Freddie Laker. BBC News website at http://news.bbc.co.uk, accessed 22 July 2005.

BBC News. (2003, 4 August). BA promises compensation. BBC News website at http://news.bbc.co.uk, accessed 29 March 2005.

BBC News. (2004a, 24 August). How did BA fly into such chaos? BBC News website at http://news.bbc.co.uk, accessed 29 March 2005.

BBC News. (2004b, 22 September). Losses continue for Thomas Cook. BBC News website at http://news.bbc.co.uk, accessed 5 April 2005.

BBC News. (2004c, 24 November). Q&A: MyTravel's crisis. BBC News website at http://newsvote.bbc.co.uk, accessed 15 March 2005.

BBC News. (2004d, 30 September). UK travel firms to shed 800 jobs. BBC News website at http://news.bbc.co.uk, accessed 5 April 2005.

BBC News. (2005a, 19 August). Disney probes China labour claims. BBC News website at http://newsvote.bbc.co.uk, accessed 4 December 2005.

BBC News. (2005b, 26 July). Dogs fate gnaws at HK Disneyland. BBC News website at http://newsvote.bbc.co.uk, accessed 4 December 2005.

BBC News. (2005c, 9 June). HK Disney answers soup critics. BBC News website at http://newsvote.bbc.co.uk, accessed 4 December 2005.

BBC News. (2005d, 4 Feburary). Q&A: How well is BA performing. BBC News website at http://news.bbc.co.uk, accessed 29 March 2005.

BBC News. (2005e, 10 September). Uniform row rocks HK Disneyland. BBC News website at http://newsvote.bbc.co.uk, accessed 4 December 2005.

Caterer-Online. (2005, 24 March). Starwood capital invests in Le Meridien. Caterer Online website at http://www.caterer-online.com, accessed 6 April 2005.

Chronicle of Aviation. (1966–1985). Assorted items on Laker Airways. http://www. hellary.co.uk/laker/history, accessed 22 July 2005.

Cushnahan, G. (2003). Crisis management in small-scale tourism. *Journal of Travel & Tourism Marketing*, *15*(4), 323–347.

Dahles, H. and Bras, K. (1999). *Tourism and small entrepreneurs: Development, national policy and entrepreneurial culture: Indonesian cases*. New York: Cognizant Communication.

The Daily Telegraph. (2005, 12 September). Rows threaten to mar Disney's arrival in Hong Kong.

Department of Transport. (2004). Aer Lingus affairs. Department of Transport website at http://www.transport.ie, accessed 6 April 2005.

Donne, M. (2000). The growth and long-term potential of the low-cost airlines. *Travel & Tourism Intelligence*, *4*, 1–10.

Dow Jones. (2005, 2 August). Rivalry, oil prices may thin herd of Asia's budget carriers. *Dow Jones Newswires*.

The Edge. (2004, 22 November). Snapshots of LCCs in Singapore, 16.

EUROPA. (2004). European employment strategy. European Commission website at http://www.europa.eu.int/comm/employment, accessed 30 October 2004.

Evans, N. and Elphick, S. (2005). Models of crisis management: An evaluation of their value for strategic planning in the international travel industry. *International Journal of Tourism Research*, *7*, 135–150.

The Financial Times. (2005, 25 July). Jetstar Asia snaps up rival Valuair, 21.

Francis, G., Humphreys, I., Ison, S., and Aicken, M. (2006). Where next for low cost airlines? A spatial and temporal comparative study. *Journal of Transport Geography*, *14*(2), 83–94.

Franke, M. (2004). Competition between network carriers and low-cost carriers: Retreat battle or breakthrough to a new level of efficiency? *Journal of Air Transport Management*, *10*, 15–21.

Fullbrook, D. (2005, 10 August). Rush to get airborne in Asia's crowded skies. *South China Morning Post*, 9.

Gammack, J., Molinar, C.A., Chu, K., and Chanpayom, B. (2003). *Development needs of small to medium size tourism businesses*. Queensland: Asia Pacific Economic Cooperation International Centre for Sustainable Tourism.

Getz, D. and Carlsen, J. (2005). Family business in tourism: State of the art. *Annals of Tourism Research*, *32*(1), 237–258.

Getz, D. and Petersen, T. (2005). Growth and profit-oriented entrepreneurship among family business owners in the tourism and hospitality industry. *International Journal of Hospitality Management*, *24*, 219–242.

Gillen, D. and Morrison, W. (2003). Bundling, integration and the delivered price of air travel: Are low cost carriers full service competitors? *Journal of Air Transport Management*, *9*, 15–23.

Go, F.M. and Pine, R. (1995). *Globalization strategy in the hotel industry*. London and New York: Routledge.

Henderson, J.C. (2002). *Flying through turbulent times: Cathay Pacific*. Singapore: The Asian Business Case Centre.

Hotel Online. (2004, June). Le Meridien revs up the momentum. Hotel Online website at http://www.hotel-online.com, accessed 6 April 2005.

IATA. (2004). *World air transport statistics*. Montreal: International Air Transport Association.

The Independent. (2005, 6 October). No-frills airlines are accused over safety. The Independent website at http://news.independent.co.uk, accessed 13 October 2005.

The International Herald Tribune. (2005, 2 December). Will layoffs leave British Airways short?, 16.

Jetstar Asia. (2005). Jetstar Asia website at http://www.jetstarasia.com, accessed 10 October.

Lawton, T.C. (2002). *Cleared for take off: Structure and strategy in low fare airline business*. Aldershot: Ashgate.

Leiper, N. (2004). *Tourism management*. NSW: Pearson.

The Manager. (1996). Survival and revival: The lessons and relaunch of Disneyland in Europe. *The Manager*. Travel and Tourism Supplement, 24–25.

Meyers, G.C. (1986). *When it hits the fan: Managing the nine crises of business*. New York: Mentor.

Mills, R., Debono, J.D., and Debono, V.D. (1994). Euro Disney: A Mickey Mouse project? *European Management Journal, 12*(3), 306–314.

Mitroff, I. (1988, Winter). Crisis management: Cutting through the confusion. *Sloan Management Review*, 15–20.

Morrison, A. and Teixeira, R. (2004). Small business performance: A tourism sector focus. *Journal of Small Business and Enterprise Development, 11*(2), 166–173.

MyTravel. (2005). Annual General Meeting Statement. My Travel Group website at http://www.mytravelgroup.com, accessed 5 April 2005.

OECD. (1998). *Trends in international migration*. Geneva: Organization for Economic Cooperation and Development.

Page, S., Forer, P., and Lawton, G.R. (1999). Small business development and tourism: Terra incognita? *Tourism Management, 20*, 435–459.

PATA. (1999, June–July). When the hammer comes down. *PATA Compass*, 20–21.

Pine, R. and Qi, P. (2004). Barriers to hotel chain development in China. *International Journal of Contemporary Hospitality Management, 16*(1), 37–44.

RSA Migration Commission. (2005). Migration: A welcome opportunity. RSA Migration Commission website at www.migrationcommission.org, accessed 3 December 2005.

Sadi, M.A. and Henderson, J.C. (2005). Local versus foreign workers in the hospitality and tourism industry: A Saudi Arabian perspective. *The Cornell Hotel and Restaurant Administration Quarterly, 46*(2), 247–257.

The Scotsman. (2004, 25 November). MyTravel wins High Court battle. The Scotsman website at http://thescotsman.scotsman.com, accessed 29 March 2005.

Shaw, G. and Williams, A. (1998). Entrepreneurship, small business culture and tourism development. In D. Ioannides and K. Debbage (Eds.), *The economic geography of the tourist industry: A supply side analysis* (pp. 235–255). London: Routledge.

ST Interactive. (2003, 1 August). BA counts cost of strike. The Straits Times Interactive website at http://straitstimes.asia1.com.sg, accessed 2 August 2003.

The Straits Times. (2005a, 27 August). Air Asia profits double while rest struggle.

The Straits Times. (2005b, 22 September). Low-cost carriers take other routes to success.

The Straits Times. (2005c, 5 May). Valuair: Bumpy flight a year after take-off, H6.

Strategic Direction. (2003). Ryanair and Southwest play for higher stakes. *Strategic Direction, 19*(5), 29–32.

The Sunday Times. (2005, 25 March). First Choice conjures travel for a new age: Inside the city, 18.

Timothy, D.J. and Wall, G. (1997). Selling to tourists: Indonesian street vendors. *Annals of Tourism Research, 24,* 322–340.

Tinsley, R. and Lynch, P. (2001). Small tourism business networks and destination development. *International Journal of Hospitality Management, 20,* 367–378.

Unisys. (2003). The Aer Lingus "reversal of fortune." Unisys website at http://www.unisys.com, accessed 6 April 2005.

USA Today. (2005, 10 November). Miscues mar opening of Hong Kong Disney: Labor leaders, pop stars end up irked B5.

Valuair. (2005). Valuair website at http://www.valuair.com.sg, accessed 10 October.

The Wall Street Journal Europe. (2004, 18 November). Will Aer Lingus's strategy still fly?

Wikipedia. (2005). Freddie Laker. Wikipedia web site at http://en.wikipedia.org, accessed 22 July 2005.

WTO. (2005). *Tsunami relief for the tourism sector: Phuket action plan.* Madrid: World Tourism Organization.

10

Crisis, Tourism and Tourism Crisis Management

Introduction

The final chapter briefly reviews the main themes of the book and conclusions to be derived from earlier chapters, highlighting the significance of crisis management in which planning is a core ingredient. Elements of plans and the parties with a role in their creation and implementation are then examined, followed by some comments about the future and directions for further research. Case studies are devoted to a tourism crisis management plan and an interesting example of one company's endeavors to manage the dual challenge of a destination and commercial crisis following a natural disaster.

Review

Previous chapters have shown how tourism crises can originate in the domains of economics, politics, societies and cultures, the physical environment, technology and the industry itself. Crises assume a variety of forms and display differences regarding cause, length, scope and gravity with a range of complexity and severity. Every crisis is unique and their characteristics, evolution and resolution are shaped by a multiplicity of forces both internal and external to the organization and industry. Despite considerable variety and diversity, some common types and features are discernible and lessons learned from particular experiences of crises may have a general applicability.

While all industries are subject to crisis, it would seem that the tourism sector is unusually exposed because of the nature of its services, markets and operations. There are signs of a greater awareness of this vulnerability and an appreciation of the risks of crises, especially those related to terrorism and natural disasters as a result of the increasing frequency of such events. A number of agencies, including government bodies, are involved in dealing with the consequences of more serious crises and the process of resolution is a dynamic one which can be prolonged. Tourism crises attract intense media interest and modern communications technology assists in the collection and distribution of information about occurrences and their aftermath, including images recorded by victims.

Importance of Tourism Crisis Management

Given the above factors, the management of crises is an activity of great significance which is being allocated a higher priority as discussed in the opening chapter. Preparing and planning for crises were described there as central to their effective management, an observation confirmed by analysis of the cases cited in the book which reveal the way in which the costs of crises can escalate when institutions and places are ill equipped and unready.

Crisis management is a term which describes the responses to a crisis by organizations affected and their attempts to exercise some control over its progress and outcomes. It can be conceived of as a special campaign in which human, financial and other available resources are made use of in order to combat a situation of great difficulty. The ultimate aims are to overcome the dangers posed by the crisis and minimize damage.

This interpretation suggests a reactive stance, illustrations of which have been discussed throughout the book, but crisis management is becoming more proactive and extends to the anticipation of threats and preparations to avert or meet them. Such an exercise commences prior to the onset of crisis conditions and incorporates plans which can be executed should threats materialize. It also looks ahead to final resolution and a return to normality or near-normality. A more positive approach incorporates the notion of crises as a chance for beneficial change and growth, as well as a time for solving urgent problems, and Asian commentators frequently observe that the two Chinese characters for the word symbolize firstly crisis or danger and then opportunity.

Plans come in an assortment of forms, from those about fire at hotel properties to extreme weather at destinations, and crisis communications may be the theme of a separate and complementary document in recognition of its importance. The focus tends to be on external shocks arising from natural phenomena and malicious acts, rather than crises induced by commercial pressures or organizational deficiencies. However, companies often wish to preserve confidentiality and are reluctant to allow any plans to enter the public domain for reasons of security and competitive advantage.

Stages in Tourism Crisis Management

Stages in crisis management can be summarized under the four headings of reduction, readiness, response and recovery. These are key components of a model strategy presented by the PATA which is supported by a series of checklists (see Case One). The steps parallel those of rescue, relief and recovery which are recommended for dealing with disasters (IBLF, 2005). Disaster management has its own academic and practitioner literature which the tourism industry has drawn from and is relevant in the worst of tourism crises when physical infrastructure and people are harmed by disastrous events. Each crisis stage encompasses several aspects and tasks requiring the management of information, operations and communications.

The devising and documenting of formal plans are elements of the readiness stage and can cover a destination, industry sector or business unit and the crisis context could be general or specific. For example, the Caribbean island of Saint Lucia has a National Emergency Management Organization (NEMO) with responsibility for natural and man-made disasters, a potentially devastating hazard being that of hurricanes. The Hospitality Industry Crisis Management Plan was produced jointly by NEMO, the Tourism Board and Hotel and Tourism and Ground Handlers Associations of Saint Lucia (NEMO, 1997). It established a structure consisting of a Hospitality Industry Crisis Management Committee to take charge, liaising with NEMO and overseeing a Crisis Management Centre (CMC). The CMC comprises Crisis Management and Communications Units. They have been provided with guidelines and hotels and ground handlers have been issued with procedures to follow to try and ensure visitor well-being should a tropical storm hit the island.

The plan gives precedence to operational matters and the personal safety of staff and customers is deemed to be an immediate priority, as well as securing and protecting property. Some reference is made to communications with various audiences and, as previously noted, this dimension often merits a discrete plan in acknowledgment of its pivotal contribution. Information has to be gathered and circulated internally and among partners and then conveyed to other parties with an interest. Facts should reach friends and relatives of tourists caught up in the crisis, industry representatives, government at home and abroad and the media without undue delay.

Crisis plans further highlight the need to cultivate good relations with the media and public prior to any disturbance so that there is a store of goodwill and favorable reputation for organizations and destinations to draw on. Failure to do so and inept management of external communications at the height of the crisis and subsequently may mar a company's standing and even jeopardize its existence, similarly tarnishing destination image. Perceptions of a lack of transparency can lead to suspicions that there is something to hide, thereby creating distrust, and it is equally important to convincingly convey what is being done right with displays of care and concern for customer inconvenience and personal suffering. It is advised that one person be appointed as spokesperson in advance, working closely with the leader of the crisis task force and is as open and honest as circumstances permit. Senior figures should also be seen to be actively involved and committed to action to address the causes of the crisis and deal with its consequences.

Marketing in the short, medium and longer term is allocated space in crisis management plans and is another core tool in recovery efforts. Plans suggest that its emphasis shifts with the evolution of the crisis. Initial stress on the dissemination of factual details, accompanied by reassurance where realistic, should give way to more positive messages and an eventual restoration of conventional promotion.

Table 10.1 proposes a model plan, adapted from those of Faulkner's (2001) and Faulkner and Faulkner and Vikulov (2001), which contains guidance pertaining to each step of a crisis for hotels exposed to an outbreak of infectious disease. It is

Table 10.1: **Managing a crisis of infections disease: guidelines for hotels**

Stage of crisis	Actions
Pre-event	■ Appointment of a crisis team manager who will be in charge of environmental scanning, identifying and assessing the risk of potential disasters or threats
	■ Establishment of a crisis management team and allocation of specific responsibilities and duties to relevant individuals
	■ Brainstorming on possible scenarios and preparation of contingency crisis management plans
	■ Assessment of capability to cope with the impacts of crisis
	■ Development and documentation of crisis management strategies which are aligned to overall mission and objectives
	■ Identification of relevant external agencies and ascertainment of desired and likely level of cooperation in times of crisis
	■ Determination of procedures for the procurement and allocation of necessary resources
	■ Communication of the crisis management plans to all levels of employees, making sure that individuals are certain of their roles in the event of a crisis
	■ Development of a corporate culture of crisis awareness and preparedness
	■ Establishment of media communication strategies and management policies to be used at all times
Prodromal	■ Establishment of crisis management command center
	■ Activation of selected procedures
	■ Raising of level of preparedness across the organization
	■ Determination of primary objectives in the management of the crisis so as to focus the direction of all actions to be taken
	■ Review and revision of marketing
Emergency	■ Assurance of the safety and well-being of guests and staff
	■ Protection of property
	■ Commencement of evacuation procedures if necessary
	■ Activation of emergency services
	■ Introduction of health screening of staff and guests
	■ Intensification of existing routines of cleaning and disinfecting
	■ Contacting of partners and implementation of systems of cooperation
	■ Adherence to official directives
	■ Maintenance of open communication channels to reassure guests and employees
	■ Employment of media communications strategy
	■ Monitoring of marketing activity
	■ Application for official aid if appropriate

Table 10.1: *Continued*

Stage of crisis	Actions
Intermediate	■ Assistance to guests and employees in meeting their medium-term needs ■ Assessment of the impacts of the crisis and extent of damage ■ Cleaning up the residual impacts of the crisis ■ Beginning of the restoration of normal business operations ■ Modification of marketing
Recovery	■ Full restoration of normal business operations ■ Improvement of facilities and customer service ■ Conducting of extensive advertising and promotional campaigns ■ Entering into cooperative and collaborative initiatives
Resolution	■ Closure of crisis management command center and debriefing of all parties involved in managing the crisis ■ Collation of feedback from all parties ■ Review and enhancement of crisis management strategy, gathering knowledge from lessons learned and applying it

Sources: Henderson, J.C. and Ng, A. (2004). Responding to crisis: Severe Acute Respiratory Syndrome (SARS) and hotels in Singapore. *International Journal of Tourism Research, 6,* 411–419. Copyright John Wiley & Sons Limited. Reproduced with permission.

based on actual experiences during the SARS epidemic and of contemporary relevance for the industry worldwide which is confronting the predicted avian influenza pandemic mentioned in Chapter 7.

Planning recovery within a destination, compared to organization, framework is a much broader concept and arduous endeavor which embraces community initiatives illustrated by the Phuket Action Plan. Although reactive and written after the 2004 tsunami to facilitate rehabilitation in Indonesia, the Maldives, Sri Lanka and Thailand, it affords insights into the problems of destination recovery. Strategies which can be employed are classed under the five "action areas" of "marketing communications, community relief, professional training, sustainable redevelopment and risk management" (WTO, 2005, p. 2). The plan serves as a reminder that crisis management can and should be informed by the philosophies and practices of sustainable tourism (BEST, 2005) and corporate social responsibility. Many companies did attempt to pursue these goals in the Indian Ocean region and achieved some success, even without a pre-existing formal plan (see Case Two).

The London Development Agency and Visit London, the city's tourism promotion agency, also developed a guide in response to the 2005 terrorist bombings in the British capital with the intention of aiding tourism businesses. It offers advice about managing customers, trade, staff, the media, marketing and sources of additional help (LDA, 2005). Such a publication is again of value for other locations and could be replicated in their crisis management plans. These plans would be of particular interest to small ventures as most transnational, national and larger local companies will already possess instructions about how to proceed during and after emergencies.

The recurrence of terrorist outrages and natural disasters is likely to accelerate moves from a reactive to a proactive position and more such materials will be assembled prior to crises rather than in their aftermath. This trend is evident in the growing volume of "preparedness programs," manuals and conferences dedicated to staff training, installation of safety equipment and routines and monitoring regimes to enable businesses to manage the unexpected (Holland, 2000).

A final phase, or perhaps a facet of recovery, is the measurement of success which is indicated by the pace of recovery and the degree of permanent damage inflicted by the crisis. This closing period is also a time for reflection and evaluation, leading to appropriate revisions to existing plans so that those responsible are better prepared for future crises. Plans must therefore be flexible enough to accommodate changes outside and within the industry and destinations, as should organizations and their workforces.

Distinctive Features of Tourism Crisis Management Plans

The requirements of planning and plan contents depend on spatial boundaries which can extend from national or even international, in the case of a globally rampant infectious disease, to the premises of a single enterprise. Context is another consideration and plans can be general or more specific, subjects for the latter easier to identify in certain circumstances such as an earthquake in a zone of seismic instability. Authorship also dictates the composition of plans which may be prepared by managers of individual businesses, teams at corporate headquarters, governments and semi-official agencies, private consultants or sometimes a combination of these. There is perhaps a tendency toward cumbersome bureaucracy regarding plans and task forces with an extensive remit which should be guarded against, although partnership is a key to effectiveness in managing crises as outlined in the next section.

Many tourism crisis management plans appear somewhat over-general and may not be best suited to actual situations of crisis while there might be obstacles when it comes to implementation of plans as a whole. Resources of finance and manpower must be invested and new administrative systems, command structures and communication channels introduced which depend on varying degrees of cooperation internally and externally. Plans drawn up by consultants, especially with regard to destinations, may fail to take local conditions sufficiently into account and be too ambitious so that prevailing realities hinder execution.

The plans discussed also indicate the particular demands of planning for crises within a tourism industry setting, confirming again the special qualities which set it apart from other economic sectors. While selected tourism organization plans may correspond to those found in unrelated industries, the physical presence and movement of the consumer and likelihood of mass injury as a consequence of some tourism crises intensify their potential gravity and the urgency of good management. Defective products and services are not always life threatening and this gives rise to differences between the way other businesses and members of the tourism industry perceive and respond to crises.

In addition, destination crisis management planning relates to geographic location from resorts to states and its operations must be destination-wide which entails numerous participants working in collaboration. Outside threats are perhaps more pressing for tourism and the industry has been forced to accept the heightened possibility of disruption due to natural disasters and terrorist attacks because of recent successive and exceptional incidences of these. This also leads to a reliance on emergency services and other agencies of government with international, national, regional and local organizations providing support, training and guidance in the fields of crisis and disaster. Indeed, governments have obligations to protect tourists and residents at destinations and may be principal initiators and implementers of crisis management plans.

Role of Partnerships

Cooperation within the industry and beyond is fundamental to the processes of preparing, responding to and recovering from certain crises and this leads to formal and informal partnership agreements. Those with a part to play in managing a destination crisis are identified in the PATA strategy such as the police, fire and medical authorities as well as tourism and non-tourism enterprises and community groups. Government Ministries of Tourism and Tourism Boards, airlines and other transport suppliers, tour operators and travel agents in host and generating countries, trade associations and media at all levels from global to local are involved. Partnerships can also be of value in resolving single-issue and more confined crises and the network of linkages is less dense in such circumstances.

It is not only official bodies which participate in clearing up after destination crises; there are private businesses which specialize in tasks that might be seen as a government function, but which the latter do not have the capability to fully undertake. They could comprise the provision of mobile mortuaries and taking care of the dead (The Straits Times, 2005c). Whether the privatization and commercialization of disaster management is desirable is a matter for debate, but it does mean another party to consider regarding crisis planning, coordination and communications.

There are also commercial partners outside the tourism sector, an important one being the insurance industry. The question of insurance is a concern for both the tourism industry and tourist, with uncertainties about coverage should particular types of crisis occur perhaps deterring some movement and investment. Many policies have exemption clauses pertaining to terrorist attacks and certain "acts of God" and there was difficulty obtaining comprehensive policies for travel to SARS-affected countries. Airlines have also had to meet additional insurance burdens following 11

September 2001, compounding their financial woes, and the tourism industry overall must be mindful of its legal duties regarding liability issues. Insurance and reinsurance companies are faced with their own crises, due to exceptionally high claims for property damage by weather, which are having repercussions for those seeking insurance. Insured losses exceeded US$70 billion in 2005, making it the most expensive year ever and there were reports that eight insurers had withdrawn from Florida (The Montreal Gazette, 2005).

Tourism businesses in the developing world are sometimes uninsured or under-insured by choice because of a lack of funds or awareness and this can add to the impacts of crises and impede recovery. Disaster mitigation strategies stress the need to encourage the purchase of commercial insurance among poorer communities and stricter official controls on building and land use in order to avoid damage from construction too near to the water's edge in coastal centers, for example. Hazard taxes and initiatives to simplify insurance arrangements and make them more affordable have also been urged (IBLF, 2005).

Crisis prevention, management and recovery therefore necessitate a team effort among and between the public and private sectors. These teams grow in size with the scale and scope of the crisis and may assume national and international responsibilities. At the same time, strong centralized authority and direction are required to lead organizations and destinations out of crisis.

Looking Ahead

Crises are by definition unpredictable and the future is unknown, although many causes of crises will undoubtedly persist and types of crises will repeat themselves. Extreme economic volatility, violent social upheaval, disease, political dislocation, terrorist atrocities, tropical storms and environmental pollution are present or constantly threatened in several parts of the world and can precipitate tourism crises. The industry will continue to be highly competitive and subject to commercial pressures capable of triggering crises, although it has some control over those crises which are a result of adverse developments of its own creation. There may also be new forms of crises as the industry expands its geographical reach, technology of all manifestations advances and tourist volumes rise.

Such a background illuminates the importance of the study of tourism crises in order to improve understanding of their root causes, dynamics and consequences as a basis for better management. Case histories yield valuable lessons and can be a foundation for theories explaining the evolution of tourism crises which permit insightful comparisons across companies, destinations and industries. Analyses can also generate strategic and practical tools for use by managers at the heart of a tourism crisis, especially those from smaller businesses who may be disadvantaged in terms of resources. These represent directions for research journeys, many of which appear to be already embarked upon with more publications on the topic anticipated in the near future.

Conclusion

The book has discussed a wide range of tourism crises and demonstrated the many types to which tourism is prone. Responses have been examined and they have been both reactive and proactive with a trend toward the latter as the tourism industry acknowledges its vulnerability, especially regarding natural disasters and terrorist attacks, and is moving to prepare. Crisis management encompasses a multiplicity of activities and is a cooperative effort for destinations where authorities are expressing greater interest in the subject, a reflection of the perceived economic rewards of tourism. While more tourism crises are inevitable, it is possible to learn from past experiences so that some situations can be avoided or at least ameliorated through appropriate attitudes and actions by the parties involved.

Review Questions

1. What are the principal types of crises that the tourism industry is likely to face in the next decade?
2. What barriers might hinder the effective implementation of the PATA plan and is it suitable for adoption outside the Asia Pacific region?
3. What responsibilities to local communities and economies do tourism businesses based in generating countries have in times of destination crises?
4. Might there be conflicts between the exercise of any such responsibilities and commercial objectives?
5. What factors are critical to the success of an organization crisis management plan?

Case One: PATA Crisis Management Strategy

Phase one: reduction

1.1 Crisis Awareness	1.1.1 Identify Risks and Hazards
	1.1.2 Identify Possible Impacts
	1.1.3 Intelligence Collection
1.2 Political Awareness	1.2.1 Secure Political Cooperation
	1.2.2 Increase Political Involvement
	1.2.3 Link Tourism and Peace
1.3 Standard Operating Procedures	1.3.1 Anticipate Problems
	1.3.2 Revise Procedures
	1.3.3 Enhance Staff Awareness

Phase two: readiness

2.1 Crisis Management Plan	2.1.1 Establish Crisis Management Team
	2.1.2 Crisis Management Plan
	2.1.3 Simulation Exercises
2.2 Tourism Planning	2.2.1 Create Awareness among Industry
	2.2.2 Train Staff
	2.2.3 Advance Decision-Making
2.3 Health and Safety Measures	2.3.1 Establish a Local Network
	2.3.2 Emergency Services
	2.3.3 Hazards Handling Systems

Phase three: response

3.1 Emergency Response Procedures	3.1.1 Leadership
	3.1.2 Crisis Response
	3.1.3 Internal-External Communications
	3.1.4 External Suppliers Handling
	3.1.5 Hospital(s)
	3.1.6 Morgue(s)
3.2 Investigation	3.2.1 Crime
	3.2.2 Legal and Political
	3.2.3 Insurance
3.3 Family Assistance	3.3.1 Information Handling
	3.3.2 Transportation
	3.3.3 Accommodation
	3.3.4 On-site Support
3.4 Communication	3.4.1 Media
	3.4.2 Hospital(s)
	3.4.3 Morgue(s)
	3.4.4 Investigation
	3.4.5 Government

Phase four: recovery

4.1 Business Continuity Plan	4.1.1 Rehabilitation
	4.1.2 Normalisation
	4.1.3 Expansion
4.2 Human Resources	4.2.1 Impact of Reduced Labour Needs
	4.2.2 Motivation and Training
	4.2.3 Increase Crisis Awareness
4.3 Debriefing	4.3.1 Thank All Involved
	4.3.2 Follow-up with Victims
	4.3.3 Update Crisis Management Plan

Reduction checklist

This checklist is only a guide. It does not contain all of the components, contingencies or options required by each organisation or destination for its specific crisis planning process.

	Done	**To be done**
1 We agree that prevention is better than cure	____	_____
2 We have defined "crisis" for our organisation/destination	____	_____
3 We have a business impact analysis for each anticipated crisis	____	_____
4 We have identified all potential hazards and their particular locations	____	_____
5 We involve suppliers, vendors and channel partners in crisis reduction activities	____	_____
6 We train specific stakeholders/staff in security awareness	____	_____
7 We train specific stakeholders/staff in standard crime prevention behaviour	____	_____
8 We educate stakeholders/staff in preventive crisis reduction techniques	____	_____
9 We have proactive Standard Operating Procedures that take the avoidance of possible hazards and crises into consideration	____	_____
10 We are soliciting advice from emergency agencies to reduce possible hazards and crises	____	_____
11 We have assured proactive cooperation with the relevant insurance companies	____	_____
12 We have adequate disaster procedures for application in routine emergencies	____	_____
13 We have created awareness among elected and appointed officials and organisational leaders about community involvement during a disaster	____	_____
14 We have set up an emergency services liaison panel	____	_____
15 We have organised meetings to promote informal contact between all those likely to be involved in a major crisis	____	_____
16 We have communicated the need to have a crisis management plan to all stakeholders	____	_____
17 We have initiated a steering committee to assist all stakeholders to develop crisis management plans	____	_____
18 We have produced public or organisation education material	____	_____
19 We, in our destination, have the full cooperation of all political parties and movements	____	_____
20 We, in our destination, are actively linking tourism with the peace movement	____	_____
21 We, in our destination, have the full cooperation of all tourism associations and organisations	____	_____
22 We, in our destination, have created community, consumer, retailer and wholesaler awareness of our proactive efforts through public relations	____	_____
23 We have introduced legislation to increase awareness for the need to proactively reduce the chances of crisis	____	_____
24 We have introduced legislation to increase the readiness of the organisation or destination	____	_____
25 We realise that every crisis has its opportunities	____	_____

Readiness checklist

This checklist is only a guide. It does not contain all of the components, contingencies or options required by each organisation or destination for its specific crisis planning process.

	Done	**To be done**
1 We have a crisis management plan	____	_____
2 We identified a crisis management coordinator and alternate	____	_____
3 We assigned responsibilities to each stakeholder and alternates	____	_____
4 We have a multi-network notification system in place to alert all stakeholders	____	_____
5 We have a trained crisis response team	____	_____
6 We established a law enforcement, fire department and emergency services liaison	____	_____
7 We are aware of the law enforcement, fire department and emergency services command and control structure and their crisis-scene management plans	____	_____
8 We established a media liaison and plan for communication	____	_____
9 We have an inventory of internal and external skills that may be helpful	____	_____
10 We placed crisis management toolboxes (necessary items assembled in advance) in several easily accessible locations	____	_____
11 We have an emergency "dark" Web site designed that can be activated on short notice	____	_____
12 We developed all necessary forms to assist in crisis management	____	_____
13 We made suppliers, vendors and channel partners aware of the plan	____	_____
14 We designated a safe and secure crisis centre (and an alternative area)	____	_____
15 We have back-up procedures for critical information in an off-site location	____	_____
16 We collect, collate and disseminate appropriate information through one agreed spokesperson	____	_____
17 We make sure that the crisis plan avoids trying to change how people normally behave in crisis situations	____	_____
18 We are convinced that all those that are involved in the design of the plan accept it and will assist in its continued development	____	_____
19 We have made sure that the emergency organisations in our area have adopted standard terminology and procedures	____	_____
20 We ensured with all stakeholders that the responsibility for common disaster tasks is now predetermined on a mutually agreed basis	____	_____
21 We practice crisis alerts periodically throughout the year	____	_____
22 We established procedures for annual inclusion of new staff/stakeholders	____	_____
23 We established procedures for annual update/review for all stakeholders	____	_____
24 We obtained a professional review of our crisis response procedures	____	_____
25 We obtained a legal review of crisis response procedures	____	_____

Response checklist

This checklist is only a guide. It does not contain all of the components, contingencies or options required by each organisation or destination for its specific crisis planning process.

	Done	To be done
1 We have a plan that focuses on saving lives, preventing further damage and reducing the effects of the disaster		
2 We have given persons with expertise in emergency medical services the primary authority at the scene over patient care and transport		
3 We have a plan and associated training for disaster casualty distribution among area hospitals		
4 We can activate on and off-location emergency operation centre(s) within 30 minutes		
5 We can alert all stakeholders within 30 minutes		
6 We have a designated person (and/or alternate) in charge of the emergency operation centre		
7 We can have the complete crisis response team operational within one hour		
8 We have an independent crisis communication system		
9 We will have all appropriate public and private organisations represented at the emergency operations centre		
10 We have procedures for limiting the congestion caused by excessive responders and curious public		
11 We have procedures for incorporating and managing volunteers		
12 We have evacuation areas identified and staff assigned		
13 We have a plan for the set up of a temporary morgue and evaluation centre		
14 We can activate on- and off-location family assistance centre(s) within 30 minutes		
15 We have a designated person (and/or alternate) in charge of the family assistance centre		
16 We can activate sensitive family notification procedures		
17 We have an emergency budget available for family assistance		
18 We have religious support for the victims and their families available		
19 We can issue an initial press statement in the local language and English within 90 minutes after the crisis		
20 We can activate an off-location media centre within two hours		
21 We can have first press briefings with basic details of crisis and planned/ongoing response activities within three hours		
22 We have a designated person (and/or alternate) in charge of the media centre, as well as a designated main spokesperson		
23 We have linked the Web master(s) of the emergency Web site with the media centre for simultaneous updating		
24 We have secured an (emergency) budget to handle our response activities		

Recovery checklist

This checklist is only a guide. It does not contain all of the components, contingencies or options required by each organisation or destination for its specific crisis planning process.

		Done	To be done
1	We have plans to consult with families on memorial services and markers	_____	_____
2	We will stay in contact with recovering victims and with the families of the deceased	_____	_____
3	We will designate a leading executive as the "Destination Maker"	_____	_____
4	We have a strategic recovery plan draft involving all stakeholders	_____	_____
5	We recognise the importance of the aviation industry as a (reversed) distribution system and work closely with them	_____	_____
6	We will concentrate all possible political efforts on the reduction of travel advisories	_____	_____
7	We will update our overseas representatives on a regular basis	_____	_____
8	We will adopt branding as the platform of the joint marketing efforts	_____	_____
9	We have a recovery sales action plan draft	_____	_____
10	We will target the travel consultants in our main markets	_____	_____
11	We will consult our key customers and work together to reduce the impact of the crisis for both parties	_____	_____
12	We will use this opportunity to start relationships in new markets	_____	_____
13	We have a public relations plan on stand-by	_____	_____
14	We will prepare a new media and community relations plan	_____	_____
15	We will target the end-user in our main markets as recipients of these media efforts	_____	_____
16	We will invite (and host) as many credible journalists as we can	_____	_____
17	We have a system to review press clippings and to evaluate if perceptions in these articles were correct or incorrect	_____	_____
18	We will survey the affected public, either formally or informally, to evaluate the effects on the image of the organisation or destination	_____	_____
19	We will intensively (with all employees) work to create awareness of the importance of making our organisation or destination as safe as humanly possible	_____	_____
20	We will organise internal and external seminars on recovery activities for all staff	_____	_____
21	We will use the recovery period for intensive skill training for our staff	_____	_____
22	We will counsel and motivate all employees to overcome the emotional stress	_____	_____
23	We have plans for intensive debriefing sessions with all concerned	_____	_____
24	We will analyse the recovery efforts and use the "lessons learned" to improve our crisis management plan	_____	_____
25	We will recognise and thank those who have helped, both internally and externally	_____	_____

Source: PATA (2005). Crisis: It won't happen to us! Bangkok: Pacific Asia Travel Association. Reproduced with kind permission of the author, Bert Van Walbeek.

Case Two: Banyan Tree and the Indian Ocean Tsunami

Banyan Tree Hotels and Resorts operate a chain of luxury hotel resorts which were largely spared by the tsunami. There was minor damage to a beach bar in Thailand and a jetty and a few villas in the Maldives and it was expected that the opening of a new resort in Sri Lanka would be delayed by about eight months. There were no casualties among staff or clientele and the company was covered by insurance for any physical destruction. Nevertheless, the crisis for the region was also a corporate crisis.

Attention was initially given to cleaning up and undertaking any repairs. The public, media, travel trade and guests were informed and reassured about the situation and arrangements were made regarding any cancellations or postponements of bookings. Those customers with bookings who were reluctant to visit stricken areas were offered various options and 90% agreed to a postponement of their stay to a date within seven months. Alternatively, they could transfer their booking to any of the resorts owned and managed by Banyan Tree. Requests for cancellations were considered individually from those who had booked at the resorts directly affected in Thailand, the Maldives and Sri Lanka. Guests with bookings elsewhere were allowed to delay their visit by three months or choose a transfer. Less than 5% shortened their stay and those who did so could use up remaining nights at another resort, if they had paid in advance, or were not charged for the remaining nights in cases where payment was outstanding.

However, the group's chairman said in an interview that the most important consideration was "helping the local communities to recover." He spoke about concentrating on the "medium to long term recovery process of restoring shattered communities—providing trauma counselling, sponsoring orphans, rebuilding homes and schools, rebuilding boatyards to build fishing boats for villagers."

Banyan Tree announced in early January 2005 that it was setting up an Asian Tsunami Recovery Fund to "assist recovery and livelihood rehabilitation efforts through sustainable and long term support." The focus was on Indonesia, the Maldives and Sri Lanka with a separate fund for Phuket in Thailand. Staff members contributed 5% of their monthly salary on a voluntary basis and the Green Imperative Fund or GIF (a long-standing scheme dedicated to "community based environmental action in the Asia Pacific region") was redirected to the tsunami funds from January until March 2005. The GIF amount, charged daily automatically unless guests opted out, was raised from US$1 to US$2 and Banyan Tree matched staff and guest donations. Banyan Tree also called for financial aid from commercial partners, making use of its website. Money raised was passed to local community organizations and international non-governmental agencies with human resources also made available in the form of Banyan Tree staff.

The Phuket Tsunami Recovery Fund was launched by Laguna Resorts and Hotels (LRH) to provide direct assistance to tsunami victims in Thailand. The intention was to work with local authorities to determine requirements and ensure aid reached the neediest. New Year celebrations at the resort hotels were canceled and the money allocated was channeled into the fund. The GIF increases were introduced and a total of 3,000 staff was invited to donate 5% of their January salary, with equal sums given by LRH. Staff were released to take part in community cleanup and recovery efforts. A group of 67 displaced families from a destroyed village near the resort received emergency clothing and food supplies in one instance.

Staff in Sri Lanka helped in the distribution of food and medicines and Banyan Tree adopted two villages in the worst hit Indonesian province of Aceh. A number of recovery and rehabilitation priorities were identified, such as the repair of fishing boats and school buildings and provision of medical supplies and farming equipment, and 10 staff were sent to work on these projects. In the Maldives, the company partnered the United Nations Development Programme (UNDP) and some voluntary groups to help repair and rebuild 77 houses on one island. It also funded the purchase and transportation of materials and sent 15 engineers from its resort. Volunteers from among the staff, including carpenters and plumbers, were given paid leave to spend three-week periods as part of the team and Banyan Tree's Director of Conservation was also involved.

A newspaper advertisement at the beginning of 2005 reminded a regional audience that it was business as usual at the resorts while seeking to generate relief funds. A photograph showed three local fishermen on a jetty and was headed "We survived the tsunami. Now we must help others." Readers were encouraged to "stay with us and let someone else feel the healing this time."

Sources: Banyan Tree undated, 2004, 2005a, 2005b and 2005c; Muqbil, 2004; The Straits Times, 2005a and 2005b.

References

Banyan Tree. (undated). *The green imperative: Embracing the environment, empowering people.* Singapore: The Banyan Tree.

Banyan Tree. (2004, 27 December). Banyan Tree official media statement: Tsunami waves in Phuket, Maldives and Sri Lanka.

Banyan Tree. (2005a). Phuket Recovery Fund. Press Release. Banyan Tree Media Hub. Banyan Tree website at http://www.banyantree.com, accessed 1 August 2005.

Banyan Tree. (2005b). Tsunami recovery efforts by Banyan Tree Group: Extracts from media interview on 14 January. Banyan Tree Media Hub. Banyan Tree website at http://www.banyantree.com, accessed 1 August 2005.

Banyan Tree. (2005c). Tsunami relief work on the island of Naalaafushi, Maldives. Project report May 2005. Banyan Tree Media Hub. Banyan Tree website at http://www.banyantree.com, accessed 1 August 2005.

BEST. (2005). Managing risk and crisis for sustainable tourism innovation. BEST Education Network Think Tank V. At BEST Education Network website at http://www.besteducationnetwork.org/ttv, accessed 6 December 2005.

Faulkner, B. (2001). Towards a framework for tourism disaster management. *Tourism Management, 22,* 134–147.

Faulkner, B. and Vikulov, J. (2001), 101.

Henderson, J.C. and Ng, A. (2004). Responding to crisis: Severe Acute Respiratory Syndrome (SARS) and hotels in Singapore. *International Journal of Tourism Research*, *6*, 411–419.

Holland, M. (2000). Crisis management of the national tourism product: Dealing with induced or imposed catastrophe. Pannell Kerr Forster website at www.pkf.co.uk, accessed 21 February 2005.

IBLF. (2005). *Disaster management and planning: An IBLF framework for business response.* London: International Business Leaders Forum.

LDA. (2005). *Crisis management for tourism businesses.* London: London Development Agency.

The Montreal Gazette. (2005, 7 December). High risk regions face new peril: Loss of insurance: Damage this year tops $200 billion.

Muqbil, I. (2004). Postponement and cancellation policy: Banyan Tree Official Statement. worldroom.com website at www.worldroom.com/pages/travelnews/muqbil/news_archive.phtml, accessed 1 August 2005.

NEMO. (1997). *The hospitality industry crisis management plan.* St Lucia: National Emergency Management Organization.

PATA. (2005). Crisis: It won't happen to us! Bangkok: Pacific Asia Travel Association.

The Straits Times. (2005a, 19 January). Banyan Tree Hotels and Resorts advertisement.

The Straits Times. (2005b, 10 January). Public listing no longer Banyan Tree's top priority.

The Straits Times. (2005c, 30 May). Roping in private sector when disaster strikes.

WTO. (2005). *Tsunami relief for the tourism sector: Phuket action plan.* Madrid: World Tourism Organization.

Index